The Chartered Governance Institute
Study Text

Financial Reporting and Governance

Study Text

Financial Reporting and Governance

Kathryn Cearns and Jacques Colley

icsa
The Chartered Governance Institute

First published 2017
Published by ICSA Publishing Limited
Saffron House
6–10 Kirby Street
London EC1N 8TS

Typeset by Paul Barrett Book Production, Cambridge

British Cataloguing in Publication Data
A catalogue record for this book is available from the British Library.

ISBN 978-1-86072-781-8

Contents

Acknowledgements

The publisher and author would like to acknowledge the contribution made by the author of a previous version of this book, Bruce Horwood, and the technical reviewer of the text, Caroline Fox. The author thanks Marks & Spencer Group plc for the use of their *Annual Report and Financial Statements 2016* and the Financial Reporting Council for quoting from the *Corporate Governance Code*.

This text is based on the law and accounting standards without anticipating any potential changes arising from the impact of the UK leaving the European Union. [There are unlikely to be any significant changes in the near future in this area.]

Every effort has been made to locate and acknowledge sources and holders of copyright material in this study text. In the event that any have been inadvertently overlooked, please contact the publisher.

How to use this study text

The Chartered Governance Institute study texts developed to support our Level 5 International Finance and Administration Qualifications follow a standard format and include a range of navigational, self-testing and illustrative features to help you get the most out of the support materials.

Each text is divided into three main sections:

- introductory material
- the text itself
- additional reference information.

The sections below show you how to find your way around the text and make the most of its features.

Introductory material

The introductory section of each text includes a full contents list and the aims and learning outcomes for the modules in question.

Where relevant, the introductory section will also include a list of acronyms and abbreviations or a list of legal cases for reference.

The text itself

Each part opens with a list of the chapters to follow, an overview of what will be covered and learning outcomes for the part.

Every chapter opens with a list of the topics covered and an introduction specific to that chapter. Chapters are structured to allow students to break the content down into manageable sections for study. Each chapter ends with a summary of key content to reinforce understanding.

Features

The text is enhanced by a range of illustrative and self-testing features to assist understanding and to help you prepare for the examination. You will find answers to the 'test yourself' and 'worked example' questions towards the end of this text. Each feature is presented in a standard format, so that you will become familiar with how to use them in your study.

These features are identified by a series of icons.

The texts also include tables, figures and other illustrations as relevant.

Reference material

The text ends with a range of additional guidance and reference material, including a glossary of key terms, a directory of web resources and a comprehensive index.

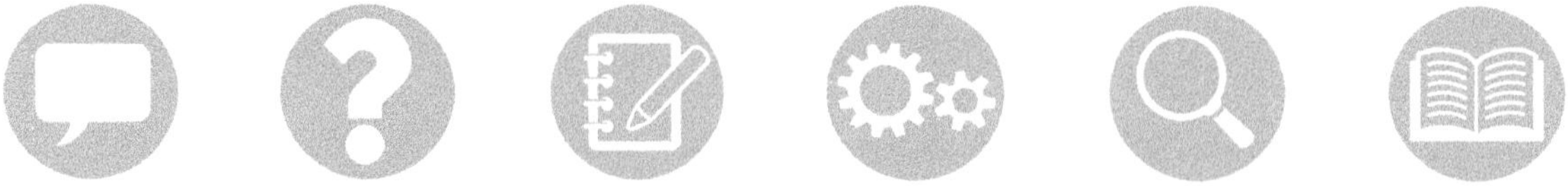

Stop and think | Test yourself | Worked examples | Making it work | Case law | Case study

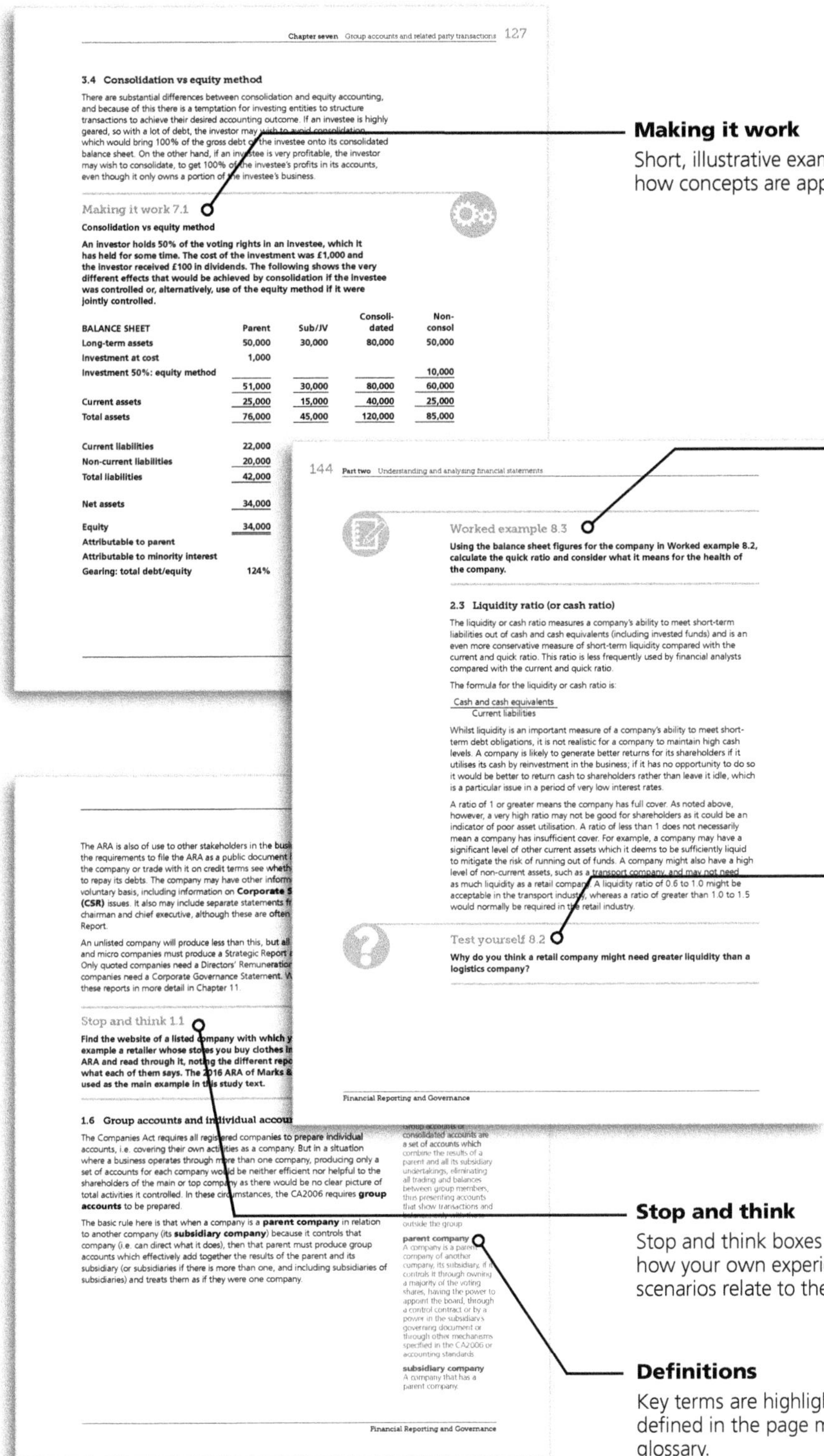

Making it work

Short, illustrative examples which look at how concepts are applied in practice.

Worked example

Crucial to an understanding of finance-based modules. Questions and answers allow you to work through a calculation as part of your study. Answers are to be found towards the end of the text.

Test yourself

Short, revision-style questions to help you re-cap on key information and core concepts. Answers are to be found towards the end of the text.

Stop and think

Stop and think boxes encourage you to reflect on how your own experiences or common business scenarios relate to the topic under discussion.

Definitions

Key terms are highlighted in bold on first use and defined in the page margins and the end of book glossary.

The Financial Reporting and Governance modules

Aims

The Financial Reporting and Governance modules are aimed specifically at those employed as administrators in junior supervisory roles, whose present or future position requires a broad knowledge and understanding of the perspective of the industry, whilst demanding a high degree of operational knowledge covering legal, regulatory and financial frameworks.

The modules aim to enable students to understand the importance of the two significant and highly relevant aspects of offshore finance, 'financial reporting and interpretation' and 'governance' and to develop knowledge, understanding and key skills within these legal, regulatory and financial frameworks.

Learning outcomes

On successful completion of these modules you will:

- Know about the financial reporting environment for different types of company
- Understand the Conceptual Framework for Financial Reporting
- Understand financial statements are prepared and presented
- Understand the application of IFRS Standards and GAAP when compiling and interpreting financial statements
- Understand how parent companies prepare accounts for the other businesses they invest in
- Understand key financial ratios and other indicators used to measure the financial performance
- of companies
- Understand the limitations of using ratios to measure financial performance
- Understand the principles of trust accounting
- Know about the types of company that may be formed in the UK and offshore jurisdictions
- Understand how companies are financed

- Understand principles and codes of good governance practice
- Know about narrative reporting and corporate social responsibility
- Know about developments in EU and US legislation and regulation to improve corporate governance practices.

Past papers

Students can access sample and past papers for these modules by logging into MyCG at www.icsa.org.uk/my_cg/login.

Acronyms and abbreviations

AIC	Association of Investment Companies
AIM	Alternative Investment Market
ARA	Annual Report and Accounts
APM	alternative performance measure
ARC	Accounting Regulatory Committee
BIS	Bank for International Settlements
BVI	British Virgin Islands
CA	current assets
CA2006	Companies Act 2006
CEO	chief executive officer
CFO	chief financial officer
CL	current liabilities
CIC	Community Interest Company
CSR	corporate social responsibility
EC	European Commission
EFRAG	European Financial Reporting Advisory Group
EPS	earnings per share
EU	European Union
ESMA	European Securities and Markets Authority
FASB	Financial Accounting Standards Board
FIFO	first in, first out
FPI	Foreign Private issuer
FRC	Financial Reporting Council
FSA	Financial Services Authority
FRED	Financial Reporting Exposure Draft
FRS	Financial Reporting Standards
FSB	Financial Stability Board
FSOC	Financial Stability Oversight Council
FVTPL	fair value through profit or loss
FVTOCI	far value through other comprehensive income
GAAP	Generally Accepted Accounting Practice (or principles)
GP	general partner
IAS	International Accounting Standards
IASB	International Accounting Standards Board
IASC	International Accounting Standards Committee
IC	incorporated cell
ICAS	Institute of Chartered Accountants of Scotland

ICAEW	Institute of Chartered Accountants in England and Wales
ICC	incorporated cell companies
IFRS	International Financial Reporting Standards
IIRC	International Integrated Reporting Council
ILP	Incorporated Limited Partnerships
ISA	International Standards on Accounting
JIT	just in time procurement
KPI	Key Performance Indicator
LLP	limited liability partnership
LTIP	Long-term incentive plan
LP	limited partnership
LPA	limited partnership agreement
M&A	mergers and acquisitions
M&S	Marks & Spencer
NED	non-executive directors
OCI	other comprehensive income
OECD	Organisation for Economic Co-operation and Development
PBIT	profit before interest and taxation
P/E	price/earnings
PIE	public interest entity
PLC	public limited company
PCAOB	Public Company Accounting Oversight Board
PCC	protected cell companies
ROA	Return on assets
ROCE	Return on capital employed
ROE	return on equity
ROI	return on investment
SEC	Securities and Exchange Commission
SIFIs	systemically important financial institutions
SLP	Separate Limited Partnerships
SOX	Sarbanes-Oxley Act 2002
TA	total assets

International Financial Reporting Standards®

International Financial Reporting Standards (and FRS 102 equivalent)

Standard	Standard name	FRS 102 chapter	Chapter in text
IFRS 1	First-time Adoption of IFRS	*	*
IFRS 2	Share-based Payment	26	4
IFRS 3	Business Combinations	19	7
IFRS 4	Insurance Contracts	*	*
IFRS 5	Non-current Assets Held for Sale and Discontinued Operations	5	3
IFRS 6	Exploration for and Evaluation of Mineral Resources	N/A	*
IFRS 7	Financial Instruments – Disclosures	*	*
IFRS 8	Operating Segments	N/A	3
IFRS 9	Financial Instruments	11, 12	5, 6
IFRS 10	Consolidated Financial Statements	9	7
IFRS 11	Joint Arrangements	15	7
IFRS 12	Disclosure of Interests in Other Entities	9	7
IFRS 13	Fair Value Measurement	*	*
IFRS 14	Regulatory Deferral Accounts	N/A	*
IFRS 15	Revenue from Contracts with Customers	23	4
IFRS 16	Leases	N/A	6
IAS 1	Presentation of Financial Statements	3, 4, 5, 6, 8	3
IAS 2	Inventories	13	5
IAS 7	Statement of Cash Flows	7	3
IAS 8	Accounting Policies, changes in Accounting Estimates and Errors	10	4
IAS 10	Events After the Reporting Period	32	3
IAS 12	Income Taxes	29	4
IAS 16	Property, Plant and Equipment	17	5
IAS 17	Leases	20	6
IAS 19	Employee Benefits	28	4
IAS 20	Accounting for Government Grants and Disclosure of Government Assistance	*	*

IAS 21	The Effects of Changes in Foreign Exchange Rates	30	3
IAS 23	Borrowing Costs	25	5
IAS 24	Related Party Disclosures	33	7, 11
IAS 26	Accounting and Reporting by Retirement Benefit Plans	*	*
IAS 27	Separate Financial Statements	9	7
IAS 28	Investments in Associates and Joint Ventures	14, 15	7
IAS 29	Reporting in Hyperinflationary Economies	*	*
IAS 32	Financial Instruments – Presentation	11, 12	6
IAS 33	Earnings Per Share	N/A	8
IAS 34	Interim Financial Reporting	N/A	*
IAS 36	Impairment of Assets	27	5
IAS 37	Provisions, Contingent Liabilities and Contingent Assets	21, 22	6
IAS 38	Intangible Assets	18	5
IAS 40	Investment Property	*	*
IAS 41	Agriculture	*	*

* Specialist or industry-specific standard not covered in this text in any detail.

Notes

Note that IFRS Standards are available by subscription from the IASB (go to www.ifrs.org). As well as individual standards, the IASB produces two bound editions on different bases, currently:

- *Red book*: containing the official pronouncements issued at 13 January 2016, including standards with an effective date after 1 January 2016 but not the standards they will replace.
- *Blue book*: consolidated without early application. Containing the official pronouncements applicable on 1 January 2016. Does not include standards with an effective date after 1 January 2016.

These books are produced annually at about the same time of year. The IASB website also offers a range of educational material.

All UK standards, including FRS 102, can be downloaded for free from the FRC website at www.frc.org.uk.

Accounting standards covered in this text

In this text we will focus on the IFRS standards, but a cross reference will be included to the relevant part of the main UK standard, FRS 102, with a note about any major differences between the standards. For example, UK GAAP equivalent: Section 2 of FRS 102 deals with pervasive concepts, covering similar issues to the Conceptual Framework.

Part one

The form and content of financial statements

Overview

In this part, you will learn about the provisions of the UK Companies Act 2006 that relate to financial reporting, as well as which accounting frameworks can or must be followed by UK companies: International Financial Reporting Standards (IFRS) and UK Generally Accepted Accounting Practice (UK GAAP). The principle of 'true and fair' will be discussed as well as the usual contents of a company's annual report. You will gain an insight into how IFRS Standards are developed by the International Accounting Standards Board (IASB) and their increasing use around the world (including the EU). You will also learn about UK GAAP, consisting of UK accounting standards and local law and regulation, how UK standards are developed by the Financial Reporting Council (FRC) and the choices companies have within UK GAAP, depending on different factors such as their size. This part also discusses the use of different accounting frameworks in offshore centres.

This part outlines the IASB's draft conceptual framework, which will underpin its standard setting in the future. The project is near completion and you will learn about the important concepts and aims of the standard setting process that are described there, including definitions of key elements of financial statements such as assets and liabilities.

You will then go on in the rest of this part to cover the reason for, and content of, each of the major statements in a full set of financial statements. Each statement, and the discussion of major elements of each statement in the following chapters, are illuminated by looking at the accounts of a real company. You will learn about other key underlying concepts, including materiality and going concern, and the treatment of events after the reporting period.

The chapters in this part will give you an insight into how revenue or turnover is calculated, the main types of company expenses, and different types of asset and liability.

Learning outcomes

At the end of this part, you will be able to:

- Outline the main legal requirements in the UK relating to financial reporting
- Describe the different types and sizes of company dealt with in UK law
- Lay out the usual contents of the Annual Report and Accounts (ARA)
- Discuss the purpose of each element of the ARA
- Describe the differences between, and use of, individual company and group accounts
- Explain what is meant by 'true and fair view'
- Explain what is meant by UK GAAP and IFRS Standards
- Summarise the process of developing IFRS Standards and UK standards and why they are used
- Discuss the benefits and drawbacks of accounting standards

- Outline the situation as regards the US and EU approaches to IFRS Standards
- Discuss the acceptability of different accounting standards in offshore centres
- Outline the advantages and disadvantages of having a conceptual framework
- Discuss in broad terms the contents of the IASB's draft conceptual framework
- Describe the qualitative characteristics of useful financial information and define the elements of financial statements
- Understand substance over form and be able to give examples in practice
- Describe recognition and derecognition as well as different measurement methods
- Understand general features of financial reporting, including accruals, going concern, materiality and aggregation and offsetting
- Describe the content of the main statements
- Explain the split between current and non-current assets and liabilities and their different types
- Outline the main income statement line items and the different methods of presenting expenses
- Appreciate the impact of discontinued operations on company results
- Explain how the statement of cash flows is presented
- Discuss the need for disclosure of operating segments and why this is useful
- Explain what happens in relation to events subsequent to the financial year
- Understand the importance of the revenue line and how revenue is accounted for under the new IFRS Standards
- Appreciate the basic approach to employee benefits, including pensions and share-based payment
- Outline the accounting for foreign currency exchange rate changes and income taxes

- Understand the accounting for property, plant and equipment
- Explain the accounting for intangible assets, including research and development
- Understand why assets become impaired and how impairments are calculated and accounted for
- Outline accounting for inventories
- Explain, at a high level, accounting for financial assets, including their impairment under the expected loss model
- Understand and describe provisions and contingent liabilities and their different accounting treatment, and the treatment of contingent assets
- Explain the treatment of financial liabilities and how they are differentiated from equity
- Understand the current treatment of leases and the potential effect on gearing of the new leasing standard.

Chapter one
The financial reporting environment

List of topics

1. Introduction
2. UK Companies Act
3. International Financial Reporting Standards
4. UK Generally Accepted Accounting Practice

1. Introduction

In this first chapter, we will cover the provisions of the UK Companies Act 2006 that relate to financial reporting, because it is the law that requires UK companies to prepare accounts. We will look at which accounting frameworks can or must be followed by different companies, namely International Financial Reporting Standards (IFRS Standards) and UK Generally Accepted Accounting Practice (UK GAAP). We will consider the principle of 'true and fair' in financial reporting, and there is also a brief summary of other legal and regulatory issues related to accounts, including share capital, reserves and distributions and taxation. An overview of the usual contents of a company's annual report is also given.

We will then consider IFRS Standards in more detail and their increasing use around the world (including the EU), whether through wholesale adoption or gradual convergence. IFRS Standards are developed by the International Accounting Standards Board (IASB), and sometimes interpretations are needed which are issued as required through an IFRS Standards Interpretations Committee of the IASB®. IFRS Standards and Interpretations have to be adopted formally into EU law before they can be applied.

UK GAAP, consisting of UK accounting standards and local law and regulation, is the alternative to IFRS Standards. UK standards, issued by the Financial Reporting Council (FRC), are now based on a simplified version of IFRS Standards and companies have choices within UK GAAP depending on different factors such as their size.

2. UK Companies Act

The principal Act of Parliament relating to companies in the UK is the Companies Act 2006, although there are other more minor pieces of legislation.

2.1 The Companies Act 2006

The Companies Act 2006 (CA2006) consolidated and replaced many of the provisions of the previous legislation, i.e. the Companies Acts of 1985 and 1989, and is made up of around 1,300 sections supplemented by **secondary legislation**.

secondary legislation
Is subordinate legislation which supplements primary law. It is enacted by a person or body, other than the legislature, who has been granted the relevant authority. This enables secondary legislation to be enacted in a more timely manner.

The CA2006 was the outcome of a long process of development and consultation which began in 1997. It was introduced with the aim of reforming company law and:

- improving shareholder communication and engagement
- enhancing a long-term investment culture
- strengthening regulation
- protecting the interests of consumers by increasing a company's disclosure requirements
- making it simpler to incorporate and run a company; and
- affording flexibility for the future.

The CA2006, which has been amended in a variety of ways since it originally came into force, sets out the statutory requirements of UK companies, including the rules over their formation, activities, relationships with shareholders and their management. Although much of the Act is a product of the development of UK law, substantial parts are based on the requirements of EU Directives, which must be transposed into UK law to be effective. These include the Accounting Directive, the Statutory Audit Directive and various older company law directives.

We are focusing on companies here, but note that requirements to prepare accounts for other types of entity, including limited liability partnerships and limited partnerships, are usually found in other specific legislation. For unincorporated businesses such as partnerships and sole traders, the requirements to prepare proper accounts are often found in tax law. What this effectively means is that, in the UK, most businesses must prepare true and fair accounts, which involves following accounting standards.

public interest entities (PIEs)
PIEs in the EU are entities that are listed on an EU-regulated market, or are credit institutions (such as banks) or insurance undertakings and any other entity that is designated as a PIE by an EU Member State because of its significant public relevance.

traded companies
Companies with securities traded on a regulated market, such as the main London Stock Exchange.

quoted companies
Companies whose equity share capital is listed on the main exchange in the UK, the EEA or the New York Stock Exchange or Nasdaq. AIM companies are not quoted.

public companies
Companies whose certificate of incorporation states they are a public company or which have converted to public company since incorporation and whose share capital is at least £50,000.

2.2 Key features of the Companies Act 2006

The CA2006 is divided into 47 Parts and has a long list of Schedules attached to it. The way it applies to companies depends on their nature or size, although many provisions apply to all companies. The main (but not only) distinctions are:

- **Public-Interest Entities (PIEs)** vs non-PIEs
- **Traded** vs untraded companies
- **Quoted** vs unquoted companies
- **Public** vs private companies
- Micro vs small vs medium-sized vs large companies (see below).

2.3 Size criteria for micro, small, medium-sized and large companies

A company's size is a key issue in determining which accounting rules it can follow by law. In effect, the smaller a company, the fewer and simpler rules it has to follow, although:

- some types of company cannot follow simpler regimes, even if they meet the size criteria, for example if they are listed or carry on insurance or banking activities; and
- companies can always choose to opt in to a more complex regime if they wish to, for example if they are just starting up but intend to grow rapidly and so will need to move reasonably soon to larger company rules.

The main limits were increased for 2015 financial years onwards and are shown in Table 1.1.

Table 1.1: Limits of a company's size

Category	Turnover	Balance sheet total	Employees
Micro	≤£632k	≤£316k	≤10
Small	≤£10.2m	≤£5.1m	≤50
Medium-sized	≤£36.0m	≤£18.0m	≤250

Anything above the medium-sized limits is classed as a large company. For each category, only two out of the three limits need to be met in any year. Balance sheet total means the total gross assets of the company (i.e. before deduction of liabilities). There are further exemptions for companies that are dormant, i.e. they have no activity to record as they are not trading.

2.4 Accounting rules in the Companies Act

Part 15 of the CA2006 covers the main accounting requirements, consisting mainly of administrative instructions such as how often to prepare accounts, who they must be sent to and so on. This part of the Act also deals with the content of accounts, but much of the detail is in secondary legislation, most importantly:

- the Large and Medium-sized Companies and Groups (Accounts and Reports) Regulations 2008; and
- the Small Companies and Groups (Accounts and Directors' Report) Regulations 2008.

Some rules on accounts apply to nearly all companies. So, for example, all companies must send their accounts to their shareholders; and for all companies, failure to maintain accounting records could lead to a criminal offence being committed by every officer of the company who is in default.

The main differences in accounting requirements arise between public and private companies or between micro or small companies and other companies. So for example:

- All limited liability company financial statements must be filed at Companies House (so making them available to the general public). For private companies this must be within nine months of the year end, but public company financial statements must be filed within six months of the year end.
- Small companies do not have to produce group accounts (see below), can produce relatively simple accounts and are exempt from audit (discussed in Chapter 11).
- Micro-entities, which are the very smallest of companies, can prepare and file extremely simplified accounts with almost no disclosures.

2.5 Content of the Annual Report and Accounts (ARA)

When companies publish their annual accounts, it is within a document which contains a wider set of information, known as the Annual Report and Accounts (ARA). The contents of this document are governed by law and – for listed and Alternative Investment Market (AIM) companies – by the relevant stock market rules. Generally, the ARA of a listed UK company will contain the following:

- Strategic Report
- Directors' Report
- Directors' Remuneration Report
- Corporate Governance Statement
- Auditor's Report
- Audited Financial Statements–
  - Statement of financial position (which is the term used by the IASB), also known as the balance sheet
  - Statement of profit and loss and/or statement of comprehensive income
  - Statement of changes in equity
  - Statement of cash flows
  - Notes to the accounts.

The ARA is a key element of companies' communication with their shareholders and, for listed companies, the market, to show what the company has been doing, how the directors have managed the business for shareholders in their stewardship role, and to some extent to indicate what the future prospects of the business are. We will look at this further in Chapter 11 when we consider corporate governance.

The ARA is also of use to other stakeholders in the business, and in particular the requirements to file the ARA as a public document helps those who lend to the company or trade with it on credit terms see whether the company is likely to repay its debts. The company may have other information in its ARA on a voluntary basis, including information on **corporate social responsibility (CSR)** issues. It also may include separate statements from the company's chairman and chief executive, although these are often placed in the Strategic Report.

corporate social responsibility (CSR)
A term used to describe the processes an organisation uses to produce a positive impact on society through its activities. It is about ongoing commitment of businesses to behave ethically and responsibly towards its employees, its customers, the environment and the community at large. It is about doing business in a responsible and sustainable manner.

An unlisted company will produce less than this, but all companies except small and micro companies must produce a Strategic Report and Directors' Report. Only quoted companies need a Directors' Remuneration Report and only listed companies need a Corporate Governance Statement. We will look at some of these reports in more detail in Chapter 11.

Stop and think 1.1

Find the website of a listed company with which you are familiar, for example a retailer whose stores you buy clothes in. Download their last ARA and read through it, noting the different reports that are there and what each of them says. The 2016 ARA of Marks & Spencer plc will be used as the main example in this study text.

2.6 Group accounts and individual accounts

The Companies Act requires all registered companies to prepare individual accounts, i.e. covering their own activities as a company. But in a situation where a business operates through more than one company, producing only a set of accounts for each company would be neither efficient nor helpful to the shareholders of the main or top company as there would be no clear picture of total activities it controlled. In these circumstances, the CA2006 requires **group accounts** to be prepared.

group accounts
Group accounts or consolidated accounts are a set of accounts which combine the results of a parent and all its subsidiary undertakings, eliminating all trading and balances between group members, thus presenting accounts that show transactions and balances only with those outside the group.

The basic rule here is that when a company is a **parent company** in relation to another company (its **subsidiary company**) because it controls that company (i.e. can direct what it does), then that parent must produce group accounts which effectively add together the results of the parent and its subsidiary (or subsidiaries if there is more than one, and including subsidiaries of subsidiaries) and treats them as if they were one company.

parent company
A company is a parent company of another company, its subsidiary, if it controls it through owning a majority of the voting shares, having the power to appoint the board, through a control contract or by a power in the subsidiary's governing document or through other mechanisms specified in the CA2006 or accounting standards.

subsidiary company
A company that has a parent company.

Figure 1.1: Individual vs group accounts

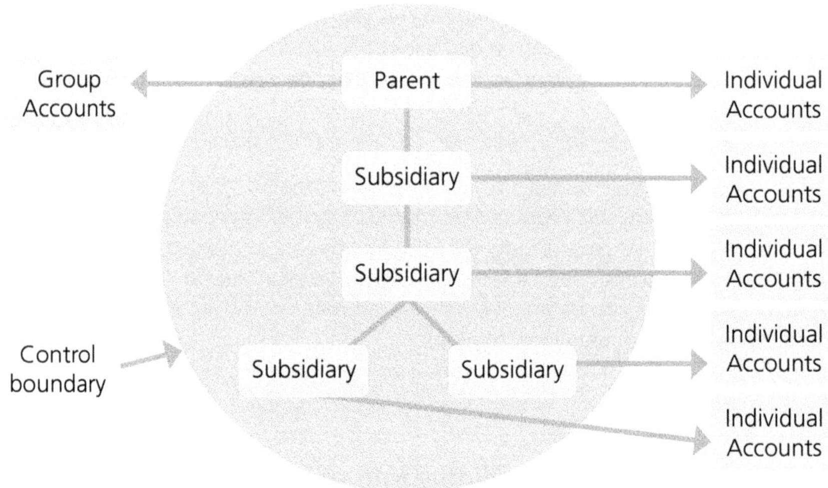

We will look at group accounts and the concept of control in more detail in Chapter 7. The main uses that are made of individual company accounts and group accounts are summarised in Table 1.2.

Table 1.2: Main uses of individual company accounts and group accounts

Use	Individual company accounts	Group accounts
Shareholder information	Accountability to direct shareholders for the parent's own activity	Accountability to parent company shareholders for all activity in the group
Taxation	Basis for actual corporation tax paid	Not used other than to show an overall tax rate for the group compared to its profit
Dividends	Dividends are paid by reference to individual company accounts	Not used

The way individual accounts are used as the basis for dividends is dealt with in another part of the CA2006. These elements of the law focus on protection of creditors when dealing with a limited liability company, i.e. where shareholders' liability extends only to the capital they put into the company and there is no recourse to them if the company cannot pay its debts. The use of individual accounts for tax purposes is covered by separate tax legislation, but it relies on the requirements in company law for the preparation of such accounts.

2.7 True and fair view

Except for micro-entity accounts (which are deemed to be true and fair in law), the directors of a company must not approve a set of financial statements that do not give a **true and fair view** of the assets, liabilities, financial position and profit or loss of the company.

true and fair view
A legal concept, but a court will usually look to compliance with generally accepted accounting practice, particularly accounting standards, in force at the time the accounts were prepared as evidence that a true and fair view has been given.

The interaction of the law and accounting standards is an important issue in financial reporting and, over the years, the authorities have obtained a series of legal opinions on the topic. These can be found on the FRC website. The key principles in relation to 'true and fair', which are effectively reproduced in IFRS Standards and UK accounting standards, are:

- Compliance with a coherent set of accounting standards will usually be expected to give a true and fair view.
- Application of accounting standards must not be mechanical and judgement has to be used to determine the best method of application.
- The information given must not be misleading and it should be free from material error or bias (although it cannot be completely accurate due to the extent of estimation involved).
- Where applying an accounting standard would give insufficient disclosure to understand the items in question, more disclosure must be given.
- Where applying an accounting standard would not give a true and fair view, the standard should not be followed (called the 'true and fair override') but full disclosure is given of what would have happened if the standard were applied.
- The use of the override is effectively limited to circumstances in which the standard did not contemplate the situation in question.

Test yourself 1.1

Go to the FRC website and, under the heading 'true and fair', read through the legal opinions there on accounting standards and true and fair. What do you think directors of a company should consider when assessing whether the company's accounts are true and fair?

2.8 Accounting standards and the law

Although some of the content of accounts is governed by law, in the UK (as in other countries) the prevailing view is that the law is not the right way to deal with the main questions of what is presented in accounts because it is too inflexible and takes too long to change. Over time, the core responsibility for this has devolved to accounting standards, which used to be produced by the accounting profession but now are generally produced by independent private sector bodies like the UK's FRC. These bodies are given authority by legislation to set standards.

Accounting standards cover the accounting treatment of balance sheet items, such as assets and liabilities, and profit and loss items such as revenue and expenses. The application of standards helps to ensure that financial information is reported consistently and objectively to enable investors, analysts, regulators and other stakeholders to make decisions based on comparable and reliable information.

The CA2006 acknowledges that companies should follow accounting standards, and has rules specifying which standards they should follow. The Act states that companies must either prepare accounts:

- under IFRS Standards as adopted for use in the EU, in which case they will be 'IAS Standards companies' under the Act; or
- under UK accounting standards and more detailed legal requirements, in which case they will be 'Companies Act companies'.

In the UK, as discussed further in Section 2, listed companies and companies on AIM must follow IFRS Standards in their group accounts, but other companies and groups have a choice between IFRS Standards and UK accounting standards (discussed in Section 3). Companies that are using IFRS Standards do not have to follow the detailed requirements of the regulations to the CA2006 where they apply to the financial statements. But they still have to follow many of the requirements that apply to reports that accompany the financial statements, such as the Directors' Report (see 'Contents of the Annual Report and Accounts' above).

Figure 1.2: Accounting frameworks available in the UK

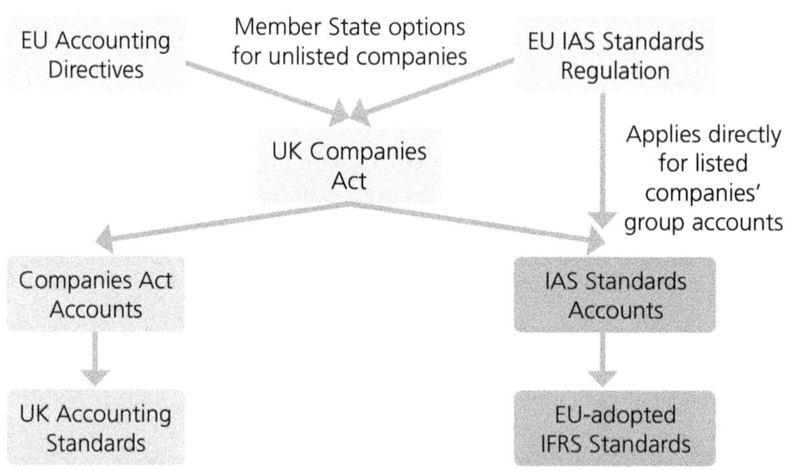

IAS = International Accounting Standards
IFRS = International Financial Reporting Standards

The main benefits of having accounting standards may be summarised as follows:

- reduced disparity and variations in accounting treatment from one reporting entity to another, and from one reporting period to another, enabling greater comparability;
- a more standardised approach, with less scope for interpretations and subjectivity;
- capacity to change to deal with urgent issues or new ways of doing business, where legal requirements may be insufficiently flexible;
- less scope for disguising liabilities and holding them off balance sheet, or using liabilities to manage earnings from year to year;
- less scope for manipulating asset valuations;
- users of accounts, such as analysts, investors and regulators, can place greater reliance on the financial statements knowing that recognised accounting standards have been applied.

Test yourself 1.2

List some of the merits of accounting standards.

3. International Financial Reporting Standards

Over the last 20 years or so it has become clear that trade globalisation has meant that it is unhelpful to have the accounts of multinational companies prepared under the local rules of their home country. The answer to this has been to develop international accounting standards, although it is up to each country whether they allow their companies to use those standards and, if they do, whether use is restricted, for example to the biggest listed companies. Those choices often reflect a country's trading history and views on global trade.

3.1 The International Accounting Standards Board

IFRS Standards are issued by the IASB. The IASB is a private sector body whose aim is to produce high quality accounting standards for use on a global basis, in the public interest.

The standards comprise:

- International Financial Reporting Standards (IFRS);
- International Accounting Standards (IAS) issued by the IASB's predecessor, the International Accounting Standards Committee (IASC); and
- **Accounting Interpretations**.

accounting interpretations
Statements issued by standard setters (e.g. IASB) to clarify how standards should be applied. Interpretations are typically published to address issues arising that were not foreseen when the standards were first set.

IFRS Standards are developed through agenda consultations to determine which areas of accounting need improvement. The IASB will then issue Discussion Papers and Exposure Drafts on a particular issue for consultation on an international basis, which leads to a final IFRS standard being published. For major subjects, the development of a final standard can take many years. The standard will usually have an implementation date some time away, to give companies affected time to prepare for its implementation.

generally accepted accounting practice or principles (GAAP)
A common set of accounting standards regulatory rules and widely-followed practices used for the preparation and presentation of an entity's financial statements.

IFRS offers a single set of globally accepted accounting standards which has now been adopted by around 130 countries around the world to replace or augment their local **Generally Accepted Accounting Practice or Principles (GAAP)**, with the notable exception of the US. In addition, Japan and India are moving only slowly towards IFRS Standards adoption. Until these important global economies adopt IFRS Standards, there will be reporting variations and disparity arising between those entities reporting under IFRS Standards and those reporting under their national standards.

3.2 The US and IFRS Standards

The US is still to make any formal recommendations on the adoption of IFRS Standards in place of US GAAP. The standard setter in the US is the Financial Accounting Standards Board (FASB), which sets accounting standards by permission of the US Securities and Exchange Commission (SEC).

The FASB and the IASB have worked jointly towards convergence of accounting standards for some years (although with mixed results), with the stated goal of achieving a single set of high-quality global accounting standards. The US SEC was expected to make a decision on the adoption of IFRS Standards by the end of 2012 but it now appears unlikely that there will be a wholesale move to adopt IFRS Standards in the US in the foreseeable future. At least part of the problem is caused by the different regulatory approach to financial reporting in the US, which has a system that is much more rules-based due to the litigious nature of its stock markets and a different legal framework for listed companies. Nevertheless, in 2007 the SEC withdrew, for non-US companies registered in the US and reporting under IFRS Standards, the requirement to reconcile their financial statements with US GAAP, a considerable benefit for foreign companies listing shares on the US markets.

The IASB and the FASB have made some progress on convergence since they signed a Memorandum of Understanding in 2006, although further convergence projects look unlikely. A few standards have been produced that are fully or almost fully converged, including one on revenue recognition (see Chapter 4). The IASB and FASB have, however, differences of opinion on certain issues, particularly on accounting for financial instruments and insurance contracts, and continuing disagreement may affect the US decision on whether to adopt IFRS Standards.

3.3 The EU and IFRS

As part of the drive to have a single market within the EU, the EU introduced the IAS Regulation in 2002 and it came into force in 2005. All companies with securities traded on an EU-regulated market must follow IFRS Standards (following formal adoption into EU law) in their group accounts. Member States may also require, permit or bar other companies from using IFRS Standards in their group or individual accounts and practice varies across member states, often depending on issues around tax or the legal basis for dividend payments.

As already noted, before any EU company can apply a standard produced by the IASB, it must first be legally endorsed for use in the EU, a formal mechanism in which the European Commission's Accounting Regulatory Committee (ARC) is advised by the European Financial Reporting Advisory Board (EFRAG). With one minor exception, all IFRS Standards have been adopted for use in the EU.

3.4 The UK and IFRS Standards

In the UK, as well as IFRS Standards applying to fully listed companies as required through the EU IAS Regulation, the Alternative Investment Market (AIM) has required IFRS Standards to be applied in group accounts since 2007.

Companies which are not listed have the option to report either under IFRS Standards or under UK GAAP. UK GAAP, which is discussed in Section 3, has become much more aligned with IFRS, but simplified to provide a more proportionate regime for unlisted companies. The FRC updates UK GAAP to reflect changes in IFRS Standards, but this is usually only every three years, to give a more stable regime. Although company law has some restrictions, UK companies have considerable choice in whether to follow IFRS Standards or UK GAAP and, within UK GAAP, whether to follow a reduced disclosure regime.

3.5 Benefits and drawbacks of one set of global standards

The main benefits of having one set of global financial reporting standards can be summarised as follows:

- Improve the standard of financial reporting worldwide where international standards aim to be high quality.
- Improve comparability of financial statements for investors who wish to invest across the world.
- Provide easier access to capital markets and enhanced globalisation of business and investment.
- Give a common global accounting framework based on a flexible, principles-based approach.
- Reduce training costs for accountants and analysts.
- Reduce costs for multinational companies as only one global reporting standard and so there is no need to reconcile local GAAPs to IFRS Standards.

There are also arguments against having one set of standards:

- One size does not fit all, particularly where countries have different histories of financial reporting.
- Cost/benefit rules suitable for the biggest companies may not be suitable for the smallest.

- Local practices continue to operate because of the flexibility of IFRS Standards, so full convergence to an international norm is not achieved.
- There is still scope to deviate from IFRS Standards (although only where the financial statements would otherwise be misleading to users), which means there can never be complete harmonisation anyway.
- The effects of convergence are not just accounting related, for example the SEC in the US is concerned that the adoption of IFRS Standards will mean an overhaul of their overall regulatory package.

Test yourself 1.3

What are the merits of having one set of global accounting standards?

4. UK Generally Accepted Accounting Practice (GAAP)

As we have seen, GAAP encompasses accounting standards, legal and other regulatory requirements, as well as practices that are accepted by custom and usage. These standards, rules and other practices are country-specific and vary from one jurisdiction to another. Examples are US GAAP and of course UK GAAP, which is used by many UK companies for financial reporting purposes. GAAP is thus not set through accounting standards in isolation. Companies must also adhere to relevant stock exchange listing requirements and any statutory requirements such as the UK CA2006, as well as widely-followed local practices that allow comparison with peer companies.

4.1 UK accounting standards

Financial Reporting Council (FRC)
The UK's independent regulator responsible for promoting high quality corporate governance and reporting to foster investment. It also sets accounting and auditing standards for the UK.

The **Financial Reporting Council (FRC)** is the standard-setting body in the UK responsible for issuing Financial Reporting Standards (FRS). In 2015 a new regime of accounting standards was introduced by the FRC, modelled on a simplified version of IFRS Standards.

Like IFRS, UK accounting standards are developed through a process which involves Discussion Papers and Financial Reporting Exposure Drafts (FREDs), issued by the FRC as a form of consultation on newly proposed concepts and standards. Once the consultation period in respect of a FRED is over, the issues raised by respondents need to be resolved before the draft standard is finalised and issued as an FRS or a modification to an FRS.

UK GAAP, like IFRS, is a principles-based approach to financial reporting. In some countries the standards are based on more detailed and rigid rules, although as countries are gradually working on convergence of accounting standards (towards a global set of accounting standards), the principles-based approach of IFRS is becoming more widely adopted.

Following a series of consultations over a 10-year period, the FRC issued a new set of standards to be applied in the UK from 2015 onwards. The new regime replaced a set of standards which over time had become inconsistent, unduly complex in places and only partly convergent with international standards. The new standards were subsequently revised to deal with changes to the rules in company law arising from a new EU Accounting Directive.

From the beginning of 2016 onwards, the new standards are as follows:

- FRS 100 – Application of Financial Reporting Requirements (September 2015)
- FRS 101 – Reduced Disclosure Framework (September 2015)
- FRS 102 – The Financial Reporting Standard Applicable in the UK and Republic of Ireland (September 2015)
- FRS 103 – Insurance Contracts (March 2014)
- FRS 104 – Interim Financial Reporting (March 2015)
- FRS 105 – The Financial Reporting Standard Applicable to the Micro-entities Regime (May 2016).

Note that the most recent versions of the standards at the time of writing are shown by the dates in brackets. Always check for updates and amendments on the FRC website to ensure you have the most recent version of any particular standard or the one that is appropriate for the accounts you are looking at.

FRS 100 gives an overview of the regime and outlines which companies can follow which standard. FRS 101 allows companies within a group that follows IFRS Standards in its group accounts to use identical standards, i.e. IFRS Standards, but with a much lower disclosure burden in the notes to the accounts.

The main standard is FRS 102, which gives guidance on how to treat all the usual major items in accounts on a subject basis by chapter. It is based on a version of IFRS Standards that has been produced to be applied to unlisted companies, called the IFRS Standards for SMEs, adjusted to deal with UK legal issues and to make certain aspects more appropriate for UK companies. Although it is based on IFRS Standards, it is much simpler and shorter than the main IFRS Standards with fewer disclosures. Most UK unlisted groups and companies will use this standard. In a group, there is a reduced disclosure regime for individual company accounts too, although the overall disclosure burden of FRS 102 is much lower than full IFRS Standards anyway.

FRS 103 is only applicable to those writing insurance contracts, a specialised area of accounting not covered in this text. Only listed companies have to issue interim or half-yearly accounts. FRS 104 therefore has limited application to those companies that have to prepare interim financial statements but are using UK GAAP, i.e. listed companies that do not prepare group accounts and are therefore not caught by the mandatory application of IFRS Standards and have chosen to use UK GAAP. FRS 105 has been designed to be applied to micro companies and other entities (such as limited liability partnerships, see Chapter 10) of a similar size and reflects the very limited requirements of the law as to preparation and publication of micro-entity accounts.

Test yourself 1.4

Describe the five UK accounting standards.

For groups there is a wide variety of choice as to which accounting standards to apply to each subsidiary. The law restricts the choice between IFRS Standards and UK GAAP: there should be consistency between the subsidiaries of a group unless the directors have good reason to allow different companies to follow different rules. However, this restriction does not apply to the different choices within UK GAAP, so for example the following would be possible:

Figure 1.3: Example of choices of GAAP within a group

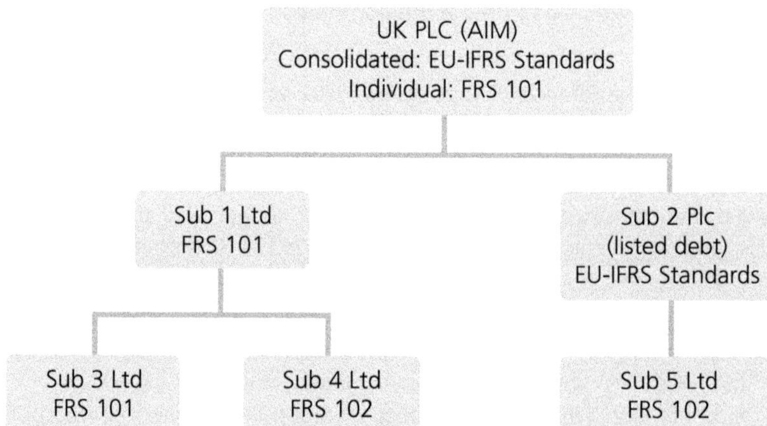

Table 1.3 shows how UK accounting standards may be applied.

Table 1.3: Extent of choice

Reporting entity	Permitted to use			
Groups listed on regulated markets and AIM	EU-adopted IFRS Standards			
Other groups (not small or micro)	EU-adopted IFRS Standards	FRS 102		
Qualifying entities (parent or subs in a group)	EU-adopted IFRS Standards	FRS 102	FRS 101 reduced disclosures	FRS 102 reduced disclosures
Small companies (per CA 2006)	EU-adopted IFRS Standards	FRS 102	Section 1A FRS 102 (modifications for small companies)	
Micro entities (per CA 2006)	EU-adopted IFRS Standards	FRS 102	Section 1A FRS 102 (modifications for small companies)	FRS 105 micro entities

4.2 Accounting standards in offshore centres

In most offshore centres IFRS Standards are permitted, but other GAAPs are usually allowed and used, particularly those with international credibility, including UK GAAP and US GAAP. For companies registered in offshore centres that wish to list securities in the EU, under the relevant EU directives they must prepare accounts under IFRS Standards or a GAAP that is deemed equivalent to IFRS Standards. Those GAAPs deemed equivalent on a permanent basis are the GAAPs of Canada, China, Japan, South Korea and the US (apart from the US, they are deemed equivalent because they are converged with or are in the process of converging with IFRS Standards). Indian GAAP has been given temporary equivalence status, which has been renewed several times, latterly until 2017, but delays in convergence to IFRS Standards mean that permanent equivalence status is yet to be given.

4.3 Accounting standards covered in this text

In the rest of this text we will focus on the IFRS Standards, but a cross reference will be included to the relevant part of the main UK standard, FRS 102, with a note about any major differences between the standards.

Chapter summary

- Company law sets the framework for the rules over preparation of accounts. Part 15 of the CA2006 covers financial reporting requirements, along with related regulations. Some requirements vary depending on whether a company is public or private, or whether it is micro, small, medium-sized or large.
- The law and other regulatory requirements govern what a company has to put in its ARA. The law also deals with when and how companies prepare accounts and deals with some issues relating to content, but accounting standards deal with the detail of how items are portrayed in accounts.
- The application of a set of accounting standards helps to ensure financial information is reported consistently and objectively to enable stakeholders to make decisions based on comparable and reliable information.
- The EU requires companies with securities traded on an EU-regulated market to use IFRS Standards in their group accounts. In the UK, companies which are not listed have the option to report either under IFRS Standards or under UK GAAP. The FRC is the standard-setting body in the UK responsible for issuing FRSs. UK accounting standards, like IFRS, follow a principles-based approach to financial reporting.
- UK GAAP is based on a simplified version of IFRS Standards, with a proportionate regime depending on the size and nature of each company. There are reduced disclosure frameworks for the individual accounts of companies within groups.
- Offshore financial centres permit the use of IFRS Standards but also other internationally-recognised GAAPs, including US and Canadian GAAPs. If companies wish to list their shares or debt in the EU, they must use IFRS Standards or an approved equivalent GAAP.

Chapter two
The conceptual framework

List of topics

1. Introduction

In this chapter we will look at the conceptual basis which underpins the international accounting framework. The IASB's Conceptual Framework for Financial Reporting, currently being comprehensively rewritten and in Exposure Draft at the time of publication, is a guide to standard setters when setting standards, preparers when they are making decisions about preparation and others with an interest in financial reporting. It contains important principles, concepts and definitions which the standard setter uses when developing accounting standards and which others use when determining how to deal with reporting problems.

An overview of the content of the IASB's Conceptual Framework as it currently stands in amended form is given. This includes outlines of the objective of financial reporting and the important concepts that are applied – relevance, faithful representation, comparability, verifiability, understandability and timeliness – when making key decisions about financial statement information.

The definitions of the key elements of financial statements – assets, liabilities, equity, income and expenses – are discussed and how recognition, measurement, presentation and disclosure principles are applied to them.

2. The need for a conceptual framework

Even though standard-setting is designed to deal with specific practical issues in accounting, standard setters would not write the most effective standards in a vacuum. In order to be coherent and consistent, it is considered useful to have a conceptual framework which underpins the standard setter's work.

UK GAAP equivalent
Section 2 of FRS 102 deals with pervasive concepts, covering similar issues to the Conceptual Framework.

As a major project, the IASB is currently rewriting and updating its conceptual framework, which has been in existence since the 1970s. Following earlier consultations, a comprehensive Exposure Draft, the Conceptual Framework for Financial Reporting (the 'Conceptual Framework') was published in May 2015. The IASB has said it wishes to complete the project by the end of 2016. As the UK's financial reporting standards are now based on a modified version of IFRS Standards, the UK FRC has a direct interest in the outcome of the conceptual framework project.

The overall purpose of the Conceptual Framework is:

1. to assist the IASB to develop standards that are based on consistent concepts;
2. to assist preparers to develop consistent accounting policies when no standard applies to a particular transaction or event; and
3. to assist all parties to understand and interpret the standards.

It is important to understand that the Conceptual Framework is not a standard and therefore if it is not consistent with existing standards when finalised, the standards will prevail. However, the Conceptual Framework is referred to by IAS 8 'Accounting Policies, Changes in Accounting Estimates and Errors' (see Chapter 3): where a particular accounting issue is not covered by an IFRS Standards, a preparing entity can look to local accounting rules if they are consistent with IFRS Standards, and also to the Conceptual Framework document for guidance. There are differing opinions about the balance between the first two purposes above, resulting in different views as to how the Conceptual Framework should be drafted in its final form.

The draft Conceptual Framework has the following Chapters:

- The objective of general purpose financial reporting.
- Qualitative characteristics of useful financial information.
- Financial statements and the reporting entity.
- The elements of financial statements.
- Recognition and derecognition.
- Measurement.
- Presentation and disclosure.
- Concepts of capital and capital maintenance.

Each of these chapters (except the last, which is beyond the scope of this text) are summarised on the next page. Together they give an important overview of how the standard setter views financial reporting and indicates the IASB's approach to setting standards. First, however, it is worth noting that there are pros and cons to having a conceptual framework.

2.1 Advantages of a conceptual framework

- A principles-based approach means an overall reduction in the number of standards required.
- It sets out the objectives of financial reporting so overall aims can be agreed.
- It describes the qualitative characteristics of meaningful information so users know what to expect.
- It can lead to greater alignment of accounting standards and consistency of approach.
- It helps users and preparers of accounts determine how items such as assets and revenue should be recognised.
- It can deal with overarching concepts, such as those on capital and capital maintenance, which could not be appropriately dealt with at standards level.

2.2 Disadvantages of a conceptual framework

- A conceptual framework may not cover all possible transactions and so gaps may still exist in the rules.
- The conceptual framework may diverge from past or future standards, which can cause confusion as to which is right or more important.
- What may be theoretically correct in the conceptual framework may not be capable of practical application at an accounting standards level, or is too costly for preparers to implement.
- If the conceptual framework focuses on one user group, such as investors, the needs of other stakeholders may not be addressed.

3. The objective of general purpose financial statements

general purpose financial reports
A particular form of general purpose financial report that provides information (about the reporting entity's assets, liabilities, equity, income and expenses) that is useful to the primary users of those statements in assessing the prospects for future net cash inflows to the entity and in assessing management's stewardship of the entity's resources.

The objective of **general purpose financial reports** is to provide financial information about the reporting entity that is useful to existing and potential investors, lenders and other creditors (users of financial statements) in making decisions about providing resources to the entity.

The IASB has made clear that this objective also encompasses helping investors in their assessment of management's stewardship of the entity's resources. This follows demands from commentators that focusing only on future cash flows did not cover all the main purposes of financial statements. Investors make decisions to buy or sell shares based on financial statements, but they also decide whether to retain management or vote for their removal.

Investors and creditors are the main providers of risk capital to businesses and yet they often cannot demand separate, bespoke information. They therefore rely on general purpose financial statements for information and they are treated as the primary users. The IASB points out the need to focus on one primary group of stakeholders with coherent needs. So although the same information will be helpful to other stakeholders, such as employees of the entity, where there are conflicting needs it is those of investors and creditors which will prevail.

In spite of the importance of financial statements, the IASB warns that there are inherent limitations to them. Investors and other users cannot gain all the information they need from financial statements and will need many other sources of information in order to make decisions about the entity.

Test yourself 2.1

What else would investors want to look at, as well as the financial statements of an entity, before making an investment decision about it?

The rest of this part of the Conceptual Framework describes in general terms how financial statements portray resources controlled by the entity, claims upon those resources by creditors or shareholders, changes in those resources and financial performance over time.

4. Qualitative characteristics of useful financial information

The Conceptual Framework has a series of concepts which are important to financial reporting and these are divided into fundamental qualitative concepts and enhancing qualitative concepts:

- Fundamental qualitative concepts–
  - relevance
  - faithful representation
- Enhancing qualitative characteristics–
  - comparability
  - verifiability
  - timeliness
  - understandability.

relevant financial information
Financial information that is capable of making a difference in the decisions made by users.

faithful representation
A faithful representation provides information about the substance of an economic phenomenon instead of merely providing information about its legal form. A perfectly faithful representation would be complete, neutral and free from error.

4.1 Fundamental qualitative concepts

If financial information is to be useful, it must be **relevant** and **faithfully represent** what it purports to represent.

material
Information whose omission or misstatement could influence decisions that the primary users of general purpose financial reports make on the basis of financial information about a specific reporting entity.

Stakeholders require financial statements to be relevant to the decisions they have to make. In determining what is relevant to users, preparers of accounts should consider whether information is **material** and the extent to which reliable information may be omitted. Information may be relevant simply because of its magnitude or because its omission from the financial statements could affect decision making. We will look at materiality again in Chapter 3.

Financial information is capable of making a difference in decision making if it has predictive value, confirmatory value or both. Predictive value and confirmatory value are interrelated in that the same information can do both: the IASB gives the example of the revenue for a company for a particular year (see Chapter 4), which can be used to confirm previous predictions about revenue for the period, as well as being used to predict next year's revenue.

The issue of faithful representation is related to the idea of 'substance over form'; to portray a true economic position, it may be necessary to override the legal form of a transaction. Leases are a good example, as we will see in Chapter 6, where the legal owner of an asset leases it to another entity and that entity records the asset as its own, even though it is not the legal owner, as it will receive most of the benefits of ownership, but also carries most of the risk, for example in relation to obsolescence of the asset. Without the concept of substance over form, accounts could be very misleading in terms of the real economic situation of the entity.

Faithful representation requires information to meet three criteria:

- Complete – all information that users need to understand the item is given;
- Neutral – there is no bias in the selection or presentation of information; and
- Free from error – there are no omissions and no errors in the process to produce the information, although this does not mean the information is necessarily completely accurate as it contains many estimates.

Test yourself 2.2

What does 'free from error' mean?

prudence
The exercise of caution when making judgements under conditions of uncertainty.

There is some controversy over the fact that the IASB has removed **prudence** as a fundamental concept, although the Framework does state that prudence supports neutrality by ensuring that assets and income are not overstated and liabilities and expenses are not understated. However, the IASB makes the point that the reverse would also not be neutral (i.e. assets and income understated and liabilities and expenses overstated) where this would lead to misleading reporting in future periods.

Test yourself 2.3

1 **Under the IASB's Conceptual Framework, what are the two fundamental qualitative characteristics of financial statements?**

2 **Why would the overstatement of liabilities not be prudent?**

4.2 Enhancing qualitative characteristics

Information that is relevant and faithfully represented can be enhanced by application of other characteristics:

Comparability means that financial statements should be comparable with prior year financial statements and with financial statements of similar entities in the same industry sector to enable users of financial statements to make informed decisions. If financial statements lack this attribute, analysts will be less equipped to assess trends and financial ratios. Not all financial statements will be easily comparable but the basic accounting concepts and policies employed often coalesce around industry norms. This enables users to see and evaluate differences within any one reporting period or over several reporting periods, whether comparing an entity's own figures over time or benchmarking against similar businesses in the same industry sector. If a reporting entity considers it is justified in changing an accounting policy from one year to the next then it should ensure that the prior year's figures are restated to enable users to have a like-for-like prior year comparative when assessing performance and changes in the financial position. We will examine this in more detail in Chapter 4.

comparability
Enables users to identify and understand similarities in, and differences among, items.

Verifiability enables different knowledgeable and independent observers to reach consensus on the treatment of an item, although complete agreement is unlikely ever to be possible.

Verifiability is not the same as being auditable, i.e. capable of being subject to audit checking, but it has similarities in the sense that if something is not verifiable, it is unlikely to be auditable and hence its reliability and usefulness is diminished.

verifiability
Enables different knowledgeable and independent observers to reach consensus, although not necessarily complete agreement, that a particular depiction is a faithful representation.

Timeliness is important as information needs to be timely to be capable of influencing the decisions of users of the accounts. Information may lose its relevance if it is not reported in a timely manner. The older the information is, the less likely it is to influence decision-making by users.

timeliness
Information is timely that is available to decision-makers in time to be capable of influencing their decisions.

Understandability is also very important as financial statements can be so complex that even accountants and other users with a good knowledge of accounts struggle to understand them. Some financial transactions, however, are inherently complex and difficult to understand, but to omit such information would not give a fair representation of the financial statements. It is therefore important that the format and layout of the financial statements, the accounting policies applied, the terminology used and other statements made within the financial statements are clear and concise. All material information should be complete and presented in a way that ensures users can understand the entity's results.

understandability
Financial information is understandable that is classified, characterised and presented clearly and concisely.

The Framework also states that there is a pervasive constraint on the information that can be provided by financial reporting, which is cost, i.e. costs need to be justified by the benefits of reporting the information. Most would interpret cost here as the cost to the entity of providing the information; however the IASB makes clear in the Framework that the entity must also consider the cost to the user of finding necessary information if the entity itself does not provide it.

Test yourself 2.4

Under the IASB's Conceptual Framework, what are the four enhancing qualitative characteristics of financial statements?

Test yourself 2.5

What are the costs of producing financial statements in your own organisation?

5. Financial information and the reporting entity

This part of the Conceptual Framework deals with the role of financial reporting, to portray the economic resources controlled by the entity, the claims upon it, transactions it undertakes and other events that cause changes to resources and claims. Importantly, there is an underlying assumption that the entity is a **going concern**.

going concern
An entity should prepare its financial statements on a going concern basis, unless (i) the entity is being liquidated or has ceased trading, or (ii) the directors have no realistic alternative but to liquidate the entity or to cease trading, in which circumstances the entity may, if appropriate, prepare its financial statements on a basis other than that of a going concern.

It is quite rare to see accounts prepared on anything other than a going concern basis, because usually once a company is not a going concern it has ceased trading and may be in the process of being liquidated. If such accounts are prepared, they will be different from going concern accounts because:

- All long-term assets are shown as current assets and are valued at the lower of cost and net realisable value (i.e. estimated selling price less costs to sell).
- Any assets with no resale value are written off.
- Long-term liabilities are taken to current liabilities and any costs of early settlement are recognised.
- Any other costs associated with winding up the business are recognised as a liability, but only if an obligation exists at the balance sheet date.

To see a set of non-going concern accounts, search the internet for the accounts of African Eagle Resources plc, a company that was listed on the UK's Alternative Investment Market (AIM), for the year ended 31 December 2012.

The company is now in administration.

More importantly, however, accounting standards require a lot of disclosure where a company is still a going concern, but there are uncertainties about whether it will be able to continue to trade, for example if it relies on bank funding and the bank may be unwilling to renew overdraft facilities. The disclosures are designed to act as a warning sign that the going concern basis may not be appropriate in the future, even if it is now.

This section of the Conceptual Framework then deals with what any reporting entity should report, that is the things that are within the reporting boundary. Broadly speaking, a reporting entity accounts for things that it controls either directly or indirectly. We will consider this question in more detail in Chapter 7, but the concept of **control** is very important in accounting standards as it determines the reporting boundary and the definition of an asset, which we will consider in the next section.

control
The present ability to direct the use of an economic resource and obtain the economic benefits that flow from it.

6. The elements of financial statements

This section of the Conceptual Framework is one of the most important as it defines the building blocks from which the financial statements are constructed.

6.1 Definitions of the elements

The focus here is on the main statements, that is the Statement of Financial Position (or Balance Sheet), and the Statement of Financial Performance, also called the Profit and Loss Account or Income Statement (although as we will see in Chapter 3, it is possible to have more than one Statement of Financial Performance).

Figure 2.1: Elements of financial statements

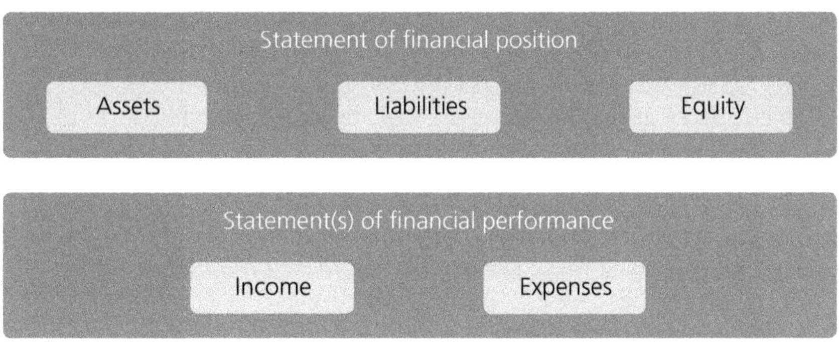

The definitions proposed in the new Conceptual Framework are refinements of those in the existing version and essentially are constructed in the same way: the definitions of an asset and a liability drive the definitions of the other elements.

Table 2.1: Conceptual Framework definitions

Element	Definition
An asset	An asset is a present economic resource controlled by the entity as a result of past events. An economic resource is a right that has the potential to produce economic benefits.
A liability	A liability is a present obligation of the entity to transfer an economic resource as a result of past events.
Equity	Equity is the residual interest in the assets of the entity after deducting all its liabilities.
Income	Income is increases in assets or decreases in liabilities that result in increases in equity, other than those relating to contributions from holders of equity claims.
Expenses	Expenses are decreases in assets or increases in liabilities that result in decreases in equity, other than those relating to distributions to holders of equity claims.

The Conceptual Framework describes various parts of these definitions in more detail. As already noted, the issue of control in relation to assets is important. And for both assets and liabilities, a past event is required to create the asset or the liability, so future events which may lead to assets or liabilities arising cannot be anticipated. As we will see in Chapter 6, this is particularly important in relation to the definition of a liability.

Equity is the residual interest in the assets of an entity once its liabilities have been deducted as shown in the accounts. Income and expenses are defined in relation to changes in assets and liabilities over time. It follows from the definitions of income and expenses that transactions with equity holders in their capacity as such do not meet the definition of income or expenses. Contributions of share capital from and share buybacks and distributions to equity shareholders are therefore not income and expenses and are instead shown separately in a Statement of Changes in Equity. For an individual company, the reserves that make up the total balance on equity will usually be required by law, and it is these that determine which elements of equity must be retained as permanent capital and which can be distributed to shareholders.

6.2 Substance over form

Many business transactions are driven by contracts and the Conceptual Framework discusses the substance of contractual rights and contractual obligations. It notes that these must be analysed carefully to ensure that their economic substance is properly understood. Although in many cases the substance will be clear, there will be circumstances where things will not be so straightforward:

1. It may be necessary to consider linked contracts if these are undertaken in conjunction with each other in order to achieve an overall commercial effect. For example, a sale of goods to a customer before the year end would be linked with a concurrent agreement to repurchase those goods after the year end. This is known as window dressing: the sale is an artificial one and should not be recorded as such because of the agreement to repurchase.
2. Contractual terms which have no commercial substance and so have no real impact on the transaction's economic effect, should be disregarded, for example if it is impossible for a party to take advantage of any particular term. An option for a company to purchase shares to give it control of another company, for example, would only be considered to have commercial substance if the company could afford to fund the purchase.
3. Implied terms should be considered as well as explicit terms, for example if a statutory warranty obligation is imposed. In many countries, for example, sales of goods to the public have statutory protection in terms of the goods being returnable if faulty.

7. Recognition and derecognition

This part of the Conceptual Framework deals with when an item should appear in the financial statements, i.e. when it should be recognised, and it should be removed, or derecognised.

Most of the discussion in this section of the Conceptual Framework deals with the criteria for **recognition** of all the elements, i.e. assets and liabilities and hence income and expenses, which are considered in the context of the fundamental qualitative characteristics of relevance and faithful representation.

recognition
The process of capturing, for inclusion in the statement of financial position or the statement(s) of financial performance, an item that meets the definition of an element. It involves depicting the item (either alone or as part of a line item) in words and by a monetary amount, and including that amount in totals in the relevant statement.

In relation to relevance, issues discussed include:

1. uncertainty of existence (for example it may not be known whether a liability exists as the facts are not clear);
2. whether items (such as customer relationships) are separable from the rest of the business or not and so should be recognised separately;
3. what the probability is of an inflow or outflow of economic resources (which may be cash or other resources); and
4. the impact of measurement uncertainty (i.e. is there a lot of uncertainty about the value that should be assigned to an item) and whether this detracts from relevance.

Many of these issues are contentious and are dealt with in more detail by individual accounting standards, as we will see in the next few chapters. In particular, when revenue (see Chapter 4) should be recognised as income – when is it actually earned? – and when liabilities (see Chapter 6) should be recognised – when is there a real obligation? – are continuing areas of debate.

Faithful representation regarding recognition has to be considered in the context of how an item is measured and presented, and any disclosures about it, which are considered in the next section. Cost constraints are also considered: sometimes the cost of recognising an item may exceed the benefits to users.

derecognition
The removal of all or a part of a previously recognised asset or liability from an entity's statement of financial position.

The discussion on **derecognition** is almost entirely focused on assets and whether an asset should be taken out of the financial statements in relation to an event subsequent to recognition. In most circumstances it will be obvious to remove an asset, because it has been sold, but other situations can be harder to deal with, particularly if some rights in an asset are retained after a sale, for example rights to a share of any subsequent profit from the asset. The analysis also applies to liabilities, but these tend to be much more straightforward to deal with, as most liabilities are derecognised when they are settled.

Test yourself 2.6

What does 'recognition' mean in the context of financial statements?

historical cost
A measure that provides monetary information about assets, liabilities, income and expenses using information derived from the transaction or event that created them. The historical cost measures of assets or liabilities do not reflect changes in prices. However, they do reflect changes such as consumption or impairment of assets and fulfilment of liabilities.

current value
A measure that provides monetary information about assets, liabilities, income and expenses using information that is updated to reflect conditions at the measurement date.

8. Measurement

Once it has been decided that something must be recognised in the financial statements, the next question is how it should be measured. There is often a choice, particularly in relation to assets, and standard setters and companies need to decide what is most useful in different situations.

We will look at measurement in relation to specific assets in different parts of this text, but broadly the choice is between:

- **historical cost**; and
- **current value**.

There are different subsets of current value, but the main one is **fair value**.

The Conceptual Framework discusses each of the measurement choices and considers when it would be best to use them, referring to the fundamental and enhancing qualitative characteristics discussed above. We will look at these choices as we go through the different parts of the accounts and consider why standard setters and companies make the choices about measurement in different situations.

Test yourself 2.7

What are the differences between historical cost and current value as forms of measurement?

9. Presentation and disclosure

fair value
The price that would be received to sell an asset or paid to transfer a liability in an orderly transaction between market participants at the measurement date.

However items are recognised and measured in financial statements, if they are not presented well or there is insufficient high quality disclosure about them, the financial statements will not be properly understood by users. The Conceptual Framework emphasises that presentation and disclosure are communication tools that are vital to financial reporting.

Efficient and effective communication includes:

1. classifying information in a structured manner that reports similar items together and reports dissimilar items separately;
2. aggregating information so that it is not obscured by unnecessary detail; and
3. using presentation and disclosure objectives and principles instead of rules that could lead to purely mechanistic compliance.

In relation to point 2 above, there have been complaints over the last few years about the length and detail in annual reports. Investors can find it hard to get to the most important information and there is a general information overload which prevents investors getting the real story about company finances. The UK's FRC is working on this issue, through its 'Clear & Concise Reporting' project, which you can look at on the FRC website.

We will look at how accounting standards deal with presentation in the next chapter. Most accounting standards set specific disclosure requirements for the subject or item they cover, but the point here is that when all the disclosures are brought together in a set of financial statements, they should be presented in a logical and understandable way.

Chapter summary

- The IASB's Conceptual Framework for Financial Reporting is under development and will replace a much older document. The Conceptual Framework helps to guide standard setters in developing new standards or changing old ones, as well as helping preparers of financial statements in deciding the right way to report things.
- The Conceptual Framework is broken down into a series of chapters, covering the overall objectives of financial reporting, the key elements of financial statements, qualitative characteristics of good financial information and how that information should be recognised, measured, presented and disclosed.
- The document also deals with important concepts such as substance over form, prudence and neutrality and going concern.
- The current revision of the Conceptual Framework document is due to be completed in late 2016 or early 2017.

Chapter three
Financial statement presentation

List of topics

1. Introduction
2. Presentation of financial statements
3. Cash flow statements
4. Operating segments
5. Events after the reporting period

1. Introduction

The key requirements governing the presentation of financial statements are explained in this chapter. We will look at the different statements required to make up a complete set of financial statements, the main components of each of the statements, their presentation and structure and what information must accompany them.

The requirement for listed companies to split their results up between operating segments, to give more insight into the make-up of the overall performance of the business, is discussed. Such companies are also required to disclose a key market measure, earnings per share, and the basis for the calculation of the measure is discussed in Chapter 8.

We will also consider how to deal with events that arise after the end of the reporting period, distinguishing those which give rise to adjustments to the financial statements compared to those which only warrant disclosure of additional information. This is an important issue and many struggle to understand the important principle of cut-off at the year end date.

2. Presentation of financial statements

2.1 The basic business model and the purpose of financial statements

Businesses are set up primarily to make a profit. But how does that actually work in practice? This is a representation of how a business operates and we will then go on to look at how this is portrayed in financial reporting:

Figure 3.1: A business model

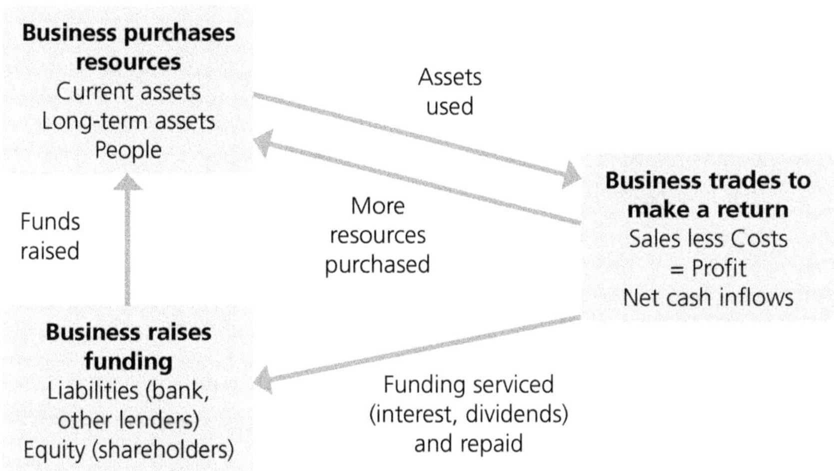

A business raises funds from its owners (in the form of equity) and if necessary debt from banks and others. If the business is carried out through a company (rather than an unincorporated sole trader or partnership (see Chapter 10)), the equity is usually in the form of shares; anyone lending to the business will usually have the right to be paid back before the equity holders and so the equity holders carry the ultimate risk of the business's failure. The business uses the funds to purchase resources to run the business, including tangible and intangible assets, but also to employ people to work in it. Employees are an asset in the broadest sense of the word, but they are not classed as assets for accounting purposes as the business does not control or own them.

The business then carries out the activity that generates profits (and cash flows). These are then used to (1) service debt and equity holders by paying them interest and dividends and ultimately repay them, and (2) reinvest in the business to replace assets and, where the business is successful, to grow the business.

Financial statements are designed to capture that cycle. They are a structured representation of the financial position (at a particular point in time) and performance (over a period of time) of an entity. The purpose of financial statements is to provide owners and other stakeholders with information on the financial position, financial performance and cash flows of the entity in which they have an interest. As the information reported is a highly-aggregated summary of a substantial number of transactions (depending on the size of the business), it is important that the financial statements are presented in such a manner that they are understandable and comparable with those of other entities.

Financial statements also reflect the stewardship of the management team who run the business and have control of its underlying assets; they are held to account for the use they have made of the resources they have.

As discussed in Chapter 2, financial statements categorise the information presented into the following elements:

- assets
- liabilities
- equity
- income and expenses (including gains and losses)
- other changes in equity (contributions by and distributions to owners)
- cash flows.

A summary of how these elements interact in the different statements required by accounting standards (other than the cash flow statement, discussed in Section 2) are summarised in Figure 3.2.

Figure 3.2: Financial statements

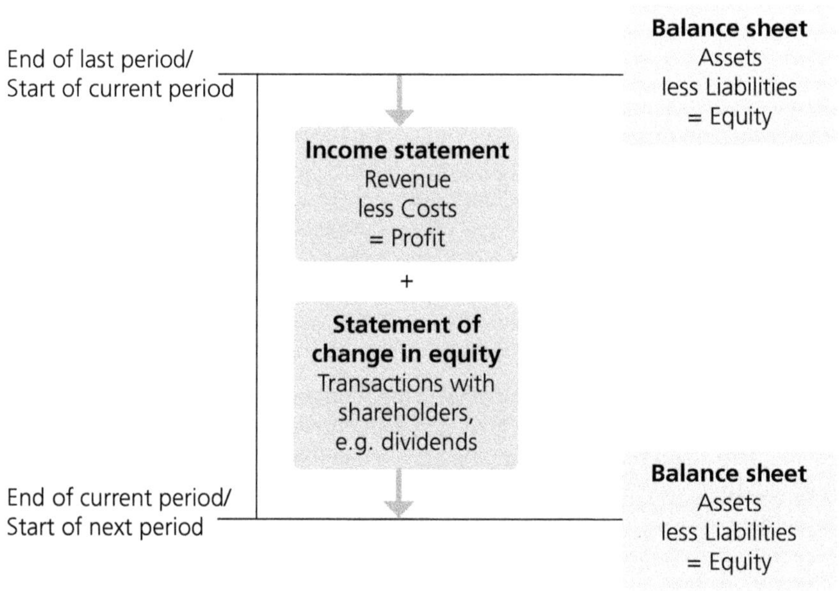

UK GAAP equivalent
Section 3 of FRS 102 deals with presentation of financial statements.

The main standard dealing with this is IAS 1 'Financial Statement Presentation'. IAS 1 is an important standard as it sets the overall objective for the preparation of financial statements, outlines the main statements required and how they are presented, as well as dealing with some important principles that apply across financial reporting.

2.2 Presentation of financial statements under IAS 1

An entity must present a complete set of financial statements (including prior period comparative information) on at least an annual basis. A complete set of financial statements should include the following components which should be given equal prominence within the annual report:

- Statement of financial position (also called a balance sheet) as at the reporting date.
- Statement of comprehensive income for the period (which can be split into two as we will see).
- Statement of changes in equity for the period.
- Cash flow statement.
- Notes (comprising a summary of significant accounting policies and other explanatory notes).

The financial statements should be clearly identified and segregated from other information within the 'annual report and accounts' document. We will use the 2016 Annual Report and Accounts of Marks & Spencer plc (M&S), the clothing and food retailer, to demonstrate each of the statements. The complete document can be found on the M&S website. Note that M&S, like many retailers, report for 52 or 53 weeks ending to the nearest date after 31 March. Most companies report on a calendar year basis, but the CA2006 is flexible in allowing a week's variation round the year end date.

Test yourself 3.1

List the components of a complete set of financial statements as required by IAS 1.

2.3 General features of financial reporting

Fair presentation and compliance with IFRS Standards

fair presentation
In the context of financial statements this means that an entity should adopt appropriate accounting policies and practices to ensure information presented in the financial statements is relevant, reliable, comparable and understandable. Where the adoption of IFRS Standards is insufficient to enable users to understand a specific transaction, additional disclosures should be given to ensure the financial statements give a fair representation of the results, financial position and cash flow.

IAS 1 states that financial statements should present the financial position, financial performance and cash flows of an entity fairly and accurately. This is presumed to be achieved by following the relevant IFRS Standards and ensuring transactions are fairly represented in accordance with the appropriate recognition criteria for assets, liabilities, income and expenses as set out in the IASB's Conceptual Framework.

In the rare circumstances where compliance with IFRS Standards might result in users being misled by the financial statements, departure from IFRS Standards is permitted provided the nature, reasons and impact of the departure is disclosed. There must be good reasons for not following the prescribed rules and departure should only occur where non-departure would conflict with the objectives of financial statements as set out in the Conceptual Framework (see Chapter 2). Even then, full disclosure must be given of the effect that would have been achieved by following accounting standards. Importantly, poor accounting (including selection of inappropriate accounting policies) cannot be rectified by disclosure of any kind of explanatory material.

This is almost identical to the requirement in UK company law to show a true and fair view, discussed in Chapter 1.

Going concern

Financial statements are prepared on a going concern basis unless management either intends to liquidate the entity or to cease trading, or has no realistic alternative but to do so. Where there are material uncertainties which cast significant doubt over the entity's ability to continue to operate in the foreseeable future, substantial disclosures are required so that users are given a clear picture of what future events might threaten the future of the company. See also the discussion in Chapter 2 for further detail.

Accruals basis of accounting

Financial statements are prepared on an accruals basis, except for cash flow information.

Under the accruals basis of accounting, transactions are accounted for when income is earned or expenses are incurred, not when cash changes hands. So in most businesses, when much trading is done on credit rather than for cash, a company will record income before cash is received and will record expenses before cash is paid. The resulting accruals are held in the balance sheet until the cash flows and discharges the debt owed to or from the company.

In Figure 3.3 a typical situation arises around the reporting year end of a company when a customer orders goods and then pays for them later:

Figure 3.3: Accruals example

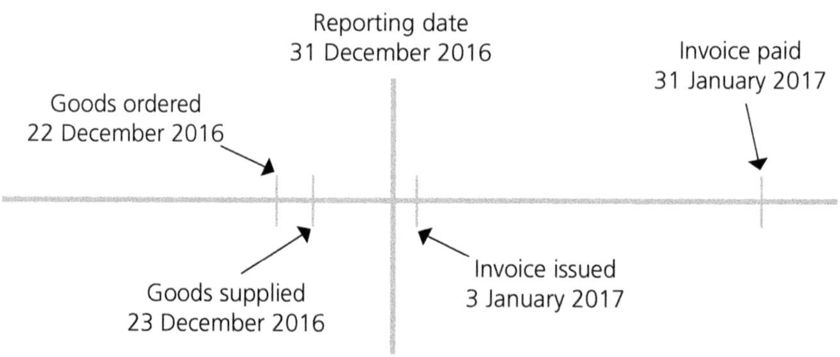

As we will see in Chapter 4, it is at the date the goods are delivered to the customer that the sale is recorded and revenue shown in the accounts. It would be too early to record revenue on the date the goods were ordered as the company has not earned the revenue by delivering the goods to the customer. But it would be too late to record the revenue only when the cash is received as it has been earned much earlier. The date of invoicing is at the choice of the preparer and it would produce random or even biased results if the date of invoicing drove the recognition of revenue.

The accruals concept is the basis for asset and liability recognition, allowing assets to be carried in the balance sheet until they have been consumed, scrapped or sold, and liabilities to be shown as amounts owing until they have been settled. Cash accounting would only show cash coming in and out, which would not indicate the true position of the business.

Materiality and aggregation

As we have already seen in Chapter 2, the concept of materiality is an important one. IAS 1 states that entities should present separately each material class of similar items. Conversely, items that are dissimilar in terms of nature or function should be presented separately unless they are immaterial. Thus, the level of **aggregation** will depend on the extent to which the entity has similar material items to report.

aggregation
The grouping of immaterial assets and presenting the total as a single line item on the face of financial statements or in the notes. Aggregation is not permitted for material items or material classes of similar items.

The concept of materiality is extremely important in financial reporting. Materiality depends on the size and nature of the omission or misstatement judged in the surrounding circumstances. The size or nature of the item, or a combination of both, could be the determining factor. In other words, it is not sufficient to say an item is small enough to be immaterial; it is also important to consider whether the item is significant just because of what it is. The most common examples of reported items that may be small in size terms compared to the company's overall net assets or profit but which are or may be very significant to the reader of the accounts are directors' remuneration (see Chapter 11) and related parties (see Chapter 7). The decision about whether an item is material or not requires the application of judgement, considered from the point of view of the reader of the accounts.

Offsetting

An important principle is that items of revenue and expense or assets and liabilities should not be offset against one another and shown on a net basis unless an accounting standard specifically permits it. A common example of where standards do allow offsetting is valuation allowances on assets. For example, if there is a provision (see Chapters 5 and 6) against a debtor asset because the debt might not be paid in full, that is used to reduce the value of the asset rather than being shown as a separate liability.

This rule is important because the netting off of assets and liabilities can disguise transactions and therefore reduce the ability of stakeholders to get a true picture of the entity's assets and liabilities and assess its future cash flows.

Comparative information

Accounting standards state that prior period comparative information should be provided in the financial statements for all amounts reported, both for amounts reported on the face of the financial statements and in the notes. At least one year of comparative information must be given for each statement and related note. If comparative figures are amended due to a change in accounting policy, then this must also be disclosed.

Test yourself 3.2

1. **How would you account for your company's electricity usage if your last electricity bill was for charges to the end of November but your year end was 31 December?**
2. **To which component of a complete set of financial statements does the accruals basis of accounting not apply?**

2.4 Content of financial statements

An entity should identify the financial statements, to distinguish them from other information published with them. Entities should also include the following information in a prominent manner:

- the name of the reporting entity;
- whether the statements are for the entity or for the group (see Chapter 7);
- the period end date or period covered;
- the **presentation currency**, as defined in IAS 21 (see Chapter 4); and
- the level of rounding used in presenting amounts (e.g. £'000 or £m).

presentation currency
Presentation currency is the currency in which the financial statements are presented.

UK GAAP equivalent
Section 4 of FRS 102 deals with presentation of the statement of financial position.

2.5 Statement of financial position (balance sheet)

The information within an entity's balance sheet is intended to provide users with an understanding of its financial position as at a specific point in time.

The statement of financial position sets out the assets and liabilities of the reporting entity and these are commonly split between current and non-current categories.

The following items are presented on the face of the statement of financial position:

Assets

- property, plant and equipment
- investment property
- intangible assets
- financial assets
- investments accounted for using the equity method
- biological assets
- inventories
- trade and other receivables
- cash and cash equivalents
- assets held for sale
- trade and other payables.

Liabilities

- provisions
- financial liabilities
- liabilities and assets for current tax
- deferred tax liabilities and deferred tax assets
- liabilities included in disposal groups.

Equity

- **non-controlling interest**, presented within equity
- issued capital and reserves attributable to owners of the parent.

non-controlling interest
Equity not attributable directly or indirectly to the parent company.

Additional items and/or subclassifications may be presented, where relevant to the understanding of the financial position.

An entity must present current and non-current assets and liabilities as separate classifications in the statement of financial position, except when a liquidity presentation is more relevant (which is often the case for banks and other financial institutions). Most ordinary trading companies will apply the current/non-current distinction. Whichever method of presentation is adopted, entities must disclose the amount expected to be recovered or settled after more than 12 months for each asset and liability line item that combines amounts expected to be recovered or settled:

- no more than 12 months after the reporting period; and
- more than 12 months after the reporting period.

An entity must classify an asset as a **current asset** when:

- it expects to realise the asset, or intends to sell or consume it, in its normal **operating cycle**;
- it holds the asset primarily for the purpose of trading;
- it expects to realise the asset within 12 months after the reporting period; or
- the asset is cash or a cash equivalent (as defined in IAS 7 – see Section 2) *unless* the asset is restricted from being exchanged or used to settle a liability for at least 12 months after the reporting period.

current assets
are assets that are readily realisable and likely to be held for less than 12 months (e.g. stock, trade debtors, investments traded on a stock exchange, cash at bank and in hand).

operating cycle
The period of time from the acquisition of assets (materials or services) to their realisation in cash receipts. For a retailer this is the length of time stock is held before receiving proceeds from its sale.

The operating cycle of an entity is the time between the acquisition of assets for processing and their realisation in cash or cash equivalents. When the entity's normal operating cycle is not clearly identifiable, it is assumed to be twelve months.

All other assets should be classified as non-current (i.e. tangible and intangible long-term assets). Assets are discussed in more detail in Chapter 5.

Test yourself 3.3

For a retail business, what are the most likely items to be classified as current?

current liabilities
are those liabilities falling due in less than 12 months such as trade creditors or bank overdrafts.

An entity must classify a liability as a **current liability** when:

- it expects to settle the liability in its normal operating cycle;
- it holds the liability primarily for the purpose of trading;
- the liability is due to be settled within 12 months after the reporting period; or
- it does not have an unconditional right to defer settlement of the liability for at least 12 months after the reporting period.

non-current liabilities
are those liabilities falling due in more than 12 months such as longer-term bank loans and other financing arrangements.

loan covenant
A restrictive clause in a loan agreement that is designed to protect the lender's interests by placing constraints on the borrower, such as limiting the borrower's ability to take on more debt without prior consent of the lender; imposing restrictions on leverage; or requiring working capital to be maintained at a minimum level.

All other liabilities are **non-current liabilities**. Liabilities are discussed in more detail in Chapter 6.

Long-term debt under an existing loan facility which is due to expire within 12 months of the year end is treated as current unless an agreement to refinance for a longer period was made before the balance sheet date. However, if the entity breaches a **loan covenant**, resulting in the loan becoming repayable on demand on or prior to the balance sheet date, the liability is treated as a current liability. This is still the case where the lender has agreed, after the balance sheet date (i.e. the date of the statement of financial position), but before the accounts sign-off, not to demand payment as a consequence of the breach. The liability is only classified as non-current if the lender agreed, on or before the balance sheet date, to provide a period of grace lasting 12 months or more from the end of the reporting period, during which the entity may remedy the breach and within which the lender is unable to enforce repayment of the loan.

Below is the consolidated statement of financial position of Marks & Spencer plc for 2016 showing the relevant line items that one would expect to see presented on the face of the statement:

shareholders' funds
are all the assets of a company less all the liabilities. It is the equity amount in a company that is due to the owners (the shareholders).

In relation to the equity or **shareholders' funds** section of the statement of financial position, certain information should be presented in either the statement of financial position, the statement of changes in equity or in the notes. For each class of share capital, the following information should be provided:

- Number of shares authorised for issue, issued and fully paid, and issued but not fully paid.
- Par (i.e. nominal) value per share, or that the shares have no par value.
- Reconciliation of the number of shares outstanding at the start and end of the period.
- Description of any rights, preferences or restrictions attached to the share class.

87
ANNUAL REPORT AND FINANCIAL STATEMENTS 2016

CONSOLIDATED STATEMENT OF FINANCIAL POSITION

	Notes	As at 2 April 2016 £m	As at 28 March 2015 £m
Assets			
Non-current assets			
Intangible assets	14	**802.8**	858.2
Property, plant and equipment	15	**5,027.1**	5,031.1
Investment property		**15.5**	15.6
Investment in joint ventures		**6.9**	12.2
Other financial assets	16	**3.0**	3.0
Retirement benefit asset	11	**851.0**	460.7
Trade and other receivables	17	**234.7**	283.3
Derivative financial instruments	21	**74.0**	75.8
Deferred tax assets	23	**–**	1.2
		7,015.0	6,741.1
Current assets			
Inventories		**799.9**	797.8
Other financial assets	16	**19.1**	11.6
Trade and other receivables	17	**321.1**	321.8
Derivative financial instruments	21	**72.1**	117.9
Current tax assets		**1.6**	–
Cash and cash equivalents	18	**247.6**	205.9
		1,461.4	1,455.0
Total assets		**8,476.4**	8,196.1
Liabilities			
Current liabilities			
Trade and other payables	19	**1,617.7**	1,642.4
Partnership liability to the Marks & Spencer UK Pension Scheme	12	**71.9**	71.9
Borrowings and other financial liabilities	20	**297.5**	279.4
Derivative financial instruments	21	**28.5**	7.7
Provisions	22	**14.0**	46.2
Current tax liabilities		**75.2**	64.0
		2,104.8	2,111.6
Non-current liabilities			
Retirement benefit deficit	11	**26.9**	11.7
Trade and other payables	19	**353.0**	319.7
Partnership liability to the Marks & Spencer UK Pension Scheme	12	**383.8**	441.0
Borrowings and other financial liabilities	20	**1,774.7**	1,745.9
Derivative financial instruments	21	**0.2**	20.0
Provisions	22	**52.0**	32.1
Deferred tax liabilities	23	**337.6**	315.3
		2,928.2	2,885.7
Total liabilities		**5,033.0**	4,997.3
Net assets		**3,443.4**	3,198.8
Equity			
Issued share capital	24	**405.8**	412.0
Share premium account		**411.3**	392.4
Capital redemption reserve		**2,210.5**	2,202.6
Hedging reserve		**32.3**	64.3
Other reserve		**(6,542.2)**	(6,542.2)
Retained earnings		**6,927.5**	6,670.5
Total shareholders' equity		**3,445.2**	3,199.6
Non-controlling interests in equity		**(1.8)**	(0.8)
Total equity		**3,443.4**	3,198.8

The financial statements were approved by the Board and authorised for issue on 24 May 2016. The financial statements also comprise the notes on pages 90 to 125.

Steve Rowe Chief Executive Officer

Helen Weir Chief Finance Officer

treasury shares
Shares in a company held in the company's own name.

- Details of **treasury shares** held by an entity and its subsidiaries and associates.
- Shares held for issue under options and other contracts.

The financial statements should also disclose the nature and purpose of each category of reserve classified as equity.

Financial statements relating to limited partnerships and unit trusts, prepared under IFRS Standards, should present the equivalent information.

2.6 Statement of comprehensive income (profit and loss account)

IAS 1 allows an entity to present either:

- a single statement of comprehensive income; or
- two statements –
  - a statement of profit or loss; and
  - a statement of comprehensive income that has the profit or loss figure from the bottom line of the income statement as the first line item and shows components of other comprehensive income underneath.

UK GAAP equivalent
Section 5 of FRS 102 deals with presentation of the statement of comprehensive income and income statement.

The reason for this choice is that accounting standards give rise to certain profits and losses that are generally viewed as not suitable to be reported within the main profit or loss figure for the period. They can be large and volatile and outside management control (see the list below), or they relate to items that will ultimately mature in a future period. As a result, the standard setter splits these out into a category called other comprehensive income or OCI and this can either be added as a category to the main statement of profit or loss, in which case it becomes a statement of comprehensive income, or shown as a separate statement in its own right.

The profit or loss section of statement of profit or loss will show the following items:

- revenue
- finance costs
- share of the results of associates and joint ventures accounted for under the equity method (see Chapter 7)
- taxation expense
- a single amount for the total of discontinued operations (see below).

A total for profit and loss is also required.

In the other comprehensive income section or statement of other comprehensive income, items must be classified according to whether they will in subsequent periods be transferred to profit or loss or not.

Items included in the 'other comprehensive income' figure include:

- changes in the revaluation surplus on long-term assets (see Chapter 5)
- actuarial gains and losses on defined benefit plans (see Chapter 4)
- gains and losses arising from the translation of the financial statements of a foreign operation (see Chapter 4)
- certain gains and losses relating to financial instruments (see Chapters 5 and 6), including on certain instruments used for **hedging**.

hedging
A risk management strategy in which an investment is undertaken to offset a position and reduce exposure to price, currency or other fluctuations, e.g. a forward contract is used to hedge against changes in foreign currency exchange rates.

Below is a copy of the income statement and statement of comprehensive income of Marks & Spencer plc for 2016. This is an example of the two-statement style of income presentation. You can see that the profit figure of £404.4m from the bottom line of the income statement is used as the first line item of the statement of comprehensive income.

86
MARKS AND SPENCER GROUP PLC
FINANCIAL STATEMENTS

CONSOLIDATED INCOME STATEMENT

		53 weeks ended 2 April 2016			52 weeks ended 28 March 2015		
	Notes	Underlying £m	Non-underlying £m	Total £m	Underlying £m	Non-underlying £m	Total £m
Revenue	2,3	**10,555.4**	**–**	**10,555.4**	10,311.4	–	10,311.4
Operating profit	2,3,5	**784.9**	**(200.8)**	**584.1**	762.5	(61.2)	701.3
Finance income	6	**21.1**	**–**	**21.1**	15.5	–	15.5
Finance costs	6	**(116.4)**	**–**	**(116.4)**	(116.8)	–	(116.8)
Profit before tax	4,5	**689.6**	**(200.8)**	**488.8**	661.2	(61.2)	600.0
Income tax expense	7	**(118.8)**	**34.4**	**(84.4)**	(124.8)	6.5	(118.3)
Profit for the year		**570.8**	**(166.4)**	**404.4**	536.4	(54.7)	481.7
Attributable to:							
Owners of the parent		**573.3**	**(166.4)**	**406.9**	541.2	(54.7)	486.5
Non-controlling interests		**(2.5)**	**–**	**(2.5)**	(4.8)	–	(4.8)
		570.8	**(166.4)**	**404.4**	536.4	(54.7)	481.7
Basic earnings per share	8	**35.0p**		**24.9p**	33.1p		29.7p
Diluted earnings per share	8	**34.9p**		**24.8p**	32.9p		29.5p

CONSOLIDATED STATEMENT OF COMPREHENSIVE INCOME

	Notes	53 weeks ended 2 April 2016 £m	52 weeks ended 28 March 2015 £m
Profit for the year		**404.4**	481.7
Other comprehensive income:			
Items that will not be reclassified to profit or loss			
Remeasurements of retirement benefit schemes	11	**346.2**	193.7
Tax charge on items that will not be reclassified		**(45.6)**	(40.2)
		300.6	153.5
Items that will be reclassified subsequently to profit or loss			
Foreign currency translation differences		**7.3**	(7.5)
Cash flow hedges and net investment hedges			
– fair value movements recognised in other comprehensive income		**(30.1)**	221.2
– reclassified and reported in profit or loss		**(22.1)**	(60.0)
– amount recognised in inventories		**5.9**	(21.6)
Tax credit/(charge) on cash flow hedges and net investment hedges		**6.5**	(21.2)
		(32.5)	110.9
Other comprehensive income for the year, net of tax		**268.1**	264.4
Total comprehensive income for the year		**672.5**	746.1
Attributable to:			
Owners of the parent		**675.0**	750.9
Non-controlling interests		**(2.5)**	(4.8)
		672.5	746.1

In order to give a fair presentation of results, entities may present additional items in the statements provided these separate items are shown within the category to which they relate. This is because the classification of extraordinary items, i.e. shown net of tax after the profit after tax line, is not permitted under IFRS Standards. You can see from the Marks & Spencer example that they have chosen to do this in a columnar format to strip out things that they do not think are part of the underlying results of the business. We will look at this further in Chapter 8.

With regard to such material items, these should be separately disclosed, for example material amounts arising as a result of:

- write-downs of inventories to net realisable value or of property, plant and equipment to recoverable amount, as well as reversals of such write-downs;
- restructurings of the activities of an entity and reversals of any provisions for the costs of restructuring;
- disposals of items of property, plant and equipment;
- disposals of investments;
- discontinued operations;
- litigation settlements; or
- other reversals of provisions.

The standard requires entities to provide an analysis of expenses recognised in profit or loss using a classification based on either their *nature* or their *function* within the entity, whichever provides information that is reliable and more relevant. These two methods are demonstrated in the examples in the following tables:

Table 3.1: Nature of expense method

Nature of expense method		
Revenue		X
Other income		X
Changes in inventories of finished goods and work in progress	X	
Raw materials and consumables used	X	
Employee benefits expense	X	
Depreciation and amortisation expense	X	
Other expenses	X	
Total expenses		(X)
Profit before tax		X

Expenses are analysed according to their nature (for example, depreciation, purchase of materials, transport costs, employee benefits and marketing costs) and not allocated to their function.

Table 3.2: Function of expense or cost of sales method

Function of expense or cost of sales method	
Revenue	X
Cost of sales	(X)
Gross profit	X
Other income	X
Distribution costs	(X)
Administrative expenses	(X)
Other expenses	(X)
Profit before tax	X

Expenses are allocated to their function, at a minimum to cost of sales and other functions such as distribution and administration expenses.

An entity should disclose the expense analysis in a way that is most suited to its business and that will give the most useful information to the user of accounts. The function of expense method tends to be the one used by most non-financial corporates in the UK.

The main rules governing revenue and some major cost lines are discussed in Chapter 4.

Test yourself 3.4

1 **What is the difference between the classification of expenses by function and by nature?**

2 **Which do you think is most useful?**

2.7 Statement of cash flows

The preparation and presentation of cash flow statements is governed by IAS 7 and is covered below.

2.8 Statement of changes in equity

UK GAAP equivalent
Section 6 of FRS 102 deals with presentation of the statement of changes in equity.

The statement of changes in equity provides an analysis of the composition of equity at the beginning and end of the reporting period and how this has changed during the period. Typical components of the statement include as a minimum share capital, share premium and retained earnings (the accumulated income and expenses of the entity that have not been distributed to owners). The formation and content of many of these are driven by legal requirements as we will see in Chapter 10.

The Marks & Spencer plc statement of changes in equity below gives an example of the key information available to users such as equity movement and dividends paid during the year.

2.9 Notes to the financial statements

UK GAAP equivalent
Section 8 of FRS 102 deals with presentation of the notes to the financial statements.

The disclosure notes provide more detailed information in respect of items presented in the financial statements, such as a break-down of figures and supporting narrative. The notes also provide information on items that are not present on the face of the main statements. The notes are very important as it is not possible to understand the main statements without the further detail given in the supporting notes. IAS 1 therefore requires the notes to be properly structured in a systematic manner, to make them understandable and easy to follow.

The kind of detailed and additional information that is required to be presented in the notes under IAS 1 includes:

- Confirmation of the basis of preparation of the financial statements and compliance with accounting standards, stating the standards applied, e.g. IFRS Standards.
- Accounting policies adopted, significant judgements made and measurement basis applied and sources of estimation uncertainty (see Chapter 4).
- Information required by other standards that is not presented on the face of the main statements.

88
MARKS AND SPENCER GROUP PLC
FINANCIAL STATEMENTS

CONSOLIDATED STATEMENT OF CHANGES IN EQUITY

	Ordinary share capital £m	Share premium account £m	Capital redemption reserve £m	Hedging reserve £m	Other reserve[1] £m	Retained earnings[2] £m	Total £m	Non-controlling interest £m	Total £m
As at 30 March 2014	408.1	355.5	2,202.6	(41.8)	(6,542.2)	6,325.1	2,707.3	(0.6)	2,706.7
Profit/(loss) for the year	–	–	–	–	–	486.5	486.5	(4.8)	481.7
Other comprehensive (expense)/income:									
Foreign currency translation	–	–	–	(2.0)	–	(5.5)	(7.5)	–	(7.5)
Remeasurements of retirement benefit schemes	–	–	–	–	–	193.7	193.7	–	193.7
Tax charge on items that will not be reclassified	–	–	–	–	–	(40.2)	(40.2)	–	(40.2)
Cash flow hedges and net investment hedges									
– fair value movements recognised in other comprehensive income	–	–	–	210.9	–	10.3	221.2	–	221.2
– reclassified and reported in profit or loss[3]	–	–	–	(60.0)	–	–	(60.0)	–	(60.0)
– amount recognised in inventories	–	–	–	(21.6)	–	–	(21.6)	–	(21.6)
Tax on cash flow hedges and net investment hedges	–	–	–	(21.2)	–	–	(21.2)	–	(21.2)
Other comprehensive income	–	–	–	106.1	–	158.3	264.4	–	264.4
Total comprehensive income/(expense)	–	–	–	106.1	–	644.8	750.9	(4.8)	746.1
Transactions with owners:									
Dividends	–	–	–	–	–	(280.7)	(280.7)	–	(280.7)
Transactions with non-controlling shareholders	–	–	–	–	–	–	–	4.6	4.6
Shares issued on exercise of employee share options	3.9	36.9	–	–	–	–	40.8	–	40.8
Purchase of own shares held by employee trusts	–	–	–	–	–	(24.2)	(24.2)	–	(24.2)
Release of share-based payments	–	–	–	–	–	(1.1)	(1.1)	–	(1.1)
Deferred tax on share schemes	–	–	–	–	–	6.6	6.6	–	6.6
As at 28 March 2015	412.0	392.4	2,202.6	64.3	(6,542.2)	6,670.5	3,199.6	(0.8)	3,198.8
As at 29 March 2015	**412.0**	**392.4**	**2,202.6**	**64.3**	**(6,542.2)**	**6,670.5**	**3,199.6**	**(0.8)**	**3,198.8**
Profit/(loss) for the year	**–**	**–**	**–**	**–**	**–**	**406.9**	**406.9**	**(2.5)**	**404.4**
Other comprehensive (expense)/income:									
Foreign currency translation	**–**	**–**	**–**	**(0.5)**	**–**	**7.8**	**7.3**	**–**	**7.3**
Remeasurements of retirement benefit schemes	**–**	**–**	**–**	**–**	**–**	**346.2**	**346.2**	**–**	**346.2**
Tax charge on items that will not be reclassified	**–**	**–**	**–**	**–**	**–**	**(45.6)**	**(45.6)**	**–**	**(45.6)**
Cash flow hedges and net investment hedges									
– fair value movements recognised in other comprehensive income	**–**	**–**	**–**	**(21.8)**	**–**	**(8.3)**	**(30.1)**	**–**	**(30.1)**
– reclassified and reported in profit or loss[3]	**–**	**–**	**–**	**(22.1)**	**–**	**–**	**(22.1)**	**–**	**(22.1)**
– amount recognised in inventories[3]	**–**	**–**	**–**	**5.9**	**–**	**–**	**5.9**	**–**	**5.9**
Tax on cash flow hedges and net investment hedges	**–**	**–**	**–**	**6.5**	**–**	**–**	**6.5**	**–**	**6.5**
Other comprehensive income/(expense)	**–**	**–**	**–**	**(32.0)**	**–**	**300.1**	**268.1**	**–**	**268.1**
Total comprehensive income/(expense)	**–**	**–**	**–**	**(32.0)**	**–**	**707.0**	**675.0**	**(2.5)**	**672.5**
Transactions with owners:									
Dividends	**–**	**–**	**–**	**–**	**–**	**(301.7)**	**(301.7)**	**–**	**(301.7)**
Transactions with non-controlling shareholders	**–**	**–**	**–**	**–**	**–**	**–**	**–**	**1.5**	**1.5**
Shares issued on exercise of employee share options	**1.7**	**18.9**	**–**	**–**	**–**	**–**	**20.6**	**–**	**20.6**
Purchase of own shares held by employee trusts	**–**	**–**	**–**	**–**	**–**	**(10.9)**	**(10.9)**	**–**	**(10.9)**
Shares purchased in buyback	**(7.9)**	**–**	**7.9**	**–**	**–**	**(150.7)**	**(150.7)**	**–**	**(150.7)**
Credit for share-based payments	**–**	**–**	**–**	**–**	**–**	**17.2**	**17.2**	**–**	**17.2**
Deferred tax on share schemes	**–**	**–**	**–**	**–**	**–**	**(3.9)**	**(3.9)**	**–**	**(3.9)**
As at 2 April 2016	**405.8**	**411.3**	**2,210.5**	**32.3**	**(6,542.2)**	**6,927.5**	**3,445.2**	**(1.8)**	**3,443.4**

1. The 'Other reserve' was originally created as part of the capital restructuring that took place in 2002. It represents the difference between the nominal value of the shares issued prior to the capital reduction by the Company (being the carrying value of the investment in Marks and Spencer plc) and the share capital, share premium and capital redemption reserve of Marks and Spencer plc at the date of the transaction.
2. The 'Retained earnings reserve' includes a cumulative £4.8m loss (last year £12.6m loss) in the currency reserve.
3. Amounts 'reclassified and reported in profit or loss' are presented within finance costs offsetting the revaluation of the hedged bonds (last year £4.4m was presented in cost of sales and £55.6m in finance costs). 'Amount recognised in inventories' includes £(93.7)m included cost of sales for the year and £87.8m (last year £21.6m) that remains in inventory at the balance sheet date.

- Information that is not presented elsewhere in the financial statements, but is relevant and helps users understand them.
- Disclosures in connection with contingent liabilities (see Chapter 6) and contractual commitments not yet required to be shown in the financial statements.
- Disclosures in respect of dividends, confirming–
  - dividends proposed or declared before the financial statements were authorised for issue but not recognised as a distribution to shareholders during the period, and the related amount per share; and
  - the amount of any cumulative preference dividends not recognised.
- Information that enables users of financial statements to evaluate the entity's objectives, policies and processes for managing capital and risk, including a confirmation of whether capital requirements are met (for example for financial institutions such as banks).

If not cited elsewhere in the financial statements, e.g. in the opening pages of the annual report and accounts, the reporting entity should also include the following information about itself in the disclosure notes:

- The domicile and legal form of the business, its country of incorporation and its registered office address or, if different, principal place of business.
- A description of the nature of the entity's operations and principal activities.
- If part of a group, the name of its parent and the ultimate parent of the group.
- If it is a limited life entity, information regarding the length of its life.

UK GAAP equivalent
Section 5 of FRS 102 deals with presentation of discontinued operations.

The notes should always be cross referenced to the relevant item in the financial statements, where appropriate.

2.10 Discontinued operations

Businesses often sell major assets or sell or close down areas of business activity, but this can take time and at the end of a reporting period the process of sale or closure may still be in progress. If it has been completed, there may be significant gains or losses to report on the transaction. When this happens, accounting standards require the discontinued operations to be disclosed separately and in a specific way, so that users of accounts can see which parts of the business will not be part of the future of the remaining business. The main standard dealing with this is IFRS 5 'Discontinued Operations'.

non-current assets
Assets that do not meet the definition of a current asset, so they will usually expected to be held and realised for more than 12 months (e.g. property, plant and equipment, intellectual property rights).

disposal group
A group of assets to be disposed of, by sale or otherwise, together as a group in a single transaction, and liabilities directly associated with those assets that will be transferred in the transaction.

IFRS 5 requires entities to measure a **non-current asset** (or **disposal group**) classified as held for sale at the lower of its carrying amount (see Chapter 5) and fair value less costs to sell and information must be given that enables users of the financial statements to evaluate the financial effects of discontinued operations and disposals of non-current assets (or disposal groups).

The presentation of the profits and losses arising from disposal groups and **discontinued operations** are particularly important, because users of the accounts need a clear picture of what components of the year's performance will not be repeated as the relevant assets or parts of the business are being sold (or even closed down or scrapped). This is because users need to understand what the ongoing parts are of an entity's business.

An entity must therefore disclose a single amount in the statement of comprehensive income comprising the total of:

1. the post-tax profit or loss of discontinued operations; and
2. the post-tax gain or loss recognised on the measurement to fair value less costs to sell or on the disposal of the assets or disposal group(s) constituting the discontinued operation.

discontinued operation
A component of an entity that either has been disposed of or is classified as held for sale and: represents a separate major line of business or geographical area of operations, is part of a single co-ordinated plan to dispose of a separate major line of business or geographical area of operations or is a subsidiary acquired exclusively with a view to resale.

A breakdown of the above amounts must be disclosed, as well as the net cash flows attributable to the operating, investing and financing activities of discontinued operations (presented either in the notes or in the financial statements; see Section 2).

The entity must also present a non-current asset classified as held for sale and the assets of a disposal group classified as held for sale separately from other assets in the statement of financial position. The liabilities of a disposal group classified as held for sale must also be presented separately from other liabilities in the statement of financial position.

Stop and think 3.1

Tesco plc has reported discontinued operations for several of the last few years. Go to the Tesco plc website and take a look at the disclosures they have made around discontinued operations.

3. Cash flow statements

The statement of cash flows shows changes in **cash** and **cash equivalents** over a financial period and therefore serves as an analytical tool to enable users of accounts to review the past year's cash movements and year end cash position assess the viability of a business in terms of liquidity, solvency and financial adaptability. Unlike the statement of comprehensive income, the statement of cash flows is not prepared on an accruals basis. Accordingly, the statement of cash flows provides additional information to supplement the other two primary financial statements, giving a different view on the performance of the business. The preparation of cash flow statements is governed by IAS 7 'Statement of Cash Flows'.

UK GAAP equivalent
Section 7 of FRS 102 deals with presentation of the statement of cash flows.

cash
Comprises cash on hand and demand deposits.

cash equivalents
Short-term, highly liquid investments that are readily convertible to known amounts of cash and which are subject to an insignificant risk of changes in value.

Test yourself 3.5

Why would investors be interested in seeing cash flow numbers and not just profit and balance sheet information?

3.1 Structure of the statement of cash flows

A statement of cash flows comprises three main sections showing all the cash items which generate the net increase or decrease in cash and cash equivalents:

- Net cash generated from/(used in) **operating activities**.
- Net cash generated from/(used in) **investing activities**.
- Net cash generated from/(used in) **financing activities**.

operating activities
The main income producing activities of a business and other activities that are not investing or financing activities.

investing activities
The acquisition and disposal of long-term assets and other investments not included in cash equivalents.

financing activities
Activities that result in changes in the size and composition of the contributed equity and borrowings of the entity.

3.2 Cash flows from operating activities

The first main section of the statement of cash flows deals primarily with cash flows derived from the principal revenue-producing activities of the entity. Examples of cash flows from operating activities are:

1. cash receipts from the sale of goods and the rendering of services;
2. cash receipts from royalties, fees, commissions and other revenue;
3. cash payments to suppliers for goods and services; cash payments to and on behalf of employees;
4. cash payments or refunds of income taxes unless they can be specifically identified with financing and investing activities; and
5. cash receipts and payments from contracts held for dealing or trading purposes.

IAS 7 permits cash flows from operating activities to be shown on a direct or indirect basis. Both lead to the same total result of net cash flows from operations, but the presentation is very different. Cash flows on a direct basis would show the gross receipts and payments in the sorts of categories indicated above. The indirect method, by comparison, adjusts profit or loss for the effects of transactions of a non-cash nature, i.e. any deferrals or accruals of past or future operating cash receipts or payments, and items of income or expense associated with investing or financing cash flows, resulting in a net cash flow number from operating activities. The indirect method is easier for businesses to prepare because it derives substantially from the existing accrual accounting records, so it is historically the method most commonly used, at least in the UK.

IAS 7 contains some useful examples, but the main adjustments required are seen in Table 3.3.

Table 3.3: Main adjustments

Operating profit		X
Depreciation	X	
Increase/decrease in stock	X/(X)	
Increase/decrease in debtors	X/(X)	
Decrease/increase in creditors	X/(X)	
Net adjustment for non-cash movements		X/(X)
Cash flow from operating activities		X

Taxes attributable to income, such as corporation tax, are usually treated as operating cash flows unless they specifically relate to an investing or financing activity. Cash flows relating to dividends and interest received and paid may be classified as operating activities provided the classification remains consistent from one reporting period to the next, although presenting such cash flows in the operating category tends to be restricted to financial institutions.

Cash flows from investing activities, the second main section of the cash flow statement, include the acquisition and disposal of long-term assets, including property, plant and equipment and intangible assets and acquisitions and disposals of shares in joint ventures, associates and other investments (see Chapter 7).

Financing activities include the issuance of ordinary shares to raise equity finance, repayment of short- and long-term borrowings, proceeds from short and long-term borrowings and finance leases. Cash flows relating to dividends paid to equity holders are also generally included in the financing activities section of the statement. As noted above, however, dividends received could be classified as either operating activities or investing activities depending on the business activities of the recipient.

Entities must disclose the components of cash and cash equivalents and present a reconciliation of the amounts in its statement of cash flows with the equivalent items reported in the statement of financial position. There is a tendency in the UK, recommended by the FRC although it is not compulsory, to give an analysis of net debt as part of the reconciliation, i.e. the gross debt of the company less its cash and cash equivalents, as M&S does in the example below. As required by IAS 1, the previous year comparative figures should be provided for all disclosures.

Following on from the main statements shown in Section 1, here is the cash flow statement for Marks & Spencer plc for 2016:

89
ANNUAL REPORT AND FINANCIAL STATEMENTS 2016

CONSOLIDATED STATEMENT OF CASH FLOWS

	Notes	53 weeks ended 2 April 2016 £m	52 weeks ended 28 March 2015 £m
Cash flows from operating activities			
Cash generated from operations	27	**1,311.3**	1,349.1
Income tax paid		**(99.3)**	(71.1)
Net cash inflow from operating activities		**1,212.0**	1,278.0
Cash flows from investing activities			
Proceeds on property disposals		**30.6**	35.4
Purchase of property, plant and equipment		**(363.3)**	(521.8)
Purchase of intangible assets		**(186.8)**	(178.0)
(Purchase)/reduction of current financial assets		**(7.2)**	6.0
Interest received		**6.8**	9.3
Acquisition of subsidiary	25	**(56.2)**	–
Net cash used in investing activities		**(576.1)**	(649.1)
Cash flows from financing activities			
Interest paid[1]		**(113.5)**	(115.3)
Cash inflow/(outflow) from borrowings		**3.1**	(165.7)
Repayment of syndicated loan notes		**(19.9)**	(10.2)
Decrease in obligations under finance leases		**(2.4)**	(4.8)
Payment of liability to the Marks & Spencer UK Pension Scheme		**(56.0)**	(54.4)
Equity dividends paid		**(301.7)**	(280.7)
Shares issued on exercise of employee share options		**20.6**	40.8
Purchase of own shares held by employee trust		**(10.9)**	(24.2)
Share buyback		**(150.7)**	–
Net cash used in financing activities		**(631.4)**	(614.5)
Net cash inflow from activities		**4.5**	14.4
Effects of exchange rate changes		**3.7**	(2.3)
Opening net cash		**187.8**	175.7
Closing net cash	28	**196.0**	187.8

1. Includes interest on the partnership liability to the Marks & Spencer UK Pension Scheme.

	Notes	53 weeks ended 2 April 2016 £m	52 weeks ended 28 March 2015 £m
Reconciliation of net cash flow to movement in net debt			
Opening net debt		**(2,223.2)**	(2,463.6)
Net cash inflow from activities		**4.5**	14.4
Increase/(decrease) in current financial assets		**7.2**	(6.0)
Decrease in debt financing		**75.2**	235.1
Exchange and other non-cash movements		**(2.0)**	(3.1)
Movement in net debt		**84.9**	240.4
Closing net debt	28	**(2,138.3)**	(2,223.2)

Test yourself 3.6

How are corporation tax payments treated in the statement of cash flows?

4. Operating segments

Larger companies often have a number of business lines and operations in many different places geographically. It is helpful for the users of the accounts to see the results broken down into different segments in order to aid analysis, because they often have different profit characteristics, asset bases and potential for future growth. Accounting standards require such an analysis to be given, but only by certain entities, which tend to be the largest, i.e. those that are listed. The standard covering the presentation of operating segments, IFRS 8, works on a management model, i.e. the segments that are reported are those that are reported internally to the decision-making management of the entity.

4.1 Scope of IFRS 8

IFRS 8 applies to the financial statements of an entity or group:

1. whose debt or equity instruments are traded in a public market; or
2. that files, or is in the process of filing, the financial statements with a securities commission or other regulatory organisation for the purpose of issuing any class of instruments in a public market.

4.2 Operating segments

The definition of an operating segment is key. The standard describes an operating segment as a component of an entity:

1. that engages in business activities from which it may earn revenues and incur expenses (including revenues and expenses relating to transactions with other components of the same entity);
2. whose operating results are regularly reviewed by the entity's chief operating decision maker to make decisions about resources to be allocated to the segment and assess its performance; and
3. for which discrete financial information is available.

4.3 Presentation of operating segments

Information for each operating segment must be presented separately, unless the characteristics of any operating segments are so similar (by reference to the nature of their products, production processes, customers etc) that they ought to be aggregated. However, any operating segment representing over 10% of gross revenue, profits or assets of the entity must always be presented separately.

4.4 Disclosures for operating segments

Disclosures must be given about how the entity has identified operating segments and their general nature. Generally speaking, information on operating segment assets and liabilities and profits and losses only need be disclosed if reported to the chief decision maker of the entity and the information disclosed may be measured in a different way to the primary or main statements, if that how it is reported internally. However, the standard does list out what would normally be expected to be shown in relation to revenues, profits and losses if these are reported to the chief decision maker, including revenue (broken down between revenue to external customers and other operating segments), interest revenue and expense, depreciation and amortisation (see Chapter 5) and other major non-cash items, material items disclosed separately as required by IAS 1 (see Section 1 above) and income taxes.

The entity must also provide reconciliations for the amounts disclosed by operating segment to the total amounts for the entity as shown in its main statements. Such reconciliations will highlight if the operating segment amounts have been measured differently to the primary or main statements of the entity, but will also show any results outside the operating segments reported, for example head office costs, assets and liabilities.

The standard also requires further disclosures, broken down as follows, unless it would involve undue cost or effort:

1. Information about products or services: revenues from external customers for each product or service line.
2. Information about geographical areas: revenues from external customers and major non-current assets.
3. Information about major customers: when any individual customer revenue represents 10% or more of total revenue.

These amounts are calculated according to how the primary or main statements are prepared, not in the way operating segment information is measured, if different.

The Marks & Spencer plc segmental information can be found on page 95 of the 2016 ARA.

5. Events after the reporting period

UK GAAP equivalent
Section 32 of FRS 102 deals with events after the end of the reporting period.

It is often very difficult to decide how cut-off works in terms of the reporting period end and whether anything that happens after that date should be taken into account in the period. So for example, if an entity's year end is 31 December, but there is a major fire in a factory in the following January before the accounts are approved, or a major customer becomes insolvent and cannot pay a debt, what should happen in the accounts? These issues are dealt with by IAS 10 'Events After the Reporting Period'.

The standard defines '**events after the reporting period**' as those events, favourable and unfavourable, that occur between the date of the statement of financial position (i.e. the balance sheet date) and the date when the financial statements are authorised for issue.

events after the reporting period
Events, whether favourable or unfavourable, that have occurred between the date of the statement of financial position (i.e. the balance sheet date) and the date when the financial statements were authorised for issue.

adjusting event
An event after the reporting period that provides further evidence of conditions that existed at the end of the reporting period. An event that raises going concern issues for the entity is an adjusting event.

non-adjusting event
An event after the reporting period that is indicative of a condition that arose after the end of the reporting period.

5.1 Adjusting and non-adjusting events

The standard classifies events after the reporting event as either:

- those that show evidence of conditions that existed at the date of the statement of financial position which are **adjusting events** for the reporting period; or
- those that are indicative of conditions that arose after the date of the statement of financial position which are **non-adjusting events** for the reporting period.

Material adjusting events should be reflected in the financial statements by adjusting the amounts recognised. An adjusting event includes an event that provides evidence that the reporting entity is no longer a going concern. If this is the case, the entity should not prepare its accounts on a going concern basis.

Non-adjusting events, as the name suggests, do not trigger a change in accounting treatment. This is because the events occurred after the reporting period and there is no evidence to justify a change in accounting treatment as at the balance sheet date. Non-adjusting events also include dividends declared after the reporting period. This is because the liability to make the dividend payments did not exist at the balance sheet date.

Non-adjusting events thus fall to be recognised in the following accounting period. However, they may require disclosure if material and if it is expected that they would affect the economic decisions made by users of the financial statements. The disclosures under IAS 10 are:

1. the nature of the event; and
2. an estimate of the financial effect (or, more rarely) a statement that a reasonable estimate of the financial effect cannot be made.

Disclosures in the financial statements should also be updated to reflect conditions existing at the reporting date in relation to which new information exists.

5.2 Examples of adjusting and non-adjusting events

Examples of material adjusting events after the reporting period include:

- a court case settlement confirming the existence of a present obligation as at the end of the reporting period, in which case a provision will need to be recognised in accordance with IAS 37 'Provisions, Contingent Liabilities and Contingent Assets' instead of the disclosure of a contingent liability in the notes (see Chapter 6);

- the discovery of material misstatements or fraud that show the financial statements to be inaccurate;
- the bankruptcy of a major customer which results in trade debtors being non-recoverable; and
- the presence of persuasive evidence that the entity can no longer continue as a going concern.

Examples of non-adjusting events after the reporting period include:

- a fall in the market value of investments between the balance sheet date and the date when the financial statements are approved for issue;
- an announcement that part of the business is no longer viable and will cease to operate;
- the sale of a major subsidiary; and
- flood damage to material assets.

Test yourself 3.7

Why should the decline in the market value of investments not be treated as an adjusting event after the reporting period?

Chapter summary

- IAS 1 is a key accounting standard as it lays out the requirement for financial statements to fairly represent the position, performance and cash flows of an entity, a broadly similar concept to the true and fair view required by UK company law. The standard is an overarching one, describing the statements and notes that are required for a complete set of financial statements and giving high-level guidance on the content and presentation of those statements and on the notes to the accounts. It prescribes some basic information that should be disclosed about the reporting entity.
- IAS 1 lays out the minimum line items and format of the statements of financial position, comprehensive income and changes in equity, which are all prepared on an accruals basis. The standard is not completely prescriptive and there is some leeway for companies to produce variations in format, particularly in the statement of comprehensive income.
- IFRS 5 deals with discontinued operations and disposals of assets or businesses, requiring segregation of such items from the results of continuing operations so that users' view of the accounts is not skewed by results which will not be present in future years.
- Entities must present a cash flow statement, which shows the flows of cash (and cash equivalents) during the year. This helps users to see how profits are converted into cash and provides information on how much

cash is reinvested and how much is used to service and settle debt or pay out to shareholders. This is important as even highly profitable businesses can run out of cash, which leads to insolvency.

- It is sometimes appropriate for accounts to be adjusted for events that occur after the reporting period but before the accounts are authorised and published. Even when it is not necessary to adjust amount reported, it may be necessary to make disclosures in the accounts for significant events. IAS 10 therefore distinguish between two types of event: adjusting events and non-adjusting events.

Chapter four
Reporting financial performance

List of topics

1. Introduction
2. Accounting policies, estimates and errors
3. Revenue
4. Employee benefits
5. Share-based payments
6. Foreign currency exchange rate changes
7. Income taxes

1. Introduction

It is vital that an entity adopts appropriate accounting policies in order to present a true and fair view of its state of affairs and financial performance. We will look at how an entity should judge the appropriateness of accounting policies and the distinction between accounting policies, changes in estimation techniques and the correction of errors by considering another major overarching standard, IAS 8.

We looked at the complete set of financial statements in the last chapter. This chapter goes on to consider some of the key items affecting the statement of comprehensive income and the accounting standards that govern them. The importance of revenue – the top line income figure that drives financial performance – will be discussed and the way accounting standards require revenue to be recognised in the accounts depending on performance under contracts to customers. For some types of business, recognising and measuring revenue is relatively straightforward, whereas for others it is a more complicated process.

Many business expenses require only simple accounting and there is no need to provide any specific guidance above and beyond overarching standards such as IAS 1 (see Chapter 3) and IAS 8. However, there are often more complicated issues around remunerating employees, so we will look at accounting for employee benefits, including pensions, and also accounting for share-based compensation, which has become very common over recent years as a means of incentivising employees.

We will look at the impact of foreign currency exchange rate changes on performance, including what is meant by functional currency and presentational currency, the rules that govern foreign currency translation and how foreign exchange differences are accounted for.

Finally, this chapter will look at the rules around reporting taxes on income, which in the UK is corporation tax, but which the IFRS standard calls, generically, income taxes. We will consider the differences between current tax and deferred tax.

2. Accounting policies, estimates and errors

There are lots of choices in accounting in terms of how to recognise, measure, present and disclose information about any item of economic relevance. Because of these choices, it is vital that users of financial statements understand the choices that have been made.

Accounting standards have rules around selection and application of **accounting policies** and their consistent application.

Accounts are also full of estimates because not all information will be known about an item at the time the accounts are prepared, usually because uncertain future events may affect the item in question, for example the amount that should be recorded for a debt due to the business as a receivable when there are doubts about the debtor's ability to pay. Accounting standards deal with **changes in accounting estimates** and also correction of **prior period errors**, when something has gone wrong with accounting in prior years.

The main standard dealing with these issues is IAS 8 'Accounting Policies, Changes in Accounting Estimates and Errors'. Like IAS 1, discussed in Chapter 3, it is an important, overarching standard, covering issues that are relevant across all aspects of financial reporting. The objective of IAS 8 is to prescribe the criteria for selecting and changing accounting policies, together with the accounting treatment and disclosure of changes in accounting policies, changes in accounting estimates and correction of errors.

2.1 Selection of accounting policies

The selection criteria for choosing accounting policies depend on what is suitable and appropriate to an entity's specific set of circumstances. There are a number of choices in accounting standards to cater for the fact that all businesses are different; some policies tend to get adopted across industries where companies are doing similar things, but in other cases the choice is very specific to the entity in question.

When selecting an accounting policy, an entity must first apply any relevant IFRS Standards (which as noted may itself allow choices). In the absence of an IFRS Standards that specifically applies to a transaction, other event or condition, an entity's management must use its judgement in developing and applying an accounting policy that results in information that is:

accounting policies
The specific principles, bases, conventions, rules and practices applied by an entity in preparing and presenting financial statements.

change in accounting estimate
An adjustment of the carrying amount of an asset or a liability, or the amount of the periodic consumption of an asset, that results from the assessment of the present status of, and expected future benefits and obligations associated with, assets and liabilities. Changes in accounting estimates result from new information or new developments and, accordingly, are not corrections of errors.

prior period errors
Omissions from, and misstatements in, the entity's financial statements for one or more prior periods arising from a failure to use, or misuse of, reliable information that: (i) was available when financial statements for those periods were authorised for issue; and (ii) could reasonably be expected to have been obtained and taken into account in the preparation and presentation of those financial statements. Such errors include the effects of mathematical mistakes, mistakes in applying accounting policies, oversights or misinterpretations of facts, and fraud.

UK GAAP equivalent
Section 10 of FRS 102 deals with accounting policies, estimates and errors.

- relevant to the economic decision-making needs of users; and
- reliable, in that the financial statements:
  - represent faithfully the financial position, financial performance and cash flows of the entity;
  - reflect the economic substance of transactions, other events and conditions, and not merely the legal form;
  - are neutral, i.e. free from bias;
  - are prudent; and
  - are complete in all material respects.

In making such judgements, an entity is required to consider the applicability of the following sources in descending order:

1. the requirements in IFRS Standards dealing with similar and related issues; and
2. the definitions, recognition criteria and measurement concepts for assets, liabilities, income and expenses in the Conceptual Framework.

An entity can also consider the most recent pronouncements of other standard-setting bodies that use a similar conceptual framework to develop accounting standards, other accounting literature and accepted industry practices, to the extent that these do not conflict with the sources above.

An entity must select and apply its accounting policies consistently for similar transactions, other events and conditions, unless an IFRS Standards specifically requires or permits categorisation of items for which different policies may be appropriate.

Test yourself 4.1

A reporting entity's management may make various judgements when applying accounting policies to ensure the substance of a transaction, circumstance or event is properly reflected in the entity's financial statements. These judgements, which must be explained in the disclosure notes, may have a significant bearing on the amounts recognised in the financial statements. What kinds of judgements might be made by management when applying accounting policies?

2.2 Changes of accounting policy

retrospective application is applying a new accounting policy to transactions, other events and conditions as if that policy had always been applied.

Given that accounting policies ought to be chosen carefully to suit a particular entity, it should be rare for changes in policy to occur. IAS 8 states that an entity should only change an accounting policy if:

1. it is required to do so by a new or revised standard (in which case many entities are likely to be changing at the same time as a new standard comes into force); or

2. the change results in the financial statements providing reliable and more relevant information about the effects of transactions, other events or conditions on the entity's financial position, financial performance or cash flows.

Where a change of accounting policy arises from a new standard, an entity should apply the new policy according to the transitional requirements of the standard. In other circumstances, the new accounting policy should be applied retrospectively. **Retrospective application** and **retrospective restatement** of errors (see below) require restatement of prior periods but is not required to the extent that it is **impracticable**. This means that it can be applied on a limited retrospective basis. Otherwise the new policy is applied prospectively; **prospective application** affects only the current and future periods.

retrospective restatement
is correcting the recognition, measurement and disclosure of amounts of elements of financial statements as if a prior period error had never occurred.

impracticable
Applying a requirement is impracticable when the entity cannot apply it after making every reasonable effort to do so, i.e, (a) if the effects of the retrospective treatment are not determinable; (b) the retrospective treatment requires assumptions about what management's intent would have been in that period; or (c) the retrospective treatment requires significant estimates of amounts and it is impossible to distinguish objectively information about those estimates that provides evidence of circumstances that existed on the date(s) as at which those amounts are to be recognised, measured or disclosed, and would have been available when the financial statements for that prior period were authorised for issue from other information.

2.3 Changes in accounting estimates

The use of reasonable estimates is an essential part of the preparation of financial statements and does not undermine their reliability. An estimate may need to be revised, however, if changes occur in the circumstances on which the estimate was based or as a result of new information or more experience. By its nature, the revision of an estimate does not relate to prior periods and is not the correction of an error (correction of errors is covered below).

A change in the measurement basis applied is a change in an accounting policy and is not a change in an accounting estimate. When it is difficult to distinguish a change in an accounting policy from a change in an accounting estimate, the change is treated as a change in an accounting estimate. A common example in practice is a change in the depreciation method for an asset (see Chapter 5). There is no change in recognition criteria or measurement basis, but there is a new view of how the asset is being consumed, how long its useful life is or what its residual value might be when it stops being used. It is therefore a change in accounting estimate.

Changes in estimates are recognised from the period in which the change arises, i.e. the changes are applied prospectively.

Test yourself 4.2

What is the difference between a change of accounting policy and a change in accounting estimate?

2.4 Correction of errors

Errors are sometimes made when preparing financial statements. To the extent that errors are discovered before the accounts are approved, they are expected to be corrected before approval. However, any material prior period errors discovered after approval should be corrected retrospectively in the first set of financial statements authorised for issue after their discovery by:

prospective application
of a change in accounting policy and of recognising the effect of a change in an accounting estimate, respectively, are: (a) applying the new accounting policy to transactions, other events and conditions occurring after the date as at which the policy is changed; and (b) recognising the effect of the change in the accounting estimate in the current and future periods affected by the change.

1. restating the comparative amounts for the prior period(s) presented in which the error occurred; or
2. if the error occurred before the earliest prior period presented, restating the opening balances of assets, liabilities and equity for the earliest prior period presented.

If it is impracticable to allocate the error to the period or periods to which it relates, it can be corrected in the current period financial statements.

2.5 Disclosures

The standard requires substantial disclosures around accounting policies, changes in accounting policy and changes in accounting estimates, as well as correction of errors. Any comparative information that is restated must be clearly labelled as such. Changes in policies and estimates and correction of errors are not very common. The most important disclosure is usually about the significant accounting policies of the entity, as is shown in the Marks & Spencer plc 2016 financial statements at Note 1 on pages 90–94 of the statements.

3. Revenue

The top line of the statement of profit and loss – the revenue line – drives the performance of the business and is often the largest number in company financial statements. It is therefore very important that it is accounted for properly. Many accounting scandals relate to wrongful revenue recognition or measurement, usually because revenue is shown too early, and so the rules were tightened recently in a new standard issued by the IASB, IFRS 15 'Revenue'. This is due to come into force for accounting periods beginning on or after 1 January 2018.

UK GAAP equivalent
Section 23 of FRS 102 deals with recognition of revenue, although it is based on the international standard preceding IFRS 15, IAS 18.

Once IFRS 15 comes into force it will replace two existing standards: IAS 18 'Revenue' and IAS 11 'Construction Contracts'. This text deals with IFRS 15 only as the most relevant and current standard.

3.1 IFRS 15

revenue
Income arising in the course of an entity's ordinary activities.

contract
An agreement between two or more parties that creates enforceable rights and obligations.

customer
A party that has contracted with an entity to obtain goods or services that are an output of the entity's ordinary activities in exchange for consideration.

The objective of IFRS 15 is to establish the principles that an entity applies to report useful information to users of financial statements about the nature, amount, timing and uncertainty of **revenue** and cash flows arising from a **contract** with a customer. The standard requires an entity to consider the terms of the contract and all relevant facts and circumstances when applying the standard, and to apply it consistently to contracts with similar characteristics and in similar circumstances. This is important as, for practical ease of application, the standard allows the required accounting to be applied to portfolios of similar contracts.

The standard must be applied to all contracts with a **customer** except those contracts dealt with more specifically by other standards, such as leases (see Chapter 6), insurance contracts and financial instruments (see Chapters 5 and 6).

3.2 Staged approach

IFRS 15 lays out a staged approach to revenue recognition and measurement, which can be seen in Figure 4.1.

Figure 4.1: Revenue steps

1. Identify the contract with a customer
2. Identify the performance obligations in the contract
3. Determine the transaction price
4. Allocate the transaction price to the performance obligation of the contract
5. Recognise revenue when (or as) a performance obligation is satisified

Each of these stages is discussed briefly below.

3.3 Identify the contract with the customer

The standard does not rely on legal definitions of a contract as the standard must be applied internationally across different legal systems. Instead, it lays out the criteria that must be met for a contract with a customer to exist for the purposes of the standard.

All of the following criteria must be met:

1. the parties to the contract have approved the contract (in writing, orally or in accordance with other customary business practices) and are committed to perform their respective obligations;
2. the entity can identify each party's rights regarding the goods or services to be transferred;
3. the entity can identify the payment terms for the goods or services to be transferred;
4. the contract has commercial substance (i.e. the risk, timing or amount of the entity's future cash flows is expected to change as a result of the contract); and
5. it is probable that the entity will collect the consideration to which it will be entitled in exchange for the goods or services that will be transferred to the customer, taking into account whether collectability of consideration is probable (i.e. in light of the customer's ability and intention to pay that amount of consideration when it is due).

The standard deals with contracts that are connected to each other and whose effect ought to be considered in combination and how to deal with contract modifications.

performance obligation
A promise in a contract with a customer to transfer to the customer either: a good or service (or a bundle of goods or services) that is distinct; or a series of distinct goods or services that are substantially the same and that have the same pattern of transfer to the customer.

3.4 Identify the performance obligations in the contract

Where a contract consists of more than one **performance obligation**, IFRS 15 requires an entity to unbundle them and assess them separately. This is to ensure that revenue is only recognised once each performance obligation has been met and hence the revenue is truly earned.

The standard states that at the inception of a contract, an entity must assess the goods or services promised in it and identify as a performance obligation each promise to transfer to the customer either:

1. a good or service (or a bundle of goods or services) that is distinct; or
2. a series of distinct goods or services that are substantially the same and that have the same pattern of transfer to the customer.

Distinct goods or services can be very wide-ranging indeed as the standard has to cover all types of customer contract, but the more obvious examples are delivery of specified goods produced by the entity (such as a manufactured car), performing tasks as a service (such as performing an audit or preparing a tax return) or providing a standing-ready service as and when required (for example regular updates to software).

A good or service that is promised to a customer is distinct if both of the following criteria are met:

1. the customer can benefit from the good or service either on its own or together with other resources that are readily available to the customer; and
2. the entity's promise to transfer the good or service to the customer is separately identifiable from other promises in the contract.

The standard gives further guidance on how to assess these tests.

Different performance obligations will be fulfilled at different times. The standard states that an entity should recognise revenue when (or as) the entity satisfies a performance obligation by transferring a promised good or service (an asset) to the customer. An asset is transferred when (or as) the customer obtains control of that asset. This is a very important principle as it governs the timing of revenue recognition; it means that an entity cannot record revenue if it has not genuinely transferred value to a customer.

The standard deals with performance obligations that are satisfied at a point in time and which can be straightforward to deal with, for example handing over a manufactured asset like a car to a customer. In other situations, for example for major asset construction contracts (buildings, ships, tunnels or roads), the standard specifies the types of factors to be taken into account when determining whether a performance obligation has been satisfied, including (but not limited to) the following factors.

1. The entity has a present right to payment for the asset.
2. The customer has legal title to the asset.
3. The entity has transferred physical possession of the asset.

4. The customer has the significant risks and rewards of ownership of the asset.
5. The customer has accepted the asset.

Compare this, however, to performance obligations that are satisfied over a period of time. Contracts for services are generally performed over time, for example a contract to provide cleaning services over a year.

The standard states that an entity transfers control of a good or service over time and, therefore, satisfies a performance obligation and recognises revenue over time, if one of the following criteria is met:

1. the customer simultaneously receives and consumes the benefits provided by the entity's performance as the entity performs (which is what happens for many services);
2. the entity's performance creates or enhances an asset (for example, software) that the customer controls as the asset is created or enhanced; or
3. the entity's performance does not create an asset with an alternative use to the entity and the entity has an enforceable right to payment for performance completed to date.

Test yourself 4.3

A common situation where a contract will combine different performance obligations is a mobile phone contract. What will the usual performance obligations be and when do you think each performance obligation will have been satisfied, at a point in time or over time?

3.5 Determine the contract price

To the extent that a performance obligation in a contract with a customer has been satisfied, an entity should recognise the related revenue. The **transaction price** is the amount of consideration to which an entity expects to be entitled in exchange for transferring promised goods or services to a customer. The consideration promised in a contract with a customer may include fixed amounts, variable amounts, or both.

transaction price
The amount of consideration to which an entity expects to be entitled in exchange for transferring promised goods or services to a customer, excluding amounts collected on behalf of third parties.

The standard has a substantial amount of guidance on dealing with variable consideration, for example due to discounts, rebates, refunds, credits, price concessions, incentives, performance bonuses, penalties or other similar items. It places strict limits on the extent to which variable consideration can be recognised in situations of uncertainty, i.e. it can only be included in the entity's total revenue for a period if it is highly probable that there will be no significant reversal of revenue recognised once the uncertainty related to the variable consideration is resolved.

IFRS 15 also gives guidance on dealing with non-cash consideration, liabilities for refunds and how to identify if the contract involves a financing arrangement, for example if a customer pays in advance to fund say the construction of an asset and the contract effectively rewards them through a financing component for the money that has effectively been borrowed by the reporting entity.

3.6 Allocate the transaction price and recognise as obligations performed

An entity must allocate the transaction price to each performance obligation (or distinct good or service) in an amount that depicts the amount of consideration to which the entity expects to be entitled in exchange for transferring the promised goods or services to the customer. The process for doing so is to use a stand-alone selling price basis, i.e. each performance obligation is assessed as if it could be sold separately and revenue is allocated in proportion to those stand-alone selling prices. Where each performance obligation can be and is sold separately by the entity, observed prices will be used. The standard allows other methods when such prices are not available, as long as they meet the overall objective of allocation, and it discusses various methods including looking at expected cost plus a profit margin, or market prices for similar performance obligations.

Worked example 4.1

An entity signs a contract with a customer which is assessed to have three performance obligations: A, B and C. The total contract revenue is £100. The entity does sell each of A, B and C separately to customers at the respective prices of £40, £60 and £20. Allocate the contract revenue to the three performance obligations.

3.7 Contract costs

IFRS 15 requires an entity to capitalise as an asset the incremental costs of *obtaining* a contract with a customer for revenue if those costs will be recovered.

An entity should also recognise as an asset the costs incurred to *fulfil* a contract, but only if those costs meet specific criteria, including that the costs are expected to be recovered.

3.8 Presentation and disclosure

IFRS 15 requires any difference between revenue recognised and measured under the standard and payments made by the customer to be included in the balance sheet as a contract asset or liability (i.e. if the customer has paid in advance there will be a liability; if the customer is paying in arrears, there will be an asset).

The standard requires a substantial raft of disclosures, including information on key judgements made in applying the standard, so that the users of the financial statements get a clear picture of how the revenue line of the entity's statement of profit or loss has been calculated. The standard also very helpfully provides a wide range of examples.

4. Employee benefits

For most businesses, one of their major expenses is the cost of paying employees, in terms of both direct pay, but also indirect pay such as holiday pay, sickness absence, employer's national insurance and parental leave. In addition many businesses give employees cash and non-cash benefits and incentives such as bonuses, pensions, share options, gym memberships and a host of other benefits. The main accounting standard dealing with accounting for these is IAS 19 'Employee Benefits' but there is also a special standard for share-based incentives, IFRS 2 'Share-based Payments' (see Section 4). Some of the more complex aspects of IAS 19, particularly in relation to pensions, are beyond the scope of this text.

4.1 IAS 19 scope and objective

IAS 19 applies to all **employee benefits** except those to which IFRS 2 'Share-based Payments' applies (see below). In fulfilling the objective of IAS 19, which is to prescribe the accounting and disclosure for employee benefits, the standard requires an entity to recognise:

1. a liability when an employee has provided service in exchange for employee benefits to be paid in the future; and
2. an expense when the entity consumes the economic benefit arising from service provided by an employee in exchange for employee benefits.

employee benefits
are all forms of consideration given by an entity in exchange for service rendered by employees or for the termination of employment.

UK GAAP equivalent
Section 28 of FRS 102 deals with employee benefits.

4.2 Employee benefits

The definition of employee benefits encompasses a very wide range of elements that can be used to remunerate employees, but which may also be paid to their dependents or beneficiaries. The services rendered for such benefits can be in any form, whether on a full-time, part-time, temporary or casual basis.

Employee benefits include:

1. **short-term employee benefits**, such as (if expected to be settled wholly before 12 months after the end of the annual reporting period in which the employees render the related services) wages, salaries and social security contributions, paid annual leave and paid sick leave, profit-sharing and bonuses, and non-monetary benefits (such as medical care, housing, cars and free or subsidised goods or services) for current employees;

short-term employee benefits
Employee benefits (other than termination benefits) that are expected to be settled wholly before 12 months after the end of the annual reporting period in which the employees render the related service.

post-employment benefits
Employee benefits (other than termination benefits and short-term employee benefits) that are payable after the completion of employment.

other long-term employee benefits
All employee benefits other than short-term employee benefits, post-employment benefits and termination benefits.

termination benefits
Employee benefits provided in exchange for the termination of an employee's employment as a result of either: (a) an entity's decision to terminate an employee's employment before the normal retirement date; or (b) an employee's decision to accept an offer of benefits in exchange for the termination of employment.

2. **post-employment benefits**, such as retirement benefits (e.g. pensions and lump sum payments on retirement) and other post-employment benefits, such as post-employment life insurance and post-employment medical care;
3. **other long-term employee benefits**, such as long-term paid absences such as long-service leave or sabbatical leave, jubilee or other long-service benefits and long-term disability benefits; and
4. **termination benefits**.

4.3 Short-term benefits

When an employee has rendered service to an entity during an accounting period, the entity must recognise the undiscounted amount of short-term employee benefits expected to be paid in exchange for that service:

1. as a liability (accrued expense), after deducting any amount already paid. If the amount already paid exceeds the undiscounted amount of the benefits, an entity must recognise that excess as an asset (prepaid expense) to the extent that the prepayment will lead to, for example, a reduction in future payments or a cash refund; or
2. as an expense.

The standard also deals with accumulating and non-accumulating paid absences, such as holiday pay and sick pay. For non-accumulating paid absences, an expense is only recognised when the absence occurs, which is commonly the case for sick pay. For accumulating paid absences (holiday pay usually falls within this category), an obligation is recognised as employees render service that increases their entitlement to future paid absences. An entity must measure the expected cost of accumulating paid absences as the additional amount that the entity expects to pay as a result of the unused entitlement that has accumulated at the end of the reporting period.

In relation to short-term profit-sharing and bonus plans, an entity must recognise the expected cost of such payments when, but only when:

1. the entity has a present legal or constructive obligation to make such payments as a result of past events; and
2. a reliable estimate of the obligation can be made.

A present obligation exists when, and only when, the entity has no realistic alternative but to make the payments. These terms are discussed further in Chapter 6, but under normal circumstances most employees will have a contract which entitles them to payment if, for example, they have been employed for the whole of the relevant period, and this will create a legal obligation. The liability will be measured taking into account expected employee leavers who will not be entitled to some or all of the bonus. To the extent, however, that any payment is entirely at the discretion of the entity, it will not be treated as an expense until it is paid or the entity has made a commitment to pay it.

4.4 Pensions

The accounting for pensions can be complex and much of it is beyond the scope of this text. Broadly speaking there are two types of pension plan dealt with by the standard:

1. **defined contribution plans**; and
2. **defined benefit plans**.

Defined contribution pensions accounting is straightforward. The entity has no further obligation beyond the contributions it has agreed to make to a fund from which the employee will benefit, and that ultimate benefit will depend on the returns the fund makes over time. To the extent any payment is outstanding or prepaid at the end of the period, this will be shown as a liability or an asset and the contributions due are recorded as an expense.

Defined benefit pensions accounting is much more complicated as the entity has an obligation to pay an amount related to final (or sometimes career average) salary of the employee, a fraction of which is earned for each year of service (effectively the **service cost**). These very long-term liabilities are discounted to reflect the time value of money, which means there is a financing charge each year as the payment date of the pension draws closer. These pensions are often (although not always) funded by the entity making payments into a scheme vehicle which is separate from the entity. The scheme assets therefore must also be accounted for, as well as any return on those assets (which is used to offset the interest expense arising from the discount rate).

Defined benefit pensions are becoming rarer, and some companies have closed existing schemes, leading to concerns about adequacy of pension provision. Over the last 20 years or so, estimates of longevity have increased so the total cost of the pension promise has grown considerably, putting pressure on the finances of the company that sponsors the scheme as they have to pay more and more in to the scheme to meet the expected obligations. In addition, companies are exposed to a lot of volatility of measurement of the scheme obligations and assets each period.

Time value of money

The time value of money is based on the principle that money available at the present time is worth more than the same amount in the future due to its potential earning capacity. This core principle of finance holds that, provided money can earn interest, any amount of money is worth more the sooner it is received. Everyone knows that money deposited in a savings account will earn interest. Because of this, we would prefer to receive money today rather than the same amount in the future. For example, assuming a 5% interest rate, £100 invested today will be worth £105 in one year (£100 multiplied by 1.05). Conversely, £100 received one year from now is only worth £95.24 today (£100 divided by 1.05), assuming a 5% interest rate. Put another way, using common finance terminology, £95.24 is the net present value of £100 received in one year at a discount rate of 5%. Discounting is permitted or required in financial reporting when its effect is material.

defined contribution plans
Post-employment benefit plans under which an entity pays fixed contributions into a separate entity (a fund) and will have no legal or constructive obligation to pay further contributions if the fund does not hold sufficient assets to pay all employee benefits relating to employee service in the current and prior periods.

defined benefit plans
Post-employment benefit plans other than defined contribution plans.

service cost
comprises: (a) current service cost, which is the increase in the present value of the defined benefit obligation resulting from employee service in the current period; (b) past service cost, which is the change in the present value of the defined benefit obligation for employee service in prior periods, resulting from a plan amendment or a curtailment; and (c) any gain or loss on settlement.

IAS 19 does not require such pension schemes to be consolidated by the employing entity. Instead, the entity shows the net deficit or surplus in the scheme on its balance sheet, i.e.:

1. if the fair value of the pension scheme assets exceed the calculated liability, there is a surplus and therefore an asset (but only to the extent the employing company can access the surplus through reduced future contributions or refunds); or
2. if the pension scheme liability exceeds the fair value of the assets, there is a deficit and therefore a liability for the employing entity.

In the statement of profit or loss of the employer entity it will show:

1. the service cost, usually as an operating cost; and
2. a net interest expense or profit (interest expense on the discount rate less the return on scheme assets).

Measurement of the pension liability is usually carried out by an actuary and the standard lays out the methodology required to be used. The calculations are complex and because of the long-term nature of the scheme any change can create a large re-measurement gain or loss. These actuarial gains and losses, because of their size and volatility, are permitted to be shown in other comprehensive income (OCI) rather than profit or loss.

The service cost is made up of various elements:

1. current service cost, which is the increase in the present value of the defined benefit obligation resulting from employee service in the current period;
2. past service cost, which is the change in the present value of the defined benefit obligation for employee service in prior periods, resulting from a plan amendment (the introduction or withdrawal of, or changes to, a defined benefit plan) or a curtailment (a significant reduction by the entity in the number of employees covered by a plan); and
3. any gain or loss on settlement (i.e. an agreement to pay an amount that eliminates all future liability for the entity).

The disclosures around pensions, particularly defined benefit pensions, are often substantial. Look at Note 11 of the Marks & Spencer 2016 ARA on pages 102–105 for an example.

4.5 Long-term employee benefits other than pensions

For other long-term employee benefits, for example healthcare benefits, the standard requires an entity to recognise the net total of the following amounts in profit or loss:

1. service cost;
2. net interest on the net defined benefit liability or asset; and
3. re-measurements of the net defined benefit liability or asset.

These benefits, like pensions, may require an actuary to make calculations about the likely benefit payable, taking into account mortality and other expectations. The difference here compared to defined benefit pensions is that any re-measurement gains or losses go through profit or loss, not through OCI.

5. Share-based payments

Over the last 20 years or so it has become much more common for companies to pay employees, often as part of their bonus or incentive arrangements, in shares or **share options**. It is common practice to give these instruments at nil cost to employees or the legal minimum for such instruments (in the UK, for example, shares must be issued for at least their nominal value in cash or other asset). Until IFRS 2 'Share-based Payment' came into force, the difference between the fair or market value of the instrument and the amount, if any, paid by an employee, was not accounted for by the entity; it was thus remuneration that was apparently 'free' to the entity, because the employee received an instrument of some value but the entity recorded no cost for the services received in return. In some industries, the extent of share-based remuneration is substantial (e.g. in the IT sector) and there was significant concern that employee costs were being understated.

IFRS 2 requires an entity to reflect in its profit or loss and financial position the effects of **share-based payment transactions**, including expenses associated with transactions in which share options are granted to employees.

IFRS 2 covers transactions with employees that involve any payment in shares or other **equity instruments** (**equity-settled share-based payments**), or for cash where the amount payable is by reference to the value of such equity instruments (**cash-settled share-based payments**), or where goods or services are received and the terms of the arrangement give either the entity or the employee the choice of settling in equity or cash. However, it also covers any such transactions with other third parties for goods or services received and consumed.

5.1 Recognition of an asset or an expense

IFRS 2 requires an entity to recognise goods or services received or acquired in a share-based payment transaction when it obtains the goods or as the services are received. The entity recognises a corresponding increase in equity if the goods or services were received in an equity-settled share-based payment transaction, or as a liability if the goods or services were acquired in a cash-settled share-based payment transaction.

When the goods or services received or acquired in a share-based payment transaction do not qualify for recognition as assets, they must be recognised as expenses, which will apply to most employee services. If an entity issues shares to purchase an asset such as a building, it would record the building as an asset and it would be depreciated over time in much the same way as if it had been purchased for cash (see Chapter 5).

share option
A contract that gives the holder the right, but not the obligation, to subscribe to the entity's shares at a fixed or determinable price for a specified period of time.

share-based payment transaction
A transaction in which the entity receives goods or services from the supplier of those goods or services (including an employee) in a share-based payment arrangement.

UK GAAP equivalent
Section 26 of FRS 102 deals with share-based payment.

equity instrument
A contract that evidences a residual interest in the assets of an entity after deducting all of its liabilities.

equity-settled share-based payment transaction
A share-based payment transaction in which the entity receives goods or services as consideration for its own equity instruments (including shares or share options) receives goods or services but has no obligation to settle the transaction with the supplier.

cash-settled share-based payment transaction
A share-based payment transaction in which the entity acquires goods or services by incurring a liability to transfer cash or other assets to the supplier of those goods or services for amounts that are based on the price (or value) of equity instruments (including shares or share options) of the entity.

5.2 Measurement

The standard states that, for equity-settled share-based payment transactions given for employee services, the entity should measure the goods or services received (and the corresponding increase in equity) indirectly, i.e. by reference to the fair value of the equity instruments granted, as it will not be possible to measure reliably the employee services received. The instrument – shares or share options for example – will be measured at the **grant date** and will not be re-measured even if the value of the equity instrument changes, because entities do not recognise changes in the value of their own equity once the equity has been issued (i.e. granted). Where the services are rendered over time, i.e. over a **vesting period**, the expense for consuming those services will be spread over that period.

Making it work 4.1

An entity grants 100 share options, valued at £30 each at the grant date, to each of its 100 employees. The share options will vest at the end of three years, if the employees are still employed. There are no other conditions. The entity expects 20% of employees to leave by the end of three years, meaning only 80% of the options will vest.

The following amounts will be recognised as an expense over the three year vesting period:

	Annual expense	Cumulative expense
	£	£
(100 options × 100 staff × £30 × 80% × 1/3)	80,000	80,000
(100 options × 100 staff × £30 × 80% × 2/3) – £80,000	80,000	160,000
(100 options × 100 staff × £30 × 80% × 3/3) – £160,000	80,000	240,000

grant date
The date at which the entity and another party (including an employee) agree to a share-based payment arrangement, being when the entity and the counterparty have a shared understanding of the terms and conditions of the arrangement. At grant date the entity confers on the counterparty the right to cash, other assets, or equity instruments of the entity, provided the specified vesting conditions, if any, are met. If that agreement is subject to an approval process (for example, by shareholders), grant date is the date when that approval is obtained.

vesting period
The period during which all the specified vesting conditions of a share-based payment arrangement are to be satisfied.

However, if the level of leavers varies from that expected, the entity will adjust for the actual number of leavers and may also revise its expectations of total leavers during the vesting period. The total expense will therefore end up being based on the actual number of options that vest.

Usually there will be **vesting conditions** that have to be met for an employee to receive the awards. These may be limited to having to remain employed by the entity up to and including the vesting date, which is often the case with general all-employee schemes. However, vesting conditions may also include meeting target earnings over the vesting period, a target share price being achieved, or some other measure which is designed to incentivise employees, although these are often confined to schemes for directors or other managers who are more likely to be able to influence the outcome of such measures.

The measurement of shares given for employee services will often be straightforward, particularly if the entity has listed shares. For share options and unlisted shares, the standard specifies the methods of valuation, which can be complex and may require expert advice from a valuer. In particular, share options may require the use of a share option pricing model; the standard does not require any particular model to be used, but does specify the inputs required to be taken into account. Note that when an employee receives a share option and then exercises that option, the accounting for that is dealt with under the usual rules for accounting for the issue of shares; it is only the grant of the share option that is dealt with by IFRS 2.

vesting condition
A condition that determines whether the entity receives the services that entitle the counterparty to receive cash, other assets or equity instruments of the entity, under a share-based payment arrangement.

Case study 4.1

How share options work in practice

Share options often form a part of executive remuneration and are intended to incentivise directors to maximise shareholder wealth. Directors may be awarded options to purchase a specified amount of their company's shares at a specified price during a specified period of time in the future. Michael Johnson, the Herbalife CEO, for example, earned US$77 million by exercising his Herbalife share options in 2011. Most of the share options were awarded to him from 2003 to 2005 when Herbalife's shares were trading at under US$10 per share and 1.8m of them were exercised in 2011 when the price was around US$50 per share. Having purchased the shares at significantly less than market value, Johnson was able to resell the majority of the shares immediately for a gain of over US$40 per share.

If an entity uses its equity instruments to purchase services from others, e.g. a lawyer or accountant, or to purchase an asset, it is acceptable to use the fair value of the services or asset received, as long as a reliable valuation can be established, which will often be the case.

Where an entity enters into cash-settled share-based payment transactions, it must measure the goods or services acquired and the liability incurred at the fair value of the liability. Until the liability is settled, the entity will re-measure the fair value of the liability at the end of each reporting period and at the date of settlement, with any changes in fair value recognised in profit or loss for the period. This is in contrast to the valuation of equity instruments above, where the valuation is at grant date and there is no re-measurement of the equity instrument.

Finally, for share-based payment transactions where either the entity or the counterparty has the choice of whether the entity settles the transaction in cash (or other assets) or by issuing equity instruments, the accounting will depend on the overall substance of the arrangement and particularly whether any obligation has been incurred.

The standard gives detailed guidance on more complex situations that can arise in practice, for example if vesting conditions are reset or modified. There are specific rules for group arrangements, for example where a parent grants share options to the employees of a subsidiary (see Chapter 7). There are extensive disclosure requirements and you can see an example of this in Note 13 in the 2016 Marks & Spencer ARA on pages 106–107.

6. Foreign currency exchange rate changes

UK GAAP equivalent
Section 30 of FRS 102 deals with foreign currency exchange rate changes.

IAS 21 'The Effects of changes in foreign exchange rates' governs most of the accounting impact of foreign currency exchange rate changes. The purpose of the standard is to prescribe how to account for transactions in foreign currencies and foreign operations. The standards explain the applicable exchange rates and the effects of foreign currency exchange rate changes in an entity's financial statements.

IAS 21 principally deals with:

- the translation of foreign currency transactions and balances;
- the translation of results and financial position of foreign subsidiaries for consolidation purposes; and
- the translation of foreign currency results into the presentation currency (i.e. the currency in which the financial statements are reported).

6.1 Functional currency

functional currency
The currency of the primary economic environment in which an entity operates.

The **functional currency** is the currency of the primary economic environment in which an entity operates. This is usually the environment in which it generates and spends cash, so the currency in which its goods and services are denominated and paid for or the currency used to pay for labour, material and other costs associated with the provision of goods and services. The functional currency might also be determined by the country where competition and regulations largely determine the selling prices of an entity's goods and services or the currency in which funds are generated from financing activities (evidenced by the currency of an entity's debt instruments and issued equity).

An entity must determine its functional currency and measure its performance and financial position in that currency. All other currencies are treated as foreign currencies. An entity cannot change functional currency unless there is a change in circumstances, events or conditions that warrants a change in functional currency.

In contrast, an entity has a free choice over its presentation currency. Where the presentation currency differs from the functional currency, the functional currency should be translated into the presentation currency.

6.2 Foreign currency transactions

Transactions in a foreign currency should be translated into the functional currency at the **spot rate** of exchange on the date of the transaction. For practical purposes, IAS 21 allows an approximate rate to be used such as the weekly or monthly average rate, provided there have been no significant fluctuations of the currency during the relevant period.

spot rate
A foreign exchange is the market fx rate used in transactions with immediate delivery.

6.3 Translation of monetary and non-monetary items at the balance sheet date

- Foreign currency denominated **monetary items** should be converted at the closing rate of exchange.
- Non-monetary items valued on a historic cost basis should be converted at the exchange rate on the date the transaction took place (i.e. the historic rate of exchange).
- Non-monetary items held at fair value should be converted at the exchange rate prevailing at the most recent valuation date, i.e. when the fair values were last determined.

monetary items
Units of currency held and assets and liabilities to be received or paid in a fixed or determinable number of units of currency.

6.4 Recognition of foreign exchange differences

Exchange differences are recognised by an entity in the income statement in the period in which they occur with the exception of exchanges differences on monetary items forming part of a net investment in a foreign operation, which are recognised in the group accounts. The exchange gains or losses are recognised in the income statement upon disposal of the foreign entity.

Foreign currency dividends paid to a parent from its foreign subsidiary may result in exchange gains or losses in the financial statements of the parent entity. These exchange differences should be recognised in the profit and loss account of the parent entity and should not be reversed out on consolidation.

exchange differences
Gains and losses arising from settlement or from converting monetary items back to one currency from another, using different exchange rates to those used for the initial recognition.

6.5 Consolidation of group entities

Entities within a group (see Chapter 7) may have different functional currencies because the functional currency is determined at entity level and not at group level. Each entity within the group should translate its individual results and financial position into the presentation currency of the group so that consolidation may take place in the presentation currency.

accounting profit
The profit or loss for a period before deducting tax expense.

taxable profit (or tax loss)
The profit (loss) for a period, determined in accordance with the rules established by the taxation authorities, upon which income taxes are payable (recoverable).

7. Income taxes

Businesses in most developed jurisdictions pay tax on their profits. The more complex issues around accounting for such taxes are generally due to the difference between **accounting profits** and **taxable profits**. The differences are mainly due to certain factors, including:

- tax relief given on investment in assets such as plant and machinery in a way that does not match the accounting charge for depreciation (see Chapter 5);

- some expenses being not allowable for taxation; and
  - whether tax losses can be carried forward to set against future taxable profits.

UK GAAP equivalent
Section 29 of FRS 102 deals with income taxes.

IAS 12 'Income Taxes' deals with accounting for taxes on profits. It is a complicated standard in some areas and in this text we will only cover the more basic aspects.

7.1 Income taxes

IAS 12 deals with taxes on income or profits, not any other form of tax such as sales taxes (e.g. VAT) or taxes on production (e.g. petroleum revenue). In the UK, income tax for most corporate vehicles is known as corporation tax. The important principle here is that deferred taxation is not a real tax of the period which is paid to the tax authorities, but rather an accounting entry to bridge the gap between accounting and taxable profits.

Test yourself 4.4

1. **Are there any corporate entities or other types of business in the UK or in your jurisdiction that do not pay corporate taxation?**
2. **What other types of taxes would not be treated as income taxes for the purposes of the standard?**

7.2 Recognition of current and deferred taxation

current tax
The amount of income taxes payable (or recoverable) in respect of the taxable profit (tax loss) for a period.

deferred taxation
The amounts of income taxes payable in future periods in respect of taxable temporary differences.

IAS 12 deals with taxation as it relates to the reporting period, namely **current taxation**, but also tax effects that arise due to transactions in the reporting period but that will only affect the entity's taxation in a later period, i.e. **deferred taxation**.

The treatment of current taxation is generally straightforward. Current tax for current and prior periods are, to the extent unpaid, recognised as a liability. If the amount already paid in respect of current and prior periods exceeds the amount due for those periods, the excess is recognised as an asset.

Deferred taxation is more complicated and most of the requirements are beyond the scope of this text. The main principle to note is that an entity, in many but not all circumstances, must recognise deferred taxation when there is a difference between taxable profits and accounting profits. The standard lays out the relevant circumstances and gives guidance on how to determine deferred taxation balances.

7.3 Measurement

IAS 12 requires current tax liabilities or assets for the current and prior periods to be measured at the amount expected to be paid to (or recovered from) the taxation authorities, and using the tax rates (and tax laws) that have been substantively enacted by the end of the reporting period. This timing issue can be important when announcements are made about changes in tax laws or rates that will not be enacted for some time.

Deferred tax assets and liabilities should be measured at the tax rates that are expected to apply to the period when the asset is realised or the liability is settled, based on tax rates (and tax laws) that have been substantively enacted by the end of the reporting period.

deferred tax assets are the amounts of income taxes recoverable in future periods in respect of: differences between the carrying amount of an asset or liability in the statement of financial position and its tax base; the carryforward of unused tax losses; and the carryforward of unused tax credits.

7.4 Disclosures

Companies must give substantial disclosures around taxation in their financial statements. As issues around how much tax businesses pay has become more controversial over the last few years, disclosures are likely to be more substantial, including narrative information on tax and tax risks in the front part of the annual report and accounts. Marks & Spencer's 2016 ARA discloses substantial information on taxation in Note 7 to the accounts on pages 99–100.

Chapter summary

- IAS 8 is an important standard which lays out the rules for companies to select and change accounting policies. It also specifies the approach to changes of estimates and correction of errors. Unless an IFRS Standards requires a change in accounting policy, entities should only change those policies when to do so would provide more relevant and reliable information. The usual rule for changes in accounting policy and correction of errors is to restate prior period information unless it is impracticable.
- The revenue line drives an entity's overall performance and a new standard has been introduced to tighten the reporting rules around it. IFRS 15 introduces a staged approach to revenue accounting by identifying contracts with customers, breaking those down into individual performance obligations and allocating the contract price to them so that when they are performed, revenue is recognised and measured.
- Accounting for employee benefits can be complicated, particularly in relation to pensions and share-based payment. IAS 19 and IFRS 2 deal with these, but also accounting for short-term pay and related benefits and other longer-term items.
- IAS 21 governs the impact of foreign currency exchange rate changes and sets out the standard accounting practice for translating foreign currency transactions and balances, foreign subsidiaries for consolidation purposes and foreign currency results into the presentation currency for reporting purposes.

- Accounting for corporate taxes is made more complicated by the need to account for deferred taxation not just current taxes. IAS 12 deals with measurement of current tax, including the rates that should be used, as well as deferred taxation, which deals with the mismatch between taxable profits and accounting profits.

Chapter five
Assets

List of topics

1. Introduction
2. Property, plant and equipment
3. Intangible assets
4. Impairment of assets
5. Inventories
6. Financial instruments

1. Introduction

As we saw in Chapter 3, a company must report its assets in the statement of financial position or balance sheet, distinguishing between long-term, non-current and current assets. This chapter looks at the main categories of assets you would expect a company to carry. It does not deal with specialist assets such as investment property or biological assets.

Businesses hold various types of asset to generate activity and profits in the longer term, including physical assets such as property and plant and machinery, and also intangible assets such as licences, brands and patents. As the assets are used to generate profits, the costs of the assets are allocated to those profits made over the asset's useful life, through the effect of depreciation or amortisation, which are described in this chapter. This is an effect of accruals accounting. Where a business finds it will not recover the carrying value of any long-term asset, it must reduce its value in its accounts and the reduction in value is reported as an impairment expense and can be viewed as an accelerated form of depreciation.

Businesses also hold shorter term assets, which will be consumed by the business or sold on by it quite quickly, including inventories or stocks which also have rules over how they are recognised and measured. Financial assets encompass a wide range of items, including cash, so most businesses will have at least some of them. More complex financial assets also have to be accounted for, including derivatives. The main items are covered in this chapter.

2. Property, plant and equipment

Almost all businesses need property in which to house their operations, be they administrative, manufacturing or other operations. Depending on the nature of the business, they will also often have plant and machinery and other forms of equipment. Heavy industries, for example steel-makers or car manufacturers may require large factories with a lot of plant and machinery; warehouses may be needed to store goods ready for sale or raw materials that will be used by the business; and even financial services firms will need offices and office equipment such as computers, photocopiers, desks and so on.

Specialist assets are covered by other standards, for example:

- IAS 40 deals with investment property, i.e. property held for renting out, but also for capital gains through trading.
- IAS 41 deals with agriculture, i.e. biological assets such as forests, livestock.
- IFRS 6 deals with exploration assets for oil and gas.

These are not covered in this text.

2.1 IAS 16

IAS 16 'Property, Plant and Equipment' covers the generality of longer life assets held for ongoing use within a business and it will affect nearly all businesses to some extent. IAS 16 lays out the accounting treatment for **property, plant and equipment** and the principal issues are the recognition of the assets, the determination of their **carrying amounts** and the depreciation charges and impairment losses (see Section 3) to be recognised in relation to them.

property, plant and equipment
Tangible items that: (a) are held for use in the production or supply of goods or services, for rental to others, or for administrative purposes; and (b) are expected to be used during more than one period.

carrying amount
The amount at which an asset is recognised after deducting any accumulated depreciation (amortisation) and accumulated impairment losses thereon.

UK GAAP equivalent
Section 17 of FRS 102 deals with property, plant and equipment.

cost
The amount of cash or cash equivalents paid or the fair value of the other consideration given to acquire an asset at the time of its acquisition or construction.

2.2 Recognition of items of property, plant and equipment

The **cost** of an item of property, plant and equipment should be recognised as an asset if, and only if:

- it is probable that future economic benefits associated with the item will flow to the entity; and
  - the cost of the item can be measured reliably.

Items such as spare parts, stand-by equipment and servicing equipment are also accounted for under IAS 16 when they meet the definition of property, plant and equipment. Otherwise, such items are classified as inventory (see Section 4). Costs of ongoing servicing of assets are not added to the carrying amount but are recorded as an expense as they are incurred.

2.3 Measurement of cost or revaluation

On its initial recognition, an item of property, plant and equipment that qualifies for recognition as an asset must be measured at its cost. The cost of an item of property, plant and equipment comprises:

- its purchase price, including import duties and non-refundable purchase taxes, after deducting trade discounts and rebates;
- any costs directly attributable to bringing the asset to the location and condition necessary for it to be capable of operating in the manner intended by management (e.g. installation and assembly costs, site preparation); and
  - the initial estimate of the costs of dismantling and removing the item and restoring the site on which it is located.

In accounting periods after the initial recognition of an item of property, plant or equipment, there is a choice of treatment. This is an example of an accounting policy choice as discussed in Chapter 3. The choice of measurement is between:

- **The cost model**: after recognition as an asset, an item of property, plant and equipment is carried at its cost less any accumulated **depreciation** and any accumulated impairment losses.
- **The revaluation model**: after recognition as an asset, an item of property, plant and equipment whose fair value can be measured reliably is carried at a revalued amount, being its fair value at the date of the revaluation less any subsequent accumulated depreciation and subsequent accumulated impairment losses.

depreciation
The systematic allocation of the depreciable amount of an asset over its useful life.

The choice of model will usually depend on the circumstances of the business: if an asset is for continuing use and there is no interest in selling it or using its value to secure financing, then it is likely an entity would not take the trouble to revalue it. There are some restrictions and requirements in relation to the revaluation model which make it more onerous. Revaluations do not have to be made annually, but must be made with sufficient regularity to ensure that the carrying amount does not differ materially from that which would be determined using fair value at the end of the reporting period. In addition, if an item of property, plant and equipment is revalued, the entire class of property, plant and equipment to which that asset belongs must also be revalued and all the assets in that class must be revalued at the same time.

The standard specifies how increases and decreases in value should be reported:

- If an asset's carrying amount is *increased* as a result of a revaluation, the increase is recognised in other comprehensive income and accumulated in equity under the heading of 'revaluation surplus'. However, the increase is recognised in profit or loss to the extent that it reverses a revaluation decrease of the same asset previously recognised in profit or loss.
- If an asset's carrying amount is *decreased* as a result of a revaluation, the decrease is recognised in profit or loss. However, the decrease is recognised in other comprehensive income to the extent of any credit balance existing in the revaluation surplus in respect of that asset. The decrease recognised in other comprehensive income reduces the amount accumulated in equity under the heading of revaluation surplus.

2.4 Depreciation

useful life
(a) the period over which an asset is expected to be available for use by an entity; or (b) the number of production or similar units expected to be obtained from the asset by an entity.

depreciable amount
The cost of an asset, or other amount substituted for cost, less its residual value.

residual value
The residual value of an asset is the estimated amount that an entity would currently obtain from disposal of the asset, after deducting the estimated costs of disposal, if the asset were already of the age and in the condition expected at the end of its useful life.

Assets that last for more than one accounting period are still consumed by the entity and so there is a need to allocate the cost or value of the asset as an expense over time as it is used. IAS 16 deals with this by requiring depreciation to be charged, which is deducted from the cost or value of the asset and taken as an expense in each period the asset is in use, across its **useful life**.

Each part of an item of property, plant and equipment with a cost that is significant in relation to the total cost of the item is depreciated separately. The depreciation charge for each period is usually recognised in profit or loss. The **depreciable amount** of an asset is allocated on a systematic basis over its useful life. The **residual value** and the useful life of an asset must be reviewed at least at each financial year-end and, if expectations differ from previous estimates, the change(s) are accounted for as a change in an accounting estimate in accordance with IAS 8 (see Chapter 3).

The depreciation method used should reflect the pattern in which the asset's future economic benefits are expected to be consumed by the entity and this should also be reviewed at least annually (with any change again being a change in accounting estimate).

Assets may also become impaired and IAS 16 requires this to be dealt with as specified by IAS 36 (see Section 3).

Worked example 5.1

An item of plant is purchased on 1 January 2016.

Cost	**£120,000**
Residual value estimated at date of purchase	**£20,000**
Residual value estimated at 1 Jan 2017	**nil**
Total useful life estimated at date of purchase	**10 years**
Total useful life estimated at 1 Jan 2018	**8 years**

What is the depreciation charge and net book value for 2016, 2017, 2018 and 2019?

2.5 Derecognition

The carrying amount of an item of property, plant and equipment is derecognised, that is removed from the financial statements, either:

- on disposal; or
  - when no future economic benefits are expected from its use or disposal.

Any net gain or loss arising from the derecognition of an item of property, plant and equipment is included in profit or loss at the point when the item is derecognised. This is an example of where offset is allowed in financial reporting (see Chapter 3): the proceeds of sale are offset against the carrying value to produce a net gain or loss. Gains cannot be classified as revenue and in most cases, if the amounts are material, companies often disclose them separately in the statement of profit or loss so they are not confused with ongoing profits from operations.

2.6 Disclosure

To the extent that property, plant and equipment is a material asset balance for an entity, the standard requires substantial disclosures, including all movements in the year for each class of asset such as additions, disposals, depreciation, impairments and revaluations. Disclosures are also required of any restrictions of title, including pledges of assets as security for borrowings, and any contractual commitments for purchase of items of property, plant and equipment in the future.

You can see the type of disclosures required by looking at Note 15 in the Marks & Spencer 2016 ARA on page 110.

3. Intangible assets

In recent times the importance of intangible assets has grown considerably for the modern economy, with companies relying on know-how, brands and intellectual property rights to run their business and make profits, rather than tangible assets. Nevertheless the accounting for intangibles, predominantly in IAS 38 'Intangible Assets' remains restrictive in terms of what can be shown as an asset, except when that intangible is acquired on its own or within another business (see Chapter 7). This has led to calls for greater disclosure around intangible assets that are home-grown by the business and therefore not shown in the financial statements, but which are likely to have a significant contribution to future earnings.

Test yourself 5.1

Apple Inc has a market capitalisation (as at end September 2015) of £608 billion, yet its balance sheet shows net assets of only approximately £120 billion. Why is there a difference and what are the main causes?

3.1 Scope and objective of IAS 38

IAS 38 deals only with those **intangible assets** that are not covered by other standards. IAS 38 requires an entity to recognise an intangible asset if, and only if, specified criteria are met, how to measure the carrying amount of intangible assets and it also requires specified disclosures about intangible assets.

intangible asset
An identifiable non-monetary asset without physical substance.

UK GAAP equivalent
Section 18 of FRS 102 deals with intangible assets.

3.2 Recognition

IAS 38 states that an intangible asset should be recognised by an entity if, and only if:

- it is probable that the expected future economic benefits that are attributable to the asset will flow to the entity; and
- the cost of the asset can be measured reliably.

When an entity assesses the probability of expected future economic benefits, it must use reasonable and supportable assumptions that represent management's best estimate of the set of economic conditions that will exist over the useful life of the asset.

Where intangible assets are acquired as part of a business combination, the probability test in relation to expected future economic benefits is assumed to be met. This means that some intangibles will be recognised by an acquirer on an acquisition which were not recognised by the target company beforehand. We will discuss this further in Chapter 7.

3.3 Measurement

The standard distinguishes between intangibles purchased separately from intangibles that are purchased as part of a business combination (see Chapter 7).

- An intangible asset acquired separately will initially be measured at cost.
- A intangible asset acquired as part of a business combination will be measured at fair value at the date of acquisition.

As with tangible assets, an entity may follow either a cost or revaluation model for intangible assets after initial recognition. However, there are even greater restrictions placed on the revaluation model for intangible assets and it is very rare to see such revaluations in practice.

3.4 Internally generated goodwill and intangibles

Internally generated goodwill may not be recognised as an asset. This is one of the main reasons why a company's balance sheet will never reflect the total value of the business. The reason for the bar is that internally generated goodwill is not separable from the business as a whole, is not capable of being controlled or accurately measured, and therefore does not meet the definition of an asset in the Conceptual Framework.

The definition of an intangible asset requires it to be identifiable to distinguish it from goodwill. An asset is identifiable if it either:

- is separable, i.e. is capable of being separated or divided from the entity and sold, transferred, licensed, rented or exchanged (regardless of whether the entity intends to do so); or
- arises from contractual or other legal rights, regardless of whether those rights are transferable or separable from the entity or from other rights and obligations.

3.5 Research and development

IAS 38 deals specifically with **research** and **development**, key issues and major components of performance for some businesses, particularly for example in the IT, pharmaceutical and engineering sectors. The standard distinguishes between a research phase, where there is still significant uncertainty about whether any costs will be recovered through successful product launch, and the development phase, where there is much more evidence about a likely successful launch and hence recovery of costs.

research
Original and planned investigation undertaken with the prospect of gaining new scientific or technical knowledge and understanding.

development
The application of research findings or other knowledge to a plan or design for the production of new or substantially improved materials, devices, products, processes, systems or services before the start of commercial production or use.

No intangible asset arising from research may be recognised as an asset. Expenditure on research must instead be recognised as an expense when it is incurred.

In contrast, an intangible asset arising from development should be recognised as an asset if, and only if, an entity can demonstrate *all* of the following:

- the technical feasibility of completing the intangible asset so that it will be available for use or sale;
- its intention to complete the intangible asset and use or sell it;
- its ability to use or sell the intangible asset;
- how the intangible asset will generate probable future economic benefits. Among other things, the entity can demonstrate the existence of a market for the output of the intangible asset or the intangible asset itself or, if it is to be used internally, the usefulness of the intangible asset;
- the availability of adequate technical, financial and other resources to complete the development and to use or sell the intangible asset; and
- its ability to measure reliably the expenditure attributable to the intangible asset during its development.

These rules are designed to avoid the recognition of costs as assets when those costs are unlikely to be recovered.

All other internally generated brands, mastheads, publishing titles, customer lists and items similar in substance may not be recognised as intangible assets and any costs that are incurred in relation to them will be recognised as an immediate expense. Moreover, expenditure on an intangible item that was initially recognised as an expense cannot be recognised as part of the cost of an intangible asset at a later date.

3.6 Amortisation

As with tangible assets, intangible assets must be depreciated, although this is referred to as **amortisation** in relation to intangible assets. The first thing to assess is the intangible asset's useful life. Unlike most tangible assets (other than freehold land), it is possible to have an intangible asset with an infinite useful life if there is no foreseeable limit to the period over which the asset is expected to generate net cash inflows for the entity.

amortisation
The systematic allocation of the depreciable amount of an intangible asset over its useful life.

Difference with UK GAAP
Under FRS 102 all intangible assets are considered to have a finite useful life and it is not possible to claim an infinite life. Where an entity cannot make an estimate of the useful life of an intangible asset, the life used must not exceed 10 years.

The standard requires an entity to assess whether the useful life of an intangible asset is finite or indefinite and, if finite, the length of that useful life. Intangible assets with an infinite useful life are not amortised. Any intangible assets based on contractual legal rights, for example in relation to a licence, will only have a life as long as those legal rights exist. Any rights to a renewal period can only be used to extend the useful life if renewal would be at no cost.

The depreciable amount of an intangible asset with a finite useful life is allocated on a systematic basis over its useful life. The amortisation method used should reflect the pattern in which the asset's future economic benefits are expected to be consumed by the entity. If that pattern cannot be determined reliably, the straight-line method is used. The amortisation charge for each period is recognised in profit or loss as an expense.

IAS 38 is more restrictive about residual values than IAS 16 for items of property, plant and equipment. The residual value of an intangible asset with a finite useful life must be assumed to be zero unless:

- there is a commitment by a third party to purchase the asset at the end of its useful life; or
- there is an **active market** for the asset and:
  - residual value can be determined by reference to that market; and
  - it is probable that such a market will exist at the end of the asset's useful life.

active market
A market in which transactions for the asset or liability take place with sufficient frequency and volume to provide pricing information on an ongoing basis.

As with tangible assets, the standard requires frequent review of the estimated useful life of an intangible asset, its expected residual value and whether it is impaired. These reviews must be thoroughly documented and often involve considerable investigation by auditors as part of their audit work.

3.7 Derecognition

The carrying amount of an intangible asset is derecognised, that is removed from the financial statements, either:

- on disposal; or
- when no future economic benefits are expected from its use or disposal.

Any net gain or loss arising from the derecognition of an intangible asset is included in profit or loss at the point when the item is derecognised. Gains cannot be classified as revenue and in most cases, if the amounts are material, companies often disclose them separately in the statement of profit or loss so they are not confused with ongoing profits from operations.

3.8 Disclosure

To the extent that intangible assets are material for an entity, the standard requires substantial disclosures, including all movements in the year for each class of asset such as additions, disposals, amortisation, impairments and revaluations. Disclosures are also required of any restrictions of title, including pledges of assets as security for borrowings, and any contractual commitments for purchase of intangible assets in the future. You can see the types of disclosure required in Note 14 of the Marks & Spencer 2016 ARA on pages 108–109.

4. Impairment of assets

When an asset is acquired and used in a business, it is important to know that the business will get sufficient value from using the asset such that its cost will be recovered. We have seen in the first two sections of this chapter that non-current assets are depreciated or amortised to reflect the consumption of their costs as they are used to generate profits and cash flows for a business. To the extent that those future profits and cash flows are not sufficient to recompense for the remaining carrying value of the asset at any particular point in time, accounting standards require impairment charges to be made, which can be thought of as a form of accelerated depreciation or amortisation.

IAS 36 'Impairment of Assets' deals with these issues for both individual assets and also for assets, including purchased goodwill, relating to acquired businesses. The aspects of the standard that relate to business combinations and assessing acquired assets, including goodwill, are beyond the scope of this text, although we will look at them briefly in Chapter 7. The rest of this section looks at the impairment requirements for single assets.

UK GAAP equivalent
Section 27 of FRS 102 deals with impairment of assets.

4.1 Scope and objective of IAS 36

The objective of IAS 36 is to prescribe the procedures that an entity applies to ensure that its assets are carried at no more than their **recoverable amount**. An asset is carried at more than its recoverable amount if its **carrying amount** exceeds the amount to be recovered through use or sale of the asset. If this is the case, the asset is described as impaired and the standard requires the entity to recognise an **impairment loss**. IAS 36 also specifies when an entity should reverse an impairment loss and prescribes disclosures.

recoverable amount
The recoverable amount of an asset or a cash-generating unit is the higher of its fair value less costs of disposal and its value in use.

impairment loss
The amount by which the carrying amount of an asset or a cash-generating unit exceeds its recoverable amount.

The standard mainly deals with the impairment of non-current assets such as property, plant and equipment and intangible assets. Other standards deal with inventories (see Section 4), financial assets (see Section 5) and other specialised assets such as investment property.

4.2 Indicators of impairment

In most cases, IAS 36 only requires an entity to consider whether an asset is impaired if there are indicators of impairment. If this were not the case, it would be very onerous to test each asset for impairment every accounting period. Where there are indicators of impairment, the entity must estimate the recoverable amount of the asset.

The standard gives the following examples of indicators of impairment, but note that this is not exhaustive and there may be others:

External sources of information

There are observable indications that the asset's value has declined during the period significantly more than would be expected as a result of the passage of time or normal use.

Significant changes with an adverse effect on the entity have taken place during the period, or will take place in the near future, in the technological, market, economic or legal environment in which the entity operates or in the market to which an asset is dedicated.

Market interest rates or other market rates of return on investments have increased during the period, and those increases are likely to affect the discount rate used in calculating an asset's value in use and decrease the asset's recoverable amount materially.

The carrying amount of the net assets of the entity is more than its market capitalisation.

Internal sources of information

Evidence is available of obsolescence or physical damage of an asset.

Significant changes with an adverse effect on the entity have taken place during the period, or are expected to take place in the near future, in the extent to which, or manner in which, an asset is used or is expected to be used. These changes include the asset becoming idle, plans to discontinue or restructure the operation to which an asset belongs, plans to dispose of an asset before the previously expected date, and reassessing the useful life of an asset as finite rather than indefinite.

Evidence is available from internal reporting that indicates that the economic performance of an asset is, or will be, worse than expected.

Dividend from a subsidiary, joint venture or associate

For an investment in a subsidiary, joint venture or associate (see Chapter 7), the investor recognises a dividend from the investment and evidence is available that:

(i) the carrying amount of the investment in the separate financial statements exceeds the carrying amounts in the consolidated financial statements of the investee's net assets,; or

(ii) the dividend exceeds the total comprehensive income of the subsidiary, joint venture or associate in the period the dividend is declared.

4.3 Assessing recoverable amount

The recoverable amount of an asset is the higher of its fair value less **costs of disposal** and its value in use. It is not always necessary to assess both amounts as if just one of them is higher than the asset's carrying value, the asset is not impaired. The standard allows two comparators to be used because only one of the measures may not be appropriate.

costs of disposal
Incremental costs directly attributable to the disposal of an asset or cash-generating unit, excluding finance costs and income tax expense.

Examples of costs of disposal are legal costs, stamp duty and similar transaction taxes, costs of removing the asset, and direct incremental costs to bring an asset into condition for its sale.

4.4 Value in use

The most difficult part of applying the standard to apply in practice relates to the calculation of value in use. The standard requires the following elements to be reflected in the calculation:

- an estimate of the future cash flows the entity expects to derive from the asset;
- expectations about possible variations in the amount or timing of those future cash flows;
- the time value of money, represented by the current market risk-free rate of interest (on a pre-tax basis);
- the price for bearing the uncertainty inherent in the asset; and
- other factors, such as illiquidity, that market participants would reflect in pricing the future cash flows the entity expects to derive from the asset.

The standard places restrictions and rules on many of these inputs in order to ensure a prudent calculation is carried out. Even then, a great deal of judgement is often required.

The estimates of future cash flows will include:

- projections of cash inflows from the continuing use of the asset;
- projections of cash outflows incurred to generate the cash inflows from continuing use of the asset (including cash outflows to prepare the asset for use); and
- net cash flows, if any, to be received (or paid) for the disposal of the asset at the end of its useful life

Worked example 5.2

A company purchased a building for £2 million on 1 January 2015. Its estimated useful life at that date was 20 years and the company uses straight line depreciation method. On the 31 December 2019 the local authority started to construct a new road junction next to the building which reduced access to the building and increased noise, thereby

adversely affecting its value. An estate agent has told the company that it could sell the company for £1 million but it would have to incur costs of £50,000 to do so. Alternatively, it if continues to use it the present value of the net cash flows the building will generate is £1.2 million. What should the building's carrying value be in the accounts and is there an impairment loss?

4.5 Recognition and measurement

If, and only if, the recoverable amount of an asset is less than its carrying amount, the carrying amount of the asset is reduced to its recoverable amount. That reduction is an impairment loss.

An impairment loss is recognised immediately in profit or loss, unless the asset is carried at revalued amount in accordance with IAS 16 or IAS 36 (see Sections 1 and 2 above). Any impairment loss of a revalued asset is treated as a revaluation decrease.

After the recognition of an impairment loss, the depreciation (amortisation) charge for the asset is adjusted in future periods to allocate the asset's revised carrying amount, less its residual value (if any), on a systematic basis over its remaining useful life.

There are occasions when an impairment loss in one reporting period is reversed in a subsequent period. The indicators of a reversal will generally be the mirror images of the indicators of impairment noted above, but they are relatively rare in practice.

4.6 Disclosures

Where impairments have occurred there are substantial disclosure requirements, particularly in relation to the inputs into the calculation of value in use and how fair value has been derived (i.e. from observable market prices or not).

5. Inventories

UK GAAP equivalent
Section 13 of FRS 102 deals with inventories.

Most businesses that are not purely service businesses will hold inventories or stocks of some kind. For most manufacturing businesses these items turn over relatively quickly as items are bought or produced and then sold on to customers. For some more specialised businesses, inventory is held for longer as it takes longer to build, for example ships, buildings, oil rigs and so on. Accounting for most forms of inventory is dealt with by IAS 2 'Inventories'.

5.1 Scope and objective of IAS 2

Inventories are assets:

- held for sale in the ordinary course of business;
- in the process of production for such sale; or
- in the form of materials or supplies to be consumed in the production process or in the rendering of services.

The primary issue in accounting for inventories is the amount of cost to be recognised as an asset and carried forward until the related revenues are recognised. IAS 2 provides guidance on the determination of cost and its subsequent recognition as an expense, including any write-down to net realisable value. It also provides guidance on the cost formulas that are used to assign costs to inventories.

5.2 Measurement

IAS 2 does not deal with initial recognition directly, but the usual rules apply, i.e. inventories will be recognised as an asset once the entity has obtained control.

In terms of measurement, IAS 2 requires inventories to be measured at the lower of cost and net realisable value (see below).

5.3 Cost

The cost of inventories comprises all costs of purchase, costs of conversion and other costs incurred in bringing the inventories to their present location and condition.

The cost of purchase of an item of inventory will include the purchase price, import duties and other taxes (other than those subsequently recoverable by the entity from the taxing authorities), and transport, handling and other costs directly attributable to the acquisition of finished goods, materials and services. Trade discounts, rebates and other similar items are deducted in determining the costs of purchase.

Conversion costs include costs directly related to the units of production, such as direct labour. They also include a systematic allocation of **fixed and variable production overheads** that are incurred in converting materials into finished goods.

The allocation of fixed production overheads to the costs of conversion is based on the **normal capacity** of the production facilities. The amount of fixed overhead allocated to each unit of production is not increased as a consequence of low production or idle plant. Unallocated overheads are recognised as an expense in the period in which they are incurred. **Variable production overheads** are allocated to each unit of production on the basis of the actual use of the production facilities.

Other costs are included in the cost of inventories only to the extent that they are incurred in bringing the inventories to their present location and condition. For example, it may be appropriate to include non-production overheads or the costs of designing products for specific customers in the cost of inventories.

Some entities will hold items of inventory that are not ordinarily interchangeable and both these and goods or services produced and segregated for specific projects should have their costs individually assigned to them. However, specific identification of costs is inappropriate when there are large numbers of items of inventory that are ordinarily interchangeable and this will be the case for many manufacturing businesses, some of which will carry hundreds or thousands of

fixed production overheads
Those indirect costs of production that remain relatively constant regardless of the volume of production, such as depreciation and maintenance of factory buildings, equipment and right-of-use assets used in the production process, and the cost of factory management and administration.

normal capacity
The production expected to be achieved on average over a number of periods or seasons under normal circumstances, taking into account the loss of capacity resulting from planned maintenance.

variable production overheads
Those indirect costs of production that vary directly, or nearly directly, with the volume of production, such as indirect materials and indirect labour.

standard inventory items. In such circumstances, costs can be assigned by using specified formulae, namely the first-in, first-out (FIFO) or weighted average cost formula. An entity should use the same cost formula for all inventories having a similar nature and use to the entity.

Worked example 5.3

Use the following information to calculate the value of inventory on hand on at the end of January and cost of goods sold during January on a FIFO basis.

1 Jan	**Opening inventory**	**70 units @ £16.00 per unit**
5 Jan	**Purchase**	**138 units @ £16.50 per unit**
9 Jan	**Sale**	**95 units @ £20.00 per unit**
11 Jan	**Purchase**	**39 units @ £17.00 per unit**
16 Jan	**Purchase**	**78 units @ £17.50 per unit**
20 Jan	**Sale**	**118 units @ £21.50 per unit**
29 Jan	**Sale**	**62 units @ £22.00 per unit**

5.4 Net realisable value

As is the case with non-current assets becoming impaired, discussed in Section 3 above, the cost of inventories may not be recoverable if those inventories are damaged, if they have become wholly or partially obsolete, or if their selling prices have fallen. The cost of inventories may also not be recoverable if the estimated costs of completion or the estimated costs to be incurred to make the sale have increased. The practice of writing inventories down below cost to **net realisable value** is consistent with the view that assets should not be carried in excess of amounts expected to be realised from their sale or use.

net realisable value The estimated selling price in the ordinary course of business less the estimated costs of completion and the estimated costs necessary to make the sale.

Inventories are usually written down to net realisable value item by item. In some circumstances, however, it may be appropriate to group similar or related items.

5.5 Derecognition and disclosure

When inventories are sold, the carrying amount of those inventories is removed as an asset and recognised as an expense in the period in which the related revenue is recognised (see IFRS 15 in Chapter 4). The amount of any write-down of inventories to net realisable value and all losses of inventories are recognised as an expense in the period the write-down or loss occurs.

As with all accounting standards, specific disclosures are required of significant accounting policies around inventories, as well as separate disclosure of inventories carried as assets at the period end, the amount of inventories recognised as an expense and any write down of inventories, including the circumstances of the write down.

6. Financial instruments

There is no escaping from the fact that financial reporting requirements for **financial instruments** are complicated due to the inherent complexity of many types of financial instruments, derivative contracts being just one example. In addition, the kinds of businesses that hold and deal in significant numbers of financial instruments, such as banks, insurance companies and other financial institutions, often deal with these most complicated forms of instrument and so the bulk of their financial statements are often difficult to understand without expert knowledge. Because of this, if you deal with accounting for financial instruments, you may need to look to guidance beyond the scope of this text.

financial instrument
Any contract that gives rise to a financial asset of one entity and a financial liability or equity instrument of another entity.

The definition of financial instruments is wide and, on the asset side, includes a lot of basic things that most companies have, including cash, trade receivables and shares in other companies. We will cover some of the more basic issues around accounting for financial assets in this chapter; financial liabilities are dealt with in Chapter 6.

The main standard dealing with this topic is IFRS 9 'Financial Instruments'. It is effective from 1 January 2018 and was endorsed for use in the EU in June 2016. This standard has been introduced because the previous standards were considered deficient in the light of the financial crisis of 2007–2010. However, other standards (or residual parts of old standards) also cover aspects of accounting for financial instruments, including:

- IAS 32 'Financial Instruments: Presentation'
- IAS 39 'Financial Instruments: Recognition and Measurement' (most of which are replaced by IFRS 9 from 2018 but which retains some requirements in relation to hedge accounting)
- IFRS 7 'Financial Instruments: Disclosures'
- IFRS 13 'Fair Value Measurement' (applies to all items that are required to be measured at fair value).

UK GAAP equivalent
Section 11 of FRS 102 deals with basic financial instruments. Section 12 deals with more complex instruments and hedge accounting and includes some useful examples.

6.1 Scope of IFRS 9

IFRS 9 excludes some financial instruments from its scope, including leases, shareholdings in subsidiaries, joint ventures and associates (see Chapter 7), insurance contracts and many others, as these are dealt with by other, more specific standards.

6.2 Important definitions

The definitions in the relevant standards are crucial.

A financial asset is any asset that is:

- cash;
- an equity instrument of another entity;

- a contractual right–
  - to receive cash or another financial asset from another entity; or
  - to exchange financial assets or financial liabilities with another entity under conditions that are potentially favourable to the entity; or
- a contract that will or may be settled in the entity's own equity instruments and is–
  - a non-derivative for which the entity is or may be obliged to receive a variable number of the entity's own equity instruments; or
  - a derivative that will or may be settled other than by the exchange of a fixed amount of cash or another financial asset for a fixed number of the entity's own equity instruments.

A derivative is a financial instrument or other contract with all three of the following characteristics:

- Its value changes in response to the change in a specified interest rate, financial instrument price, commodity price, foreign exchange rate, index of prices or rates, credit rating or credit index, or other variable, provided in the case of a non-financial variable that the variable is not specific to a party to the contract (sometimes called the 'underlying').
- It requires no initial net investment or an initial net investment that is smaller than would be required for other types of contracts that would be expected to have a similar response to changes in market factors.
  - It is settled at a future date.

amortised cost
The amount at which a financial asset or financial liability is measured at initial recognition minus the principal repayments, plus or minus the cumulative amortisation using the effective interest method of any difference between that initial amount and the maturity amount and, for financial assets, adjusted for any loss allowance.

effective interest method
The method that is used in the calculation of the amortised cost of a financial asset or a financial liability and in the allocation and recognition of the interest revenue or interest expense in profit or loss over the relevant period.

6.3 Basic recognition and measurement rules for financial instruments

Much of the detail in the relevant standards is beyond the scope of this text. However, the main principles in relation to the reporting of financial assets are as follows.

An entity recognises a financial asset in its statement of financial position when, and only when, the entity becomes party to the contractual provisions of the instrument. On initial recognition, the financial asset is recorded at fair value. There is then a choice of category for subsequent measurement, namely:

- **Amortised cost** using the **effective interest method**; or
- Fair value through other comprehensive income (OCI), so re-measured at fair value at the end of each reporting period with gains or losses presented in OCI; or
  - Fair value through profit or loss, so re-measured at fair value at the end of each reporting period with gains and losses presented in profit or loss.

This choice is given to cater for the wide range of financial assets that entities may have and the wide variety of uses to which they are put, including hedging risks. The choice is constrained by the standards: an entity must classify a financial asset as subsequently measured at amortised cost, fair value through OCI or fair value through profit or loss on the basis of both:

- the entity's business model for managing the financial assets; and
- the contractual cash flow characteristics of the financial asset.

A financial asset must be measured at amortised cost if both of the following conditions are met:

- the financial asset is held within a business model whose objective is to hold financial assets in order to collect contractual cash flows; and
- the contractual terms of the financial asset give rise on specified dates to cash flows that are solely payments of principal and interest on the principal amount outstanding.

This means that most basic financial assets, including trade receivables, will be shown at amortised cost. All derivatives are measured at fair value and so will fall into one of the other categories.

Test yourself 5.2

Why do you think derivatives must be measured at fair value? Why does this give better information than using historical cost?

A financial asset must be measured at fair value through OCI if both of the following conditions are met:

- the financial asset is held within a business model whose objective is achieved by *both* collecting contractual cash flows and selling financial assets; and
- the contractual terms of the financial asset give rise on specified dates to cash flows that are solely payments of principal and interest on the principal amount outstanding.

Broadly speaking, all other financial assets that do not fall into the above categories must be measured at fair value through profit or loss, which therefore acts as the default category.

An entity can only change the classification of any of its financial assets if its business model changes. The business model is a matter of fact, and so there has to be a substantive change for any reclassification to occur.

The approach to categorisation of financial assets is one of the major changes from the old standard (IAS 39). That standard has four main categories whereas IFRS 9 has only three. The categories under each standard and how instruments are likely to be reclassified as IFRS 9 comes into effect, are shown in Figure 5.1.

Figure 5.1: IFRS 9 vs IAS 39 classification: how financial assets will move between categories

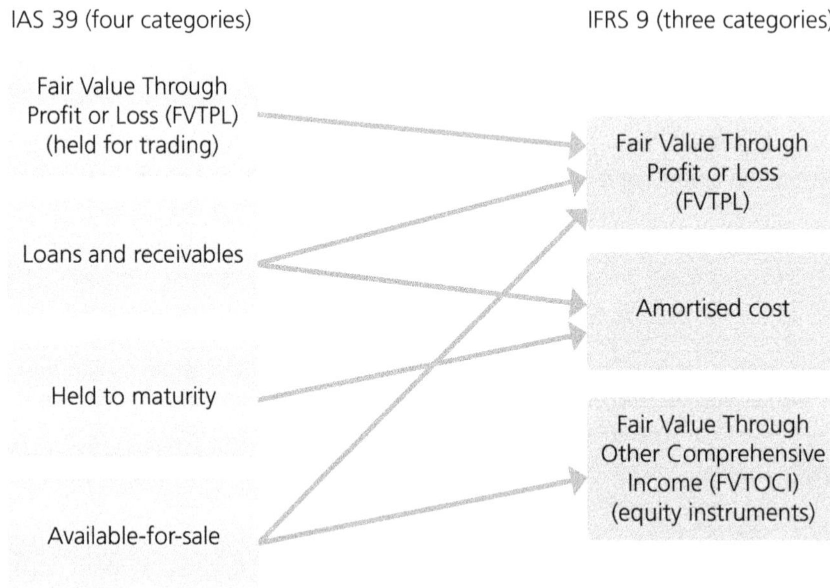

You can see Marks & Spencer's accounting policies on financial instruments under IAS 39 on pages 92–93 of the 2016 ARA.

6.4 Expected losses on financial assets at amortised cost

incurred loss model
A model that assumes that all loans will be repaid until evidence to the contrary (known as a loss or trigger event) is identified.

lifetime expected credit losses
The expected credit losses that result from all possible default events over the expected life of a financial instrument.

12-month expected credit losses
The portion of lifetime expected credit losses that represent the expected credit losses that result from default events on a financial instrument that are possible within the 12 months after the reporting date.

IFRS 9 introduces an expected loss model for assessing provisions on financial assets held at amortised cost. The previous model under IAS 39 was an **incurred loss model**, which meant that losses were only recognised when there was clear evidence that a loss event, such as a credit default of a debtor, had occurred. This model was felt to be inadequate during the financial crisis as it did not recognise losses early enough when these could be anticipated.

Under IFRS 9, at each reporting date, an entity must assess the loss allowance for a financial asset:

- If the credit risk on that asset has increased significantly since initial recognition, the loss allowance should be calculated as the **lifetime expected credit losses** on the asset.
  - If the credit risk on that asset has not increased significantly since initial recognition, the loss allowance should be calculated as equal to the **12-month expected credit losses** on the asset.

There is a simplified approach for trade receivables and contract assets arising from application of IFRS 15 (see Chapter 4) and lease receivables under IFRS 16 (see Chapter 6) where the lifetime losses can be used as the loss allowance without involving the 12-month expected losses.

An entity must measure expected credit losses of a financial instrument in a way that reflects:

- an unbiased and probability-weighted amount that is determined by evaluating a range of possible outcomes;
- the time value of money; and
- reasonable and supportable information that is available without undue cost or effort at the reporting date about past events, current conditions and forecasts of future economic conditions.

As noted above, the approach to impairment in IFRS 9 is very different to that in IAS 39. In summary, IAS 39 (replaced by IFRS 9 from 2018) uses an incurred loss model. Where a financial asset such as a debt due to the entity is held at amortised cost, the recognition of credit losses only occurs when there is evidence of a trigger event. Losses expected as a result of future events, no matter how likely, are not recognised. Objective evidence that a financial asset or group of assets is impaired includes observable data that comes to the attention of the holder of the asset about loss events such as:

- significant financial difficulty of the issuer;
- a breach of contract, such as a default in interest or principal payments;
- the lender, for reasons relating to the borrower's financial difficulty, granting to the borrower a concession that the lender would not otherwise consider; or
- it becoming probable that the borrower will enter bankruptcy or other financial reorganisation.

6.5 Dividends

The payment of **dividends** within a group is a frequent occurrence and will be important in terms of paying out profits to the ultimate shareholders of a parent company. IFRS 9 specifies that dividends are recognised in profit or loss only when:

dividends
Distributions of profits to holders of equity instruments in proportion to their holdings of a particular class of capital.

- the entity's right to receive payment of the dividend is established;
- it is probable that the economic benefits associated with the dividend will flow to the entity; and
- the amount of the dividend can be measured reliably.

These rules are important for legal purposes, because a company can only pass on a dividend to its own parent or shareholders if it has recorded the relevant profit from dividends it has received, in circumstances where its own dividend relies on such receipts.

6.6 Hedging

Companies hedge risks they face all the time. Some risks are hedged by taking out insurance contracts, but others are hedged by use of financial instruments, for example taking out a forward contract to supply a required amount of a foreign currency at a specified rate, thus taking away risk of swings in foreign exchange rates in the intervening period. Where financial instruments are used to hedge risk, accounting standards allow gains and losses on the hedging instruments to be deferred until they can be set against the mirror gains and losses arising from the hedged transaction.

IFRS 9 recognises three types of hedge:

- **fair value hedge**
- **cash flow hedge**
- Hedges of a net foreign investment (dealt with in IAS 21 'The Effects of Changes in Foreign Exchange Rates': see Chapter 4).

fair value hedge
A hedge of the exposure to changes in fair value of a recognised asset or liability or an unrecognised firm commitment or an identified portion of such an asset, liability or firm commitment that is attributable to a particular risk and could affect profit or loss.

cash flow hedge
A hedge of the exposure to variability in cash flows that is (i) attributable to a particular risk associated with a recognised asset or liability (such as all or some future interest payments on variable rate debt) or a highly probable forecast transaction and (ii) could affect profit or loss.

Many companies choose to hedge risk, but under IFRS 9 the use of hedge *accounting* is voluntary. There are rules that apply to its application, however, so entities must consider whether it is worth investing the time assessing whether to apply hedge accounting under the standard to a particular hedge. If hedge accounting is not applied, then the income statement may be exposed to greater volatility.

Much of the complexity around the hedge accounting rules are beyond the scope of this text, but the basic premise is that for hedge accounting to be applied, a hedge must be effective at inception and remain effective to a significant extent. To the extent that it does not remain effective, some or all of the gain or loss on the hedging instrument must be recognised immediately and thus the match of the hedging gain or loss against the hedged item is lost and the income statement will be more volatile.

The rules on the use of hedge accounting in IAS 39 are quite strict. In contrast, IFRS 9 allows more flexibility in the use of hedge accounting, to try to align an entity's risk management strategy, its reasons for hedging and the impact on the financial statements.

6.7 Derecognition of a financial asset

IFRS 9's basic rule in relation to when a financial asset is derecognised, i.e. removed from the financial statements, is that a financial asset should only be derecognised when:

- the contractual rights to the cash flows from the financial asset expire; or
- the entity transfers the financial asset (i.e. transfers the rights to receive the cash flows) and the transfer qualifies for derecognition because the entity no longer has the risks and rewards of ownership of the financial asset.

securitisation
The process of taking an illiquid asset, or group of assets, and through financial engineering, transforming them into a security. A typical example of securitisation is a mortgage-backed security (MBS), which is a type of asset-backed security that is secured by a collection of mortgages.

The rules in the standard go into quite a lot of additional detail as they often cover complex structured arrangements such as **securitisations**. In essence, however, to derecognise an asset, an entity must have both lost control of the asset and have no access to the benefits of the cash flows arising from it nor exposure to the risks inherent in it. In most situations this will be straightforward to assess, for example a trade debtor pays their debt in full or an option expires, but in other situations, particularly in structured transactions by financial institutions such as investment banks, it will be a complicated assessment requiring the application of judgement. The approach to derecognition in IFRS 9 is very similar to IAS 39.

Chapter summary

- Businesses use a variety of assets in their operations, some held for the long term and some which are used or sold quickly over the short term. Assets must be presented in the statement of financial position according to whether they are long-term (will be held for more than 12 months) or short-term.
- Property, plant and equipment is recorded at cost but may be revalued in subsequent periods. Apart from freehold land, such assets are depreciated over their useful lives down to their expected residual value.
- Intangible assets are of growing importance but their recognition is restricted by accounting standards unless they have been purchased. Intangible assets are amortised (which is the same as being depreciated) over their useful lives down to their expected residual value. The accounting standard on intangibles deals specifically with research and development.
- Long-term assets should not be shown at a carrying amount that is higher than the value that is expected to be made from their use or sale. Accounting standards require assets to be assessed for impairment if there are indicators of impairment. The recoverable amount of an asset is the higher of its selling value less costs of disposal and its value in use to the business.
- Inventories are usually held for the short term. They must be shown at the lower of cost and net realisable value. The costs of inventory include purchase cost, conversion costs and other production costs and such cost is written off as an expense when an item is sold and revenue is recognised.
- A broad range of items are classed as financial assets, including cash and trade receivables. The more basic instruments, held to realise cash flows, are carried at amortised cost, but derivatives and other complex instruments will be shown at fair value. Entities must assess expected losses on financial assets, particularly when there has been an impairment in the credit of the counterparty.

Chapter six
Liabilities

List of topics

1. Introduction
2. Provisions, contingent liabilities and contingent assets
3. Financial instruments
4. Leases

1. Introduction

As we saw in Chapter 3, many of an entity's liabilities are certain both as to timing and amount because they are based on contracts, for example bank debt or contracts to buy goods on credit, or based on statute, for example in relation to taxation. Other long-term obligations include pension liabilities, discussed in Chapter 4. In the shorter term, entities have to accrue for known expenses that have been incurred but where the contractual documents, such as invoices, have not yet arrived. However, companies may also be exposed to more uncertain potential liabilities which may have to be provided for or disclosed in the accounts.

The uncertainty is caused by the fact that the amount and timing of some transactions may not be known at the balance sheet date and may rely upon the occurrence or non-occurrence of uncertain future events not wholly within the company's control. Examples include legal claims, particularly if only recently notified where facts remain unclear, and environmental clean-up costs. The uncertainty is dealt with by classifying items on the liability side as either provisions or contingent liabilities: the former is recorded as a liability and expense in the accounts; the latter is merely disclosed in the notes. Contingent assets are also distinguished from assets, are only disclosed in the notes and are relatively rare, although a common example is an insurance claim where an insured loss has occurred.

Financial assets were discussed in Chapter 5. In this chapter we will look briefly at financial liabilities such as trade creditors, bank debt and derivative instruments that are liabilities. For entities that are not financial institutions, the treatment of financial liabilities is usually more straightforward than that for financial assets.

Finally, we will look at leases, which entities often choose to use in order to gain the right to use an asset rather than purchasing it outright. A new leasing standard is about to change the rules on leasing significantly and we will look briefly at both the old and the new approaches.

2. Provisions, contingent liabilities and contingent assets

IAS 37 'Provisions, Contingent Liabilities and Contingent Assets' is the standard that deals with uncertain liabilities and assets (predominantly liabilities). It is important to appreciate the reason why IAS 37 was introduced and the substantial impact it has had in practice. One might assume it was to make entities report more liabilities and therefore be more prudent. In fact, the standard is primarily aimed at stopping provisions being made when there is no actual obligation, as this allows entities to manipulate profits in current and future periods, as shown in 'Making it work 6.1'.

Making it work 6.1

Profit smoothing through the use of provisions

A listed company reports profits for the years ended 31 July 2013–2016:

	2013	2014	2015	2016
	£'000	**£'000**	**£'000**	**£'000**
Profit	**450**	**500**	**1,100**	**200**

The company likes to be in a position to report steady growth which it believes will satisfy shareholders and other stakeholders, and attract further inward investment. However, it has had exceptional results in 2015 and a relatively poor result in 2016 which may lead shareholders to believe there is volatility and undue risk.

Before the implementation of IAS 37, it would have been easy for the company to smooth the profits by creating general provisions for possible or unknown expenses in 2015. When these expenses did not arise the following year, the company could release them back to the income statement:

	2013	2014	2015	2016
	£'000	**£'000**	**£'000**	**£'000**
Original profit	**450**	**500**	**1,100**	**200**
General provision	**–**	**–**	**(500)**	**–**
Release of provision	**–**	**–**	**–**	**500**
Reported profit	**450**	**500**	**600**	**700**

The example shows that the company has achieved a steady improvement in its reported results by massaging the figures. IAS 37 prohibits irresponsible use of provisions in financial statements and stops the misrepresentation of the financial position and performance of the company. The company, in the above example, cannot simply provide for a future expense which does not exist in order to manipulate the accounts.

executory contract
A contract under which neither party has performed any of its obligations or both parties have partially performed their obligations to an equal extent.

onerous contract
A present obligation where the unavoidable costs of fulfilling the contract are higher than the economic benefits that are expected to be received. Onerous contracts can arise where a firm undertakes a contract to supply a product or service and the cost of the raw materials or human resource costs more than originally anticipated.

UK GAAP equivalent
Section 21 of FRS 102 deals with provisions and contingencies.

2.1 Scope and objective of IAS 37

The objective of IAS 37 is to ensure that appropriate recognition criteria and measurement bases are applied to provisions, contingent liabilities and contingent assets and that sufficient information is disclosed in the notes to enable users to understand their nature, timing and amount. It applies to all entities in accounting for such items, except any arising from an **executory contract**, unless the contract is onerous. **Onerous contracts** are discussed further below. The standard does not cover provisions or contingencies which are dealt with by more specific standards, for example pension obligations and income taxes. Provisions that are made to adjust the value of an asset, for example provisions for depreciation or impairment, are also not covered.

2.2 Provisions and contingent liabilities

The best way to think about how provisions and contingent liabilities fit into the overall category of liabilities and how they relate to each other is to think of a scale of uncertainty regarding liabilities. This can be seen in Figure 6.1.

Figure 6.1: Liability uncertainty

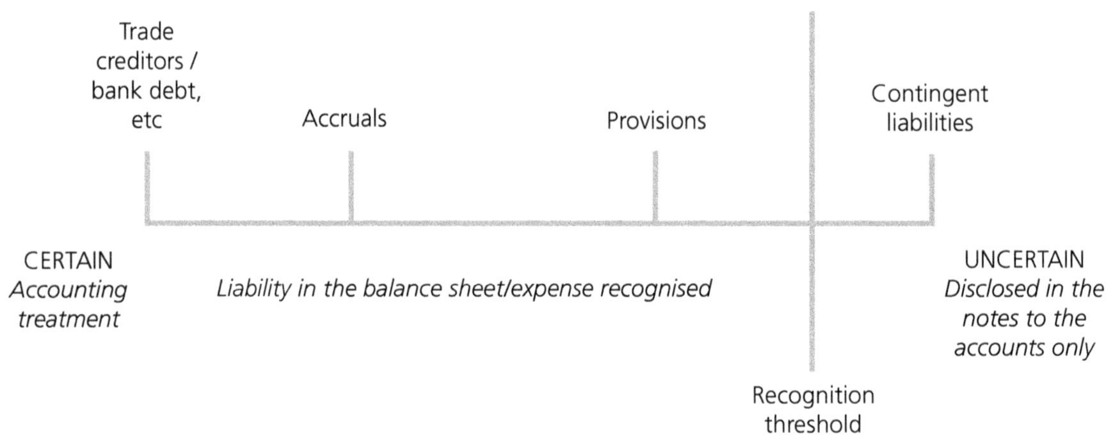

The definition of a provision as a liability of uncertain timing and amount, and the more complex definition of a contingent liability, discussed below, aim to delineate the boundary between the two. However, a great deal of judgement needs to be applied in deciding whether a provision or contingent liability exists because of the uncertainty usually surrounding the situations in which they arise.

2.3 Recognition of provisions

A **provision** should be recognised when:

- an entity has a present obligation (legal or constructive) as a result of a past event;
- it is probable that an outflow of resources embodying economic benefits will be required to settle the obligation; and
- a reliable estimate can be made of the amount of the obligation.

provision
A liability of uncertain timing or amount.

If these conditions are not met, no provision can be recognised. Where it is not clear whether there is a present obligation or not, a past event is deemed to give rise to a present obligation if, taking account of all available evidence, it is more likely than not that a present obligation exists at the end of the reporting period. In other words, it is a probability test.

The definitions of **legal obligation** and **constructive obligation** are very important. Legal obligations are usually readily identified because the relevant contractual or legislative requirement will be written down. Nevertheless, it may be hard to determine, on the facts, whether a legal requirement has actually been breached, thus creating an obligation. For example, if two parties to a joint venture operate an oil refinery, and there is an explosion and hence a possible breach of health and safety or other rules leading to a fine, it may not be clear whether one or other or both parties are liable until a process of regulatory investigation and prosecution is completed.

legal obligation
An obligation that derives from a contract (through its explicit or implicit terms), legislation or other operation of law.

constructive obligation
An obligation that derives from an entity's actions where: (a) by an established pattern of past practice, published policies or a sufficiently specific current statement, the entity has indicated to other parties that it will accept certain responsibilities; and (b) as a result, the entity has created a valid expectation on the part of those other parties that it will discharge those responsibilities.

Constructive obligations are included to deal with situations where an entity has committed to do something and that commitment is sufficient to make it very difficult, if not impossible, for the company to avoid paying out to meet it. There are many varieties of constructive obligation that can arise in practice:

- A company has previously made generous redundancy payments in excess of the statutory requirement.
- Land contamination by a chemical company if the company's policy is to clean up even if it is not legally obliged to do so.
- A retailer has a returns policy for unused and undamaged goods returned within, say, four weeks.
- A marketing company has undertaken to give out cash prizes and laptops to 10% of participants of a recent survey and the undertaking was communicated to all participants before they undertook the survey.
- A company has a restructuring plan in place and has created a valid expectation by those affected that the restructuring will be carried out.

Companies often use provisions for the restructuring of operations. Restructuring may have a significant impact on the operations of a business, be it through the sale or termination of a business, the closure of a branch, ceasing operations in a particular jurisdiction or the restructuring of a management team. A provision for restructuring costs can only be recognised where management has a legal or constructive obligation to restructure. The business must have a detailed and formal restructuring plan, which sets out the parts of the business affected, the locations concerned, details of the employees subject to termination payments, expenditure and timings. The business must have also raised a valid expectation in those affected by the restructuring, for example by communicating the plan or having already commenced the restructuring. A mere intent to restructure is insufficient.

2.4 Measurement of provisions

The amount recognised as a provision should be a best estimate of the expenditure required to settle the obligation as at the balance sheet date.

Where there is a portfolio of similar items, it may be straightforward to determine the best estimate of the outcome on the basis of expectations about the portfolio as a whole.

Worked example 6.1

An entity sells goods with a warranty under which customers are covered for the cost of repairs of any manufacturing defects that become apparent within the first six months after purchase. If minor defects were detected in all products sold, repair costs of £1m would result. If major defects were detected in all products sold, repair costs of £4m would result. The entity's past experience and future expectations indicate that, for the coming year:

- **75% of the goods sold will have no defects,**
- **20% of the goods sold will have minor defects, and**
- **5% of the goods sold will have major defects.**

What should the provision be on a best estimate basis?

Where there is a single obligation to measure, it can be much more difficult to come up with a best estimate. This is often because the potential outcomes in relation to the obligation are binary in nature, for example a court case in which the entity is being sued will be either won or lost, with respective outcomes of nil cost (particularly if legal fees will be reimbursed by the other party) or the payment of a substantial and material sum. It is also often hard to tell the likelihood of either outcome; in the court case example, the difficulty of assessing the facts and therefore the extent and nature of the obligation is what causes the parties to go to court in the first place.

The standard suggests that, where a single obligation is being measured, the individual most likely outcome may be the best estimate of the liability. However, even in such a case, the entity should consider other possible outcomes. Where other possible outcomes are either mostly higher or mostly lower than the most likely outcome, the best estimate will be a higher or lower amount. For example, if an entity has to rectify a serious fault in a major plant that it has constructed for a customer, the individual most likely outcome may be for the repair to succeed at the first attempt at a cost of £100,000, but a provision for a larger amount should be made if there is a significant chance that further attempts will be necessary.

Test yourself 6.1

What should an entity consider when determining the best estimate of a provision?

Where it is genuinely not possible to calculate a sufficiently reliable amount for a provision, the standard requires it to be treated instead as a contingent liability, so there will be no recognition of a provision and only disclosures will be made about it. The standard emphasises that this will be rare, but a court case would be a good example of where a reliable measurement might not be possible.

Where the time value of money could have a material impact on the future cash flows, the provision should be discounted to reflect the value of the expenditure that is expected to be required to settle the liability. This will depend on when the expenditure is going to be incurred. Generally, only larger and very long-term provisions are discounted, for example environmental clean-up costs on a major site which will not actually be paid out for another 20 years.

At the end of each reporting period, provisions need to be reviewed and adjusted to show the current best estimate. This might mean that some provisions are reversed as payment of the obligation is no longer probable.

Test yourself 6.2

Explain what you understand by the term 'provision' and give at least one example of a constructive obligation.

You can see the Marks & Spencer provisions at Note 22 of the 2016 financial statements on page 118.

2.5 Contingent liabilities

A **contingent liability** is a possible obligation to transfer economic benefit as a result of a past transaction or event, whose existence will be confirmed only by the occurrence or non-occurrence of uncertain future events not wholly within the entity's control. As the obligation is only possible (i.e. less likely than not to occur) then it is a contingent liability and not recognised in the accounts as a provision.

A contingent liability might also be a present obligation. However, if the amount of the present obligation cannot be reliably measured or it is unlikely that the entity will have to transfer economic benefits in order to satisfy the obligation then the contingent liability is not recognised as a provision in the accounts. Instead, disclosure should be made for each class of contingent liability as at the

Contingent liability
Is either (a) a possible obligation that arises from past events and whose existence will be confirmed only by the occurrence or non-occurrence of one or more uncertain future events not wholly within the control of the entity; or (b) a present obligation that arises from past events but is not recognised because: (i) it is not probable that an outflow of resources embodying economic benefits will be required to settle the obligation; or (ii) the amount of the obligation cannot be measured with sufficient reliability.

balance sheet date setting out the nature of the contingent liability, estimations of the possible economic outflows and timings and amounts of these outflows. If there is any possibility of reimbursement then this should also be disclosed. There is no requirement for disclosure where it is virtually certain that the business will not have to make a payment, i.e. when the contingency is remote.

Examples of contingent liabilities include court cases or regulatory action where it is not (yet) clear whether the entity has a liability (i.e. at the balance sheet date the liability is only possible, not probable) or, as discussed above, where a provision ought to be recognised but it is not possible to measure on a best estimate basis the expected amount required to settle the liability.

IAS 37 is unusual in that it is the only standard to allow a certain level of non-disclosure around both provisions and contingencies if disclosure would damage the entity and therefore cause loss to shareholders (although often if a provision has to be made, by its nature this will expose the issue). In extremely rare cases, disclosure of some or all of the information required by IAS 37 can be expected to prejudice seriously the position of the entity in a dispute with other parties. In such cases, an entity need not disclose the information, but must disclose the general nature of the dispute, together with the fact that, and reason why, the information has not been disclosed.

Test yourself 6.3

What are the key differences between a provision and a contingent liability?

2.6 Contingent assets

contingent asset
A possible asset that arises from past events and whose existence will be confirmed only by the occurrence or non-occurrence of one or more uncertain future events not wholly within the control of the entity.

A **contingent asset** is a possible asset that arises from a past transaction or event and whose existence will be confirmed only by the occurrence or non-occurrence of uncertain future events not wholly within the entity's control.

Contingent assets should not be recognised in the accounts until the realisation of income is almost certain to occur, for example the settlement of a court case resulting in compensation owing for breach of contract. At this point, the asset is no longer a contingent asset as economic benefit is probable.

Table 6.1 shows a summary of probabilities as applied to provisions, contingent liabilities and contingent assets, but note that it is very difficult to be accurate as to likelihood of outcome and in practice judgement will always be required.

Table 6.1: Summary of probabilities

Likelihood of outcome	Liability	Asset
Virtually certain	Recognise provision	Recognise asset
Probable (>50%)	Recognise provision	Disclose contingent asset
Possible (<50%)	Disclose contingent liability	No disclosure allowed
Remote (say <5%)	No disclosure required	No disclosure allowed

Stop and think 6.1

Should a provision be made in each of the following circumstances?

- **A company rewards its staff for professional level examination passes. The rewards are documented in the company's staff handbook, creating an expectation on behalf of staff that an exam pass will lead to a financial reward.**
- **A company has received a legal claim from a customer alleging that the goods it received from the company were defective and caused damage to their own equipment.**
- **A firm has a contract to provide services to a customer but now estimates that the cost of supplying the services will exceed the contract revenue.**

3. Financial instruments

Most entities will have **financial liabilities** of some sort, including trade creditors, bank debt, bonds and so on. We looked at financial instruments that are assets in Chapter 5. The same standards apply to accounting for financial liabilities.

financial liability
Any liability that is: (a) a contractual obligation: (i) to deliver cash or another financial asset to another entity; or (ii) to exchange financial assets or financial liabilities with another entity under conditions that are potentially unfavourable to the entity; or (b) a contract that will or may be settled in the entity's own equity instruments and is:(i) a non-derivative for which the entity is or may be obliged to deliver a variable number of the entity's own equity instruments; or (ii) a derivative that will or may be settled other than by the exchange of a fixed amount of cash or another financial asset for a fixed number of the entity's own equity instruments.

3.1 Recognition and derecognition

As with financial assets, an entity recognises a financial liability in its statement of financial position when, and only when, the entity becomes party to the contractual provisions of the instrument.

An entity removes a financial liability (or a part of a financial liability) from its statement of financial position (i.e. derecognises it) when, and only when, it is extinguished. In other words, when the obligation specified in the contract is discharged, cancelled or expires.

The following are accounted for as if the original financial liability has been extinguished, along with the recognition of a new financial liability.

- An exchange between an existing borrower and lender of debt instruments with substantially different terms.
- A substantial modification of the terms of an existing financial liability or a part of it (whether or not attributable to the financial difficulty of the debtor).

The difference between the carrying amount of a financial liability (or part of a financial liability) extinguished or transferred to another party and the consideration paid, including any non-cash assets transferred or liabilities assumed, is recognised in profit or loss.

3.2 Measurement

derivative
A financial instrument or other contract; (a) whose value changes in response to the change in a specified interest rate, financial instrument price, commodity price, foreign exchange rate, index of prices or rates, credit rating or credit index, or other variable, (sometimes called the 'underlying'); and (b) which requires no initial net investment or an initial net investment that is smaller than would be required for other types of contracts that would be expected to have a similar response to changes in market factors; and (c) which is settled at a future date.

Initial recognition is at fair value. Thereafter, most financial liabilities are measured at amortised cost. There are exceptions, most of which are beyond the scope of this text, but all **derivatives** that are financial liabilities must be re-measured at fair value with all gains and losses taken to profit and loss. There is an option to designate any financial liability as fair value through profit and loss. This is usually only used by financial institutions such as insurers as they often wish to match the fair value of their assets with the fair value of their liabilities so their balance sheet is matched and there is also reduced volatility in their income statement.

Financial liabilities can be used for hedging purposes and will be subject to the rules on hedge accounting in the standards.

3.3 Presentation: liabilities and equity

An important issue in financial reporting is the distinction between liabilities and equity and how they are presented. This is because the user of the accounts will want to know to what extent a company is funded by debt (which must be repaid) compared to its equity base, (where there is no obligation to repay that equity). Debt holders rank ahead of equity holders in the event of an entity being wound up. Investors use ratios to assess debt levels or gearing and we will look at this issue in terms of analysing the performance of an entity in Chapter 8.

IAS 32 states that the issuer of a financial instrument must classify the instrument, or its component parts, on initial recognition as a financial liability or an equity instrument in accordance with the substance of the contractual arrangement, and the definitions of a financial liability and an equity instrument. Those definitions are obviously therefore very important.

The overall impact of this is that, even if a financial instrument is legally a share, for example a preference share, it will be presented as a liability if it contains an obligation to deliver cash (as is usually the case with preference shares). Moreover, the amount payable on that share, while legally a dividend, will be presented as interest in the statement of profit and loss.

If a financial instrument includes both a liability and equity element, then the instrument must be split into its component parts for reporting purposes. A good example is convertible debt, where the holder has the option to be repaid in cash or in the issuing entity's shares. The instrument is split by working out the debt obligation and then taking the residual as the equity element, which is effectively an 'embedded' option. The liability element is calculated by taking the present value of the stream of future cash flows required by the contract, discounted at the rate of interest applied at that time by the market to instruments of comparable credit status and providing substantially the same cash flows, on the same terms, but without the conversion option.

Worked example 6.2

An entity issues 2,000 convertible bonds at the start of year 1. The bonds have a three-year term, and are issued at their nominal value of £1,000 per bond, giving total proceeds of £2m. Interest is payable annually in arrears at a nominal annual interest rate of 6%. Each bond is convertible at any time up to maturity into 250 ordinary shares. When the bonds are issued, the prevailing market interest rate for similar debt without conversion options is 9%. How should the bonds be accounted for?

4. Leases

An entity may not wish to purchase an asset outright or may not be able to afford to. There are advantages in not owning assets, including potential protection from technological obsolescence and other risks associated with asset ownership. Entities can instead choose to use an asset through a leasing arrangement, which is a contract between two parties; the lessor (who is the legal owner of the asset) and the lessee (who obtains the right to use the asset in exchange for rental payments).

UK GAAP equivalent
Section 20 of FRS 102 deals with leases.

It is important to note the substance of a transaction; any contract which conveys the right to control the use of a particular asset for a period of time (e.g. 12 months) In exchange for consideration (e.g. rental payments) would be considered a lease arrangement, regardless of what the face of the contract attempts to portray.

IFRS 16 'Leases' is the accounting standard that covers lease arrangements. It replaced IAS 17 'Leases', discussed briefly below.

4.1 IAS 17: key historic concepts

IAS 17 divided the accounting treatment for **leases** into two types:

- **finance leases**; if the lease transferred substantially all the risks and rewards incidental to ownership.
- **operating leases**; if the lease did not transfer substantially all the risks and rewards incidental to ownership.

lease
is an agreement whereby the lessor conveys to the lessee in return for a payment or series of payments the right to use an asset for an agreed period of time.

finance lease
A lease that transfers substantially all the risks and rewards incidental to ownership of an asset. Title may or may not eventually be transferred.

operating lease
A lease other than a finance lease.

The distinction was important as it affected how the lease was accounted for from the perspective of the lessee. The distinction has been removed by the introduction of IFRS 16.

Accounting by lessors is beyond the scope of this text, but it mirrors accounting by lessees under IAS 17, distinguishing between finance and operating leases. This has not been changed by the introduction of IFRS 16.

IAS 17 no longer applies to businesses reporting under IFRS; however, businesses reporting under UK GAAP will apply FRS 102 to lease arrangements, which is similar in concept to IAS 17.

4.2 IFRS 16: key modern concepts

IFRS 16 was issued in January 2016 and replaced IAS 17. It applies to annual periods beginning on or after 1 January 2019.

Under IAS 17, leases were classified into operating leases and/or finance leases from the perspective of the lessee. Under IFRS 16, this distinction has been removed, and the accounting treatment is similar to that as was the case for finance leases under IAS 17.

Leases are accounted for by lessees as if they had purchased the asset and borrowed money to pay for it, so the statement of financial position will show a 'right of use' asset to be depreciated, a liability for the amount 'borrowed' and interest paid over the life of the lease. This is an example of 'substance over form' in accounting as the reporting does not merely follow the legal form of the transaction, where legal ownership of the asset remains with the lessor.

4.2.1 Measurement of lease liabilities and right of use asset

The lessee will treat the lease liability as a 'financial liability' – the double entry at the commencement of the lease would be:

- Debit Right of use asset
- Credit Lease liability

The lease liability is measured at the present value of the future lease payments, which may include fixed payments, variable payments and/or any termination penalties that may be incurred.

When determining the present value, the discount factor used is the rate implicit in the lease unless it cannot be determined, in which case it is the lessee's incremental borrowing rate.

The lessee will remeasure the lease liability as regular lease payments are made by deducting the lease payments and adding any interest on the lease liability to the initial amount at commencement of the lease.

The right of use asset is initially recognised at cost. The initial cost is the amount of the lease liability plus any payments previously made (e.g. deposits), any initial direct costs, plus any costs of removing/dismantling the asset at the end of the lease (per the lease agreement). Any lease incentives received are deducted from the initial cost.

The asset will be depreciated normally over the shorter of the lease term or its useful life. If there is a reasonable certainty that the lessee will obtain ownership by the end of the lease term, then the asset should be depreciated over its useful life.

4.2.2 Low value and short term assets

The lessee can choose to account for the lease payments as an expense in its statement of profit and loss (rather than a liability in its statement of financial position) if:

- The lease is for a period of 12 months or less; or
- The underlying asset is of a low value (based on judgement).

Examples of low value assets include tables, telephones, small computers and small items of furniture. It is worth noting that IFRS 16 specifically states that cars are not low value assets.

The double entry for a low value or short term lease would therefore be:

- Debit Expense account
- Credit Cash, accruals or payables (depending on the method of payment)

Test yourself 6.4

Which stakeholders would receive more accurate information about lease commitments following the introduction of IFRS 16, and what decisions would this help them make?

4.5 Impact of IFRS 16

The change in accounting treatment of leases by the lessee is likely to have lead to greater levels of debt, increased gearing, effects on operating profit and impact on return on capital employed (ROCE). Although the lessee's asset base will also be larger as a consequence. The total costs to be expensed will be frontloaded because finance charges are higher at the beginning of the lease.

A company like M&S has substantial operating lease commitments, as shown in Note 26(C) of its 2016 financial statements (page 120). The substantial operating lease commitments in Note 26(C) indicate that the company is likely to be severely affected by the new standard: depending on the actual calculations required to apply the new standard, the company is facing adding approximately £4.7 billion in liabilities to its balance sheet (although with the same added to assets).

The following is an extract from the financial statements of M&S for the year ended 31 March 2019:

"Impact of application of IFRS 16 Leases

As a lessee, IFRS 16 removes distinctions between operating and finance leases and requires the recognition of a right of use asset and corresponding liability for future lease payables. The right of use asset will be subsequently depreciated on a straight-line basis over the life of the lease. Interest will be recognised on the lease liability.

This will result in earlier recognition of expense for leases currently classified as operating leases, although over the life of a lease the total expense recognised will not change. Right of use assets recognised by the Group comprises property, motor vehicles and equipment, including those in scope under certain logistics contracts.

The Group has elected not to recognise right of use assets and lease liabilities for leases of low-value assets, and lease payments associated with those assets will be recognised as an expense on a straight-line basis. In addition, amounts for leases with variable consideration, such as turnover leases, will continue to be recognised on a straight-line basis.

There will be a significant impact on the balance sheet as at 31 March 2019. It is expected on a pre-tax basis that a right of use asset of approximately £1.7bn and lease liability of approximately £2.6bn will be recognised, along with the derecognition of onerous lease provisions of approximately £0.2bn and other working capital balances (including lease incentives) of approximately £0.4bn, which results in an overall adjustment to retained earnings of approximately £0.3bn.

Operating profit and EBIT before adjusting items increase due to the depreciation expense being lower than the lease expense it replaces. The overall impact on profit before tax and adjusting items depends on the relative maturity of the lease portfolio. Rounded to the nearest £10m, it is estimated that for the 52 weeks ended 30 March 2019:

- Profit before tax when applying IFRS 16 is c.£10m higher than that reported in these financial statements under current accounting standards, including IAS 17 Leases.
- Profit before tax excluding adjusting items is c.£10m lower.
- Operating profit before tax and adjusting items is c.£130m higher.

Chapter summary

- IAS 37 enhances the transparency of financial statements and helps prevent misleading accounting practice and profit smoothing, because Entities cannot use provisions made when there is no real obligation to smooth out volatility.
- A provision may only be made in the financial statements where there is a legal or constructive obligation, where the outflow of economic resources is probable and if the obligation can be measured or estimated with reasonable reliability. Provisions are measured at the best estimate of the

amount needed to settle the obligation and may need to be discounted to reflect the time value of money.

- Contingent liabilities and contingent assets are not recognised but instead are disclosed in the accounts; however, contingent liabilities must be disclosed when there is a possible obligation, whereas contingent assets may only be disclosed if it is probable that the asset will be received.
- Financial liabilities are accounted for under the same standards as financial assets (discussed in Chapter 5). For most entities that are not financial institutions, financial liabilities will be measured at amortised cost rather than fair value, unless they are derivatives.
- Leases are common contracts used to obtain the right to use an asset without owning it. Under IFRS 16, leases are accounted for by the lessee in the same way as buying the asset and borrowing money to buy it.

Part two

Understanding and analysing financial statements

Overview

In this part you will learn about the different types of investment that a parent company may have in other businesses, which may be in the form of subsidiaries, joint arrangements or associates. You will get a broad understanding of how each is treated for accounting purposes and why sometimes parent companies may aim to get certain types of accounting treatment. You will see how parent companies prepare group accounts, the main rules around their preparation and the treatment of business combinations (often called mergers and acquisitions, or M&A in practice).

This part then goes on to cover the important issue of financial ratio analyses. You will learn about the key ratios used for measuring liquidity, profitability, efficiency and gearing. You will also gain an understanding of how some key ratios, such as return on capital employed and earnings per share, interlink with other performance indicators and turnover ratios. You will come to appreciate that a single performance measure, such as earnings per share, cannot tell the whole story about a company, and that ratios should be considered in aggregate and in context of the business environment and the markets in which it is operating.

Learning outcomes

At the end of this part, you will be able to:

- Understand the different types of investment a company may have in other businesses and how they are accounted for
- Describe the differences between subsidiaries, joint arrangements and associates
- Understand how a consolidation works and how it compares to equity accounting
- Explain the gearing and profit implications for the different forms of investment
- Understand how business combinations are accounted for, including the calculation of goodwill
- Appreciate the importance of understanding related party transactions and disclosures
- Discuss and explain the main profitability ratios
- Explain what is meant by the term working capital
- Assess liquidity and explain the difference between the current ratio and the quick ratio
- Calculate and explain the main efficiency ratios
- Explain the relationship between ROCE, profit margin and asset turnover
- Explain why ratios are likely to be different for companies in different industry sectors and give examples of industry sectors;
- Discuss the significance of inventory turnover and explain the benefits and disadvantages of both high and low inventory turnover
- Understand the importance of receivable and payable payment periods

- Distinguish between debt and equity and explain why a company might choose one type of financing over another
- Calculate and interpret the various gearing ratios
- Understand and explain why companies present KPIs and the regulatory concerns over their use.

Chapter seven

Group accounts and related party transactions

List of topics

1. Introduction

As we discussed in Chapter 1, many larger businesses do not operate through only one legal entity; instead they may operate through several entities, often but not always companies, for reasons relating to tax, liability limitation and regulation. For multinational firms the form and law around each entity will vary depending on which country each is based. In financial reporting terms, it would not be efficient for the ultimate shareholders in a business to have to look at each of the individual accounts of entities that were effectively operating as one business, so law and accounting standards require group accounts to be prepared.

The point of view of the ultimate shareholder is the most important one, so everything is seen from the perspective of the entity in which those shareholders have their investment; namely, a parent entity. The reporting rules consider different levels of investment and influence that a parent may have on other entities, but the most important is a parent's investment in and relationship with its subsidiaries. The definition of parent and subsidiaries is based on a control model, in other words, does the parent control the subsidiary, which might be through legal ownership rights, but can be by other means.

There are also other levels of investment and influence that a parent may have in other entities, particularly joint control with one party or more, in which case the investment is a joint operation, and a large but not controlling interest, which gives significant influence, in which case the entity is an associate. Below that, a holding in another entity will be accounted for as a simple investment.

Following the financial crisis the whole issue of group accounts, and in particular what should be classed as a subsidiary, was revisited. The most complex aspects of the accounting are beyond the scope of this text, but we will cover some of the main issues in this chapter.

We will also look at related party disclosures in this chapter. Any transactions with parties that are related to each other may not be on an arms' length basis and so accounting standards (and sometimes the law) require disclosure of such relationships and transactions, in order to ensure users of accounts are put on guard as to their economic impact. The standard on related parties also covers disclosure of remuneration of management, which is discussed in Chapter 11.

2. Different types of investment

As noted above, there are different types of investment that a parent company may have. The most important is between it and any subsidiary. A parent and all its subsidiaries make up a group. Other, lesser investments in entities are also important, but joint operations and associates are not classified as members of a group; only the parent and subsidiaries are members.

2.1 The relevant accounting standards

Figure 7.1 indicates how the choices are made about the treatment of different investments and how they are accounted for.

Figure 7.1: Investments

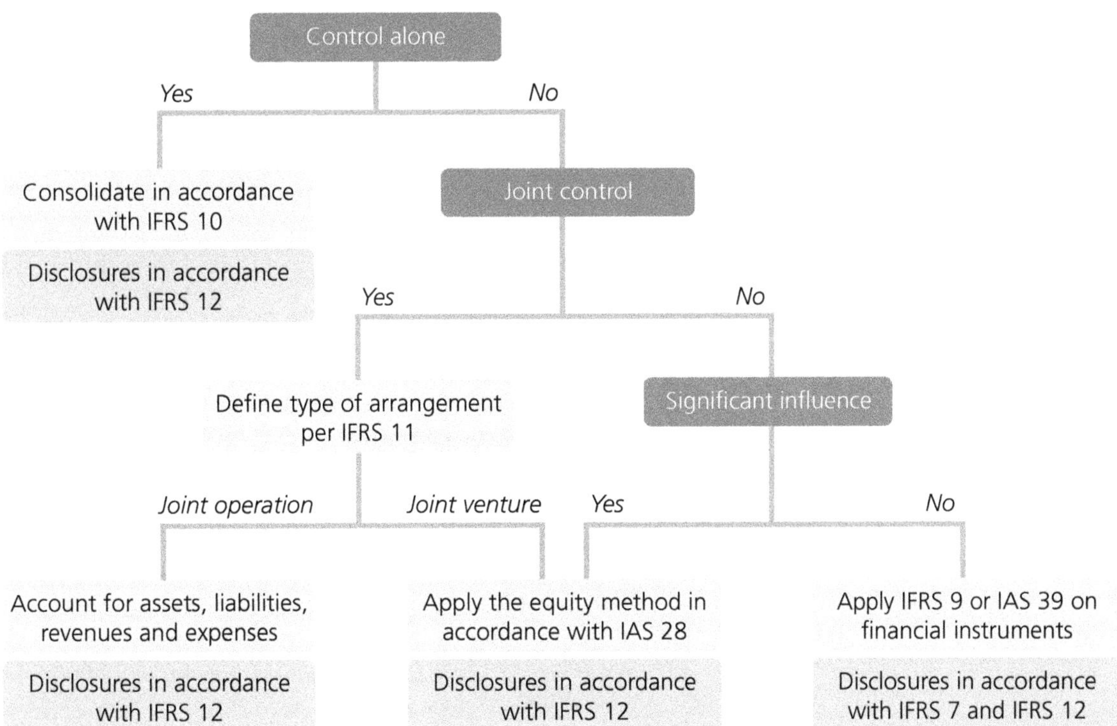

And these are the standards to which Figure 7.1 refers:

- IFRS 10 'Consolidated Financial Statements'
- IFRS 11 'Joint Arrangements'
- IFRS 12 'Disclosure of Interests in Other Entities'
- IAS 39 'Financial Instruments: Recognition and Measurement'
- IFRS 9 'Financial Instruments'.

IFRS 7 is a general disclosure standard for financial instruments. Also of relevance are:

- IAS 27 'Separate Financial Statements'
- IAS 28 'Investments in Associates and Joint Ventures'.

These last two standards deal with the treatment of the investments in the individual accounts of the parent and IAS 28 describes the equity method of accounting, outlined in Section 3. In addition, IFRS 3 'Business Combinations' deals with how to account for acquisitions of other businesses (see Section 4).

A parent company may therefore have relationships with other entities as shown in Figure 7.2, which will also mean other parties are involved:

Figure 7.2: Investment relationships of a parent for accounting purposes

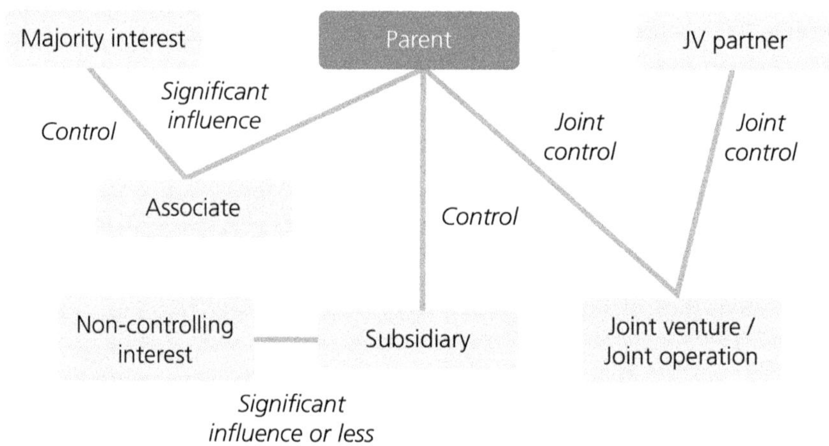

2.2 Company law and sizes of groups

Company law also governs whether group accounts should be prepared. Broadly speaking, the tests and definitions are similar to IFRS Standards in terms of types of investment and process for consolidation, but small groups are exempt from preparing group accounts. Small groups are those that can meet two out of three of the size criteria relating to turnover, balance sheet total and employees. Both turnover and balance sheet total can be judged on a net (i.e. consolidated basis, see below) or gross, by just adding up the relevant figures for each company in the group.

Two out of three of	Gross	Net
Aggregate turnover	≤£12.2m	≤£10.2m
Aggregate balance sheet total	≤£6.1m	≤£5.1m
Aggregate number of employees	≤50	≤50

It is also worth noting that in both IFRS Standards and company law there are exemptions from preparing group accounts if a parent company is also a subsidiary of another company (i.e. it is an intermediate parent company), as long as the ultimate parent of the group prepares group accounts that meet certain criteria.

Note C6 on pages 123–125 of the Marks & Spencer 2016 ARA carries a list of all the subsidiaries of the parent, as well as holdings in other related undertakings (i.e. joint ventures, associates and so on).

3. Subsidiaries and consolidated accounts

As already noted, a parent and all its subsidiaries make up a **group** and a group must prepare **consolidated financial statements**. The important thing, therefore, is to identify both a **parent** and its **subsidiaries**. This question is dealt with primarily in IFRS 10 'Consolidated Financial Statements'.

3.1 Control

IFRS 10 states that an investor (i.e. the potential parent), regardless of the nature of its involvement with an entity (the investee), must determine whether it is a parent by assessing whether it has **control of the investee**.

In particular, IFRS 10 states that control, in relation to a parent and an investee entity, comprises three elements, and all must be present:

- **Power** over the **relevant activities** of an investee from existing rights.
- Exposure or rights to variable returns of the investee.
- The ability to use that power to affect the returns of the investee.

Control can be exercised in a variety of ways, most commonly by:

- Holding voting rights attached to shares.
- Via a contract (e.g. with other vote holders).
- Through control of the board of directors or other decision-making body.
- Through 'de facto' control (see below).

It is important to bear in mind that it does not matter where subsidiaries are based (i.e. they can be registered in another country) or what legal form they take: if they are controlled by the parent, directly or indirectly, they must be consolidated.

In the vast majority of situations in practice, a parent will control its subsidiaries through direct or indirect voting rights, as seen in Figure 7.3.

group
A parent and its subsidiaries.

consolidated financial statements
The financial statements of a group in which the assets, liabilities, equity, income, expenses and cash flows of the parent and its subsidiaries are presented as those of a single economic entity.

parent
An entity that controls one or more entities.

subsidiary
An entity that is controlled by another entity.

UK GAAP equivalent
Section 9 of FRS 102 deals with consolidation.

control of an investee
An investor controls an investee when the investor is exposed, or has rights, to variable returns from its involvement with the investee and has the ability to affect those returns through its power over the investee.

power
Existing rights that give the current ability to direct the relevant activities.

relevant activities
Activities of the investee that significantly affect the investee's returns.

Figure 7.3: Group structure based on voting rights (%)

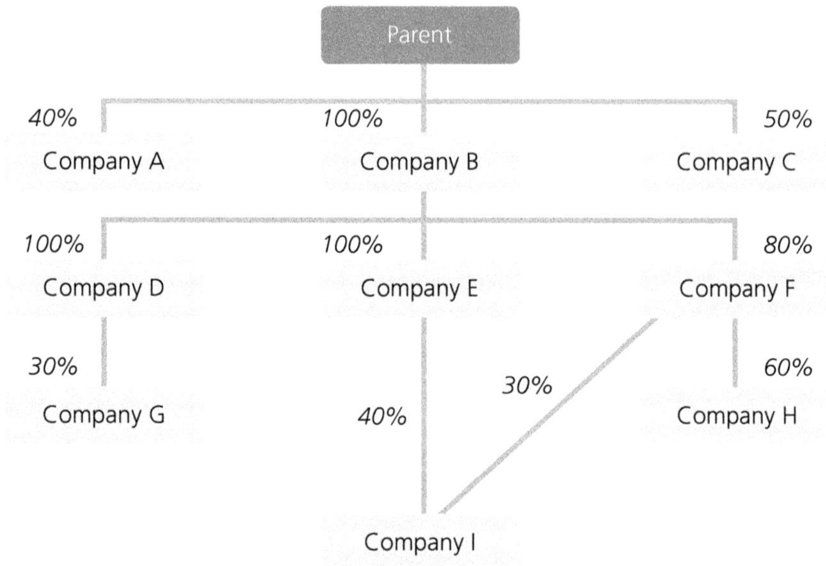

In Figure 7.3, both direct and indirect holdings are taken into account. Company A is likely to be an associate (see below) of Parent (more than 20% but less than 50% of voting shares), Company B is a subsidiary of Parent (more than 50% of voting rights) and Company C (assuming another party has 50% and there is joint control) would be a joint arrangement for Parent. However, under Company B there are other companies. Companies D, E and F would also be subsidiaries of Parent (100% × 100%; 100% × 100%; 100% × 80% of voting rights respectively). But Company I is also a subsidiary through the holdings of both Company E and Company F (100% × 100% × 40%) plus (100% × 80% × 30%) = 64%. Company H, however, is not controlled by Parent through voting rights (100% × 80% × 60% = 48%).

De facto control exists where one party has a substantial holding of voting rights and the remainder, while a majority, are held by a wide range of unconnected parties who do not act in agreement with each other.

Figure 7.4: De facto control via voting rights

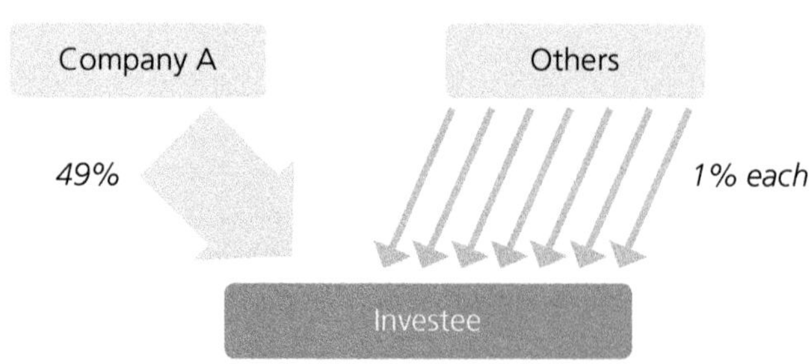

In this case, Company A will have control because it can exercise power even with a minority of the voting rights.

Potential voting rights must also be taken into account where they have substance. In the following situation, if Company A has the option to purchase 20% of the shares in the investee from Company B, the option is in the money (i.e. it is on advantageous terms for Company A) and Company A can afford the purchase, then the shares over which Company A has an option will be brought into account and Company A, not Company B, will have the requisite power and control.

Figure 7.5: Potential voting rights

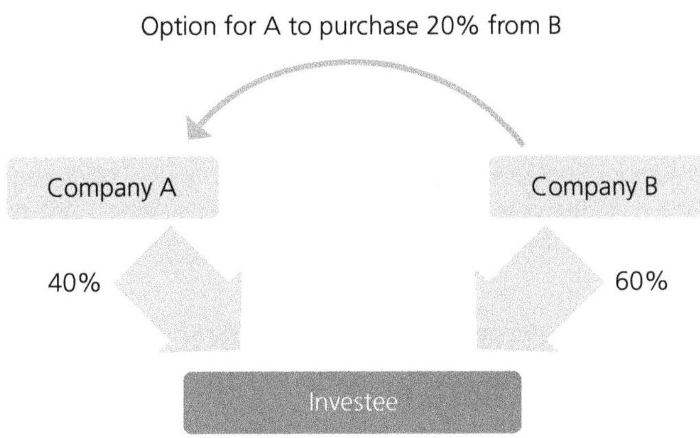

In a situation where a parent has control, if there are other investors in the subsidiary, these are known as non-controlling interests. These are sometimes called minority interests.

3.2 Consolidation

When a parent has worked out which of its investments are subsidiaries, what must it do to consolidate them? The best way of thinking about it is a big, line-by-line adding-up exercise, where the parent and subsidiary accounts are simply added up to create total figures for the group.

It is important to realise that the consolidated accounts include everything controlled by the parent on a 100% basis. This is even the case where the parent (whether directly or indirectly) owns less than 100% of the shares in the subsidiary. The share of a subsidiary's results that belongs to the non-controlling or minority interest is disclosed at the foot of the balance sheet and income statement and in the statement of changes in equity.

There are certain other things that have to be done:

- Intragroup items must be eliminated, including all transactions, balances and profits and losses. This means that the consolidated totals will consist only of transactions, balances and profits and losses created through transactions with parties outside the group, thereby avoiding double counting. The parent entity's investment in the subsidiaries, which will usually be carried at cost or (more rarely) fair value in its balance sheet as an investment, is also eliminated through the process of consolidation.

- The accounting policies of all group companies must be aligned, so that like items are treated in the same way for the group as a whole. Groups will often require their subsidiaries to follow the same accounting policies to avoid having to adjust the figures for consolidation, but sometimes subsidiaries (for example those based overseas from the parent) are required to follow local accounting rules and therefore adjustments must be made just for the consolidation.
- There are rules about non-coterminous accounting periods: if subsidiaries have a year-end more than three months away from the parent's year-end, then special accounts will need to be prepared for the consolidation.

There are other detailed rules in IFRS 10 on the consolidation process. Once a parent loses control of a subsidiary, it will cease to be consolidated from that date. This means that if control is lost during a financial year, the consolidated accounts will include the results of the subsidiary in its income statement only up to the date control was lost.

joint arrangement
An arrangement of which two or more parties have joint control.

UK GAAP equivalent
Section 15 of FRS 102 deals with joint arrangements.

significant influence
The power to participate in the financial and operating policy decisions of the investee but is not control or joint control of those policies.

associate
An entity over which the investor has significant influence.

UK GAAP equivalent
Section 14 of FRS 102 deals with associates.

joint control
The contractually agreed sharing of control of an arrangement, which exists only when decisions about the relevant activities require the unanimous consent of the parties sharing control.

joint operation
A joint arrangement whereby the parties that have joint control of the arrangement have rights to the assets, and obligations for the liabilities, relating to the arrangement.

joint venture
A joint arrangement whereby the parties that have joint control of the arrangement have rights to the net assets of the arrangement.

4. Joint arrangements, associates and equity accounting

As well as controlling other entities, businesses often go into partnership with other businesses on profit-raising ventures which may be narrow in scope or limited in timescale, where neither side wants to give the other control and where the partners need each other: both sides will make necessary contributions of money (in the form of both equity and debt) to share risk, and other assets and often expertise as well. In such circumstances the investment is usually 'deadlocked' where each party cannot do anything significant without the agreement of the other. Such situations are classified as **joint arrangements** and dealt with in IFRS 11.

Sometimes entities may have investments in other companies where they have **significant influence** but not control or joint control, usually with a voting rights investment of between 20% and 50%. These are classed as **associates** and are dealt with in IAS 28. The main method of accounting for both of these is equity accounting, although certain forms of joint arrangement are dealt with differently, as noted in Figure 7.3.

4.1 Joint arrangements

A joint arrangement is an arrangement of which two or more parties have **joint control**. In a joint arrangement the parties are bound by a contractual arrangement and the contractual arrangement gives two or more of those parties joint control of the arrangement. A joint arrangement is either a **joint operation** or a **joint venture**.

The difference between joint operations and joint ventures is important as they are accounted for very differently.

In the case of a joint operation, the reporting entity is exposed to specific assets, liabilities, income and expenses and therefore accounts for those exposures. A joint operator therefore recognises in relation to its interest in a joint operation:

- its assets, including its share of any assets held jointly;
- its liabilities, including its share of any liabilities incurred jointly;
- its revenue from the sale of its share of the output arising from the joint operation;
- its share of the revenue from the sale of the output by the joint operation; and
- its expenses, including its share of any expenses incurred jointly.

However, in the case of a joint venture, an investing entity is exposed to the net returns in the business of the joint arrangements. A joint venturer must recognise its interest in a joint venture as an investment and account for it using the equity method in accordance with IAS 28 (see below).

4.2 Associates

There are situations where entities wish to take strategic long-term stakes in other entities, without having control. In some circumstances the investor's holding is large enough, and their involvement in the investee is great enough, that the investor has a level of influence that is greater than for a more minor, arms' length investment. Usually the voting rights level of such an investment is between 20% and 50% and these investments, where there is a significant influence, are classed as associates.

IAS 28 'Investments in Associates and Joint Ventures' prescribes the accounting for investments in associates and to set out the requirements for the application of the **equity method** when accounting for investments in associates and joint ventures.

equity method
A method of accounting whereby the investment is initially recognised at cost and adjusted thereafter for the post-acquisition change in the investor's share of the investee's net assets. The investor's profit or loss includes its share of the investee's profit or loss and the investor's other comprehensive income includes its share of the investee's other comprehensive income.

In terms of identifying associates, if an entity holds 20% or more of the voting rights of an investee, it is presumed that the entity has significant influence, unless it can be clearly demonstrated that this is not the case. Conversely, if an entity holds less than 20% of the voting rights of an investee, it is presumed that the entity does not have significant influence, unless such influence can be clearly demonstrated. A substantial or majority ownership by another investor does not necessarily preclude an entity from having significant influence. So in Figure 7.5, for example, Companies A, G and H would be associates, unless it could be demonstrated that Parent did not have significant influence.

The existence of significant influence by an entity is usually evidenced in one or more of the following ways:

- representation on the board of directors or equivalent governing body of the investee;

- participation in policy-making processes, including participation in decisions about dividends or other distributions;
- material transactions between the entity and its investee;
- interchange of managerial personnel; or
- provision of essential technical information.

Test yourself 7.1

Why would a business want to hold an investment in an entity where it did not control it? What are the advantages and disadvantages of having such a holding?

4.3 Equity method

The equity method is sometimes called a 'one-line consolidation', but it is not really a consolidation at all. On initial recognition the investment in an associate or a joint venture is recognised in the investor's balance sheet at cost, and the carrying amount is increased or decreased to recognise the investor's share of the profit or loss of the investee after the date of acquisition. The investor's share of the investee's profit or loss is recognised in the investor's profit or loss. Distributions received from an investee reduce the carrying amount of the investment.

There are rules in IAS 28 about when to cease using the equity method, which will be either when significant influence or joint control is lost or if the investor's interest changes to achieve control, at which point the associate or joint venture will become a subsidiary.

As associates and joint ventures are not controlled, their financial statements may be prepared to a different date to that of the investor. The standard allows some latitude for differences in year ends, but only up to a three-month difference; if the year-end dates are more than that length apart, special accounts would be required from the associate or joint venture.

If the associate or joint venture is loss-making, this will have a negative impact on the amount shown by the investor in its balance sheet. The standard states that, after the investor's interest is reduced to zero, additional losses are provided for, and a liability is recognised, only to the extent that the entity has incurred legal or constructive obligations (see Chapter 6) or made payments on behalf of the associate or joint venture. If the associate or joint venture subsequently reports profits, the investor will resume recognising its share of those profits only after its share of the profits equals the share of losses not recognised.

4.4 Consolidation vs equity method

There are substantial differences between consolidation and equity accounting, and because of this there is a temptation for investing entities to structure transactions to achieve their desired accounting outcome. If an investee is highly geared, so with a lot of debt, the investor may wish to avoid consolidation, which would bring 100% of the gross debt of the investee onto its consolidated balance sheet. On the other hand, if an investee is very profitable, the investor may wish to consolidate, to get 100% of the investee's profits in its accounts, even though it only owns a portion of the investee's business.

Making it work 7.1

Consolidation vs equity method

An investor holds 50% of the voting rights in an investee, which it has held for some time. The cost of the investment was £1,000 and the investor received £100 in dividends. The following shows the very different effects that would be achieved by consolidation if the investee was controlled or, alternatively, use of the equity method if it were jointly controlled.

BALANCE SHEET	Parent	Sub/JV	Consoli-dated	Non-consol
Long-term assets	50,000	30,000	80,000	50,000
Investment at cost	1,000			
Investment 50%: equity method				10,000
	51,000	30,000	80,000	60,000
Current assets	25,000	15,000	40,000	25,000
Total assets	76,000	45,000	120,000	85,000
Current liabilities	22,000	5,000	27,000	22,000
Non-current liabilities	20,000	20,000	40,000	20,000
Total liabilities	42,000	25,000	67,000	42,000
Net assets	34,000	20,000	53,000	43,000
Equity	34,000	20,000	53,000	43,000
Attributable to parent			34,000	
Attributable to minority interest			10,000	
Gearing: total debt/equity	124%	125%	126%	98%

INCOME STATEMENT				
Revenue	200,000	80,000	280,000	200,000
Cost of sales	(120,000)	(30,000)	(150,000)	(120,000)
Gross profit	80,000	50,000	130,000	80,000
Other expenses	(50,000)	(30,000)	(80,000)	(50,000)
Operating Profit	30,000	20,000	50,000	30,000
Finance costs	(5,000)	(1,000)	(6,000)	(5,000)
Dividend from JV	100	0	0	0
Share of profit of JV (after tax)	0	0	0	6,000
Profit before tax	25,100	19,000	44,000	31,000
Taxation	(9,000)	(7,000)	(16,000)	(9,000)
Profit after tax	16,100	12,000	28,000	22,000
Attributable to parent			22,000	
Attributable to minority interest			6,000	
Gross profit %	40%	63%	46%	40%
Total profit %	8%	15%	10%	11%

On the positive side, consolidation gives a boost to profitability, at least at the gross profit level. However, it also means that the relatively high debt of the investee flows through into the consolidated results, increasing gearing for the group as a whole; this is avoided if the investee is treated as a joint venture and equity accounted. We will look at ratio analysis in more detail in Chapter 8.

UK GAAP equivalent
Section 19 of FRS 102 deals with business combinations and goodwill.

business
An integrated set of activities and assets that is capable of being conducted and managed for the purpose of providing a return in the form of dividends, lower costs or other economic benefits directly to investors or other owners, members or participants.

business combination
A transaction or other event in which an acquirer obtains control of one or more businesses.

5. Business combinations

Businesses do not only grow organically. They often purchase other businesses, to complement their existing operations, add to their market share or move into new areas of activity. Sometimes such transactions are driven by tax considerations. Whatever the reason, the rules on accounting for these transactions are complicated and therefore much of the detail is beyond the scope of this text. However, the basic approach is described here, mainly through coverage of the relevant standard IFRS 3 'Business Combinations'.

5.1 Identifying a business combination

IFRS 3 does not apply to the acquisition of anything other than a **business**. Therefore an entity must determine whether a transaction or other event is a **business combination** by applying the definitions in the standard, which requires that the assets acquired and liabilities assumed constitute a business. If the assets acquired are not a business, the reporting entity should instead account for the transaction or other event as an asset acquisition. In addition,

IFRS 3 does not apply to transactions under common control, for example when one subsidiary acquires another subsidiary from its parent, nor does it apply to the formation of joint arrangements.

5.2 The acquisition method

IFRS 3 requires all business combinations to be accounted for using the acquisition method. This involves:

- identifying the acquirer;
- determining the acquisition date;
- recognising and measuring the identifiable assets acquired, the liabilities assumed and any non-controlling interest in the **acquiree**; and
- recognising and measuring goodwill or a gain from a bargain purchase.

There must always be an **acquirer** in a business combination. In most circumstances this will be straightforward to determine as one entity buys another using cash or its own shares as currency, but in other situations, for example when two entities come together that are of roughly equal size to pool their resources, it may be more difficult to determine the identity of the acquirer. The standard lists various factors to be taken into account, including the relative voting rights of shareholders in the combined entity after the combination, the composition of the governing board (more from one of the combining entities than the other), the composition of senior management and also the terms of the exchange. On this latter point, the acquirer usually pays a premium on the pre-combination price of the acquired entity.

The **acquisition date** is the date control passes, which will often (but not always) be the date of the legal transfer of consideration.

As at the acquisition date, the acquirer must recognise, separately from **goodwill**, the **identifiable** assets acquired, the liabilities assumed and any non-controlling interest in the acquiree. To qualify for recognition as part of applying the acquisition method, the identifiable assets acquired and liabilities assumed must meet the definitions of assets and liabilities in the Conceptual Framework (see Chapter 2) at the acquisition date. For example, costs the acquirer expects but is not obliged to incur in the future to effect its plan to exit an activity of an acquiree or to terminate the employment of or relocate an acquiree's employees are not liabilities at the acquisition date.

There is a difference in accounting for intangible assets in a business combination, compared with those generated internally by a company. As we saw in Chapter 5, such intangibles cannot usually be recognised if they are internally developed. In a business combination, however, the assets purchased will include intangible assets such as customer lists, brands and so on which must be recognised separately from goodwill. Similarly, we saw in Chapter 6 that contingent liabilities are usually disclosed but not recognised. In a business combination, however, the total price that has been paid takes account of such contingencies and so these are recognised in the financial statements of the group.

acquiree
The business or businesses that the acquirer obtains control of in a business combination.

acquirer
The entity that obtains control of the acquiree.

acquisition date
The date on which the acquirer obtains control of the acquiree.

goodwill
An asset representing the future economic benefits arising from other assets acquired in a business combination that are not individually identified and separately recognised.

identifiable
An asset is identifiable if it either: (a) is separable, i.e. capable of being separated or divided from the entity and sold, transferred, licensed, rented or exchanged, either individually or together with a related contract, identifiable asset or liability, regardless of whether the entity intends to do so; or (b) arises from contractual or other legal rights, regardless of whether those rights are transferable or separable from the entity or from other rights and obligations.

contingent consideration
Usually, an obligation of the acquirer to transfer additional assets or equity interests to the former owners of an acquiree as part of the exchange for control of the acquiree if specified future events occur or conditions are met. However, contingent consideration also may give the acquirer the right to the return of previously transferred consideration if specified conditions are met.

Once all the acquired assets and liabilities are identified, they are then measured at fair value as at the acquisition date. The consideration given for the purchase is also measured at fair value at the acquisition date, including any **contingent consideration**. The consideration may be just cash, but if the acquirer is using its own equity shares as consideration, these will be measured using the fair value at the acquisition date. Where the shares are traded on a market, this will be straightforward to find; if they are not traded, a valuation may need to be obtained.

The difference between the fair value of the consideration given and the fair value of the identifiable assets and liabilities is goodwill where the consideration is higher than the value of the assets and liabilities acquired. Where the consideration is lower, this is a bargain purchase and the gain is recognised immediately in the statement of profit or loss.

Acquisition-related costs are costs the acquirer incurs to effect a business combination. Those costs include finder's fees; advisory, legal, accounting, valuation and other professional or consulting fees; general administrative costs; and costs of registering and issuing debt and equity securities. The acquirer must account for acquisition-related costs as expenses in the periods in which the costs are incurred and the services are received, except that the costs to issue debt or equity securities are accounted for under the relevant financial instruments standards.

After the acquisition, all assets are depreciated or amortised as required by IAS 16 and IAS 38 (see Chapter 5), including all identifiable recognised intangible assets. Some of these intangibles will be amortised over relatively short periods of time as they do not have very long useful lives, for example in the case of customer lists or relationships. Goodwill is not amortised but is tested for impairment annually. Impairment is governed by IAS 36 (see Chapter 5).

Worked example 7.1

Company X purchased 100% of the shares of Company Y. The consideration consisted of £1 million in cash and 100,000 shares in Company X. On the date of acquisition, the shares of Company X were trading at £10 per share. The total fair value of Company Y's assets and liabilities at the date of acquisition was £1.4 million. Calculate the goodwill that Company X will have to report on its acquisition of Company Y.

Stop and think 7.1

The next time you see an acquisition reported by a listed company, go to their website and look at the relevant acquisition documents (usually a prospectus and related documents). Consider the financial information given about the impact of the acquisition and how it will appear in the next set of accounts.

6. Related party transactions

Users of accounts will normally base their reading of the accounts and analysis of them on the expectation that all the transactions undertaken by the entity have been at arms' length, where both the entity and the counterparty to each transaction are trying to obtain the best deal they can and, through market prices or negotiation, transact at a fair price. However, this may not always be the case and so IAS 24 'Related Party Transactions' deals with disclosures when transactions are not at arms' length and so users may need to take a different view of such transactions. Entities are not required to disclose whether transactions are actually at a fair price or not; they must simply disclose which transactions are related party transactions, which puts the reader on alert. The standard also requires disclosure of who ultimately controls the entity, again to put users on alert about potential influence of other parties.

This standard also deals with remuneration of directors, here called **key management personnel**. In many countries, including the UK, disclosure of directors' remuneration required by law often fulfils the same function, but there may be differences between the legal requirements and IAS 24. The disclosure of remuneration of key management personnel is considered in Chapter 11. There are also substantial restrictions and safeguards in UK company law regarding other transactions between companies and directors, including restrictions on loans to directors. We will also discuss these in Chapter 11.

key management personnel
Those persons having authority and responsibility for planning, directing and controlling the activities of the entity, directly or indirectly, including any director (whether executive or otherwise) of that entity.

UK GAAP equivalent
Section 33 of FRS 102 deals with related party disclosures.

6.1 Definition of related parties

The definition of a related party is complex, but the main point to note is that related parties can be either individuals or other entities. In a group context, all group companies will be related parties:

close family members of a person
Those family members who may be expected to influence, or be influenced by, that person in their dealings with the entity and include: (a) that person's children and spouse or domestic partner; (b) children of that person's spouse or domestic partner; and (c) dependants of that person or that person's spouse or domestic partner.

A related party is a person or entity that is related to the entity that is preparing its financial statements (the 'reporting entity'):

(a) a person or a **close member** of that person's family is related to a reporting entity if that person–
   (i) has control or joint control of the reporting entity;
   (ii) has significant influence over the reporting entity; or
   (iii) is a member of the key management personnel of the reporting entity or of a parent of the reporting entity.

(b) an entity is related to a reporting entity if any of the following conditions applies–
   (i) the entity and the reporting entity are members of the same group (which means that each parent, subsidiary and fellow subsidiary is related to the others);
   (ii) one entity is an associate or joint venture of the other entity (or an associate or joint venture of a member of a group of which the other entity is a member);
   (iii) both entities are joint ventures of the same third party.
   (iv) one entity is a joint venture of a third entity and the other entity is an associate of the third entity.
   (v) the entity is a post-employment benefit plan for the benefit of employees of either the reporting entity or an entity related to the reporting entity. If the reporting entity is itself such a plan, the sponsoring employers are also related to the reporting entity.
   (vi) the entity is controlled or jointly controlled by a person identified in (a);
   (vii) a person identified in (a)(i) has significant influence over the entity or is a member of the key management personnel of the entity (or of a parent of the entity);
   (viii) the entity, or any member of a group of which it is a part, provides key management personnel services to the reporting entity or to the parent of the reporting entity.

related party transaction
A transfer of resources, services or obligations between a reporting entity and a related party, regardless of whether a price is charged.

The complexity of the definition means that the hardest part of applying the standard is to identify all related parties. Once they have been identified, the standard requires various disclosures to be made about them and any **related party transactions**.

Relationships between a parent and its subsidiaries must be disclosed irrespective of whether there have been transactions between them. An entity must disclose the name of its parent and, if different, the ultimate controlling party. If neither the entity's parent nor the ultimate controlling party produces consolidated financial statements available for public use, the name of the next most senior parent that does so must also be disclosed.

In addition, if an entity has had related party transactions during the periods covered by the financial statements, it must disclose the nature of the related party relationship as well as information about those transactions and outstanding balances, including commitments, necessary for users to understand the potential effect of the relationship on the financial statements. At a minimum, disclosures will include:

- the amount of the transactions;
- the amount of outstanding balances, including commitments–
  - their terms and conditions, including whether they are secured, and the nature of the consideration to be provided in settlement; and
  - details of any guarantees given or received;

- provisions for doubtful debts related to the amount of outstanding balances; and
- the expense recognised during the period in respect of bad or doubtful debts due from related parties.

These disclosures must be made separately for each of the following categories:

- the parent;
- entities with joint control of, or significant influence over, the entity;
- subsidiaries;
- associates;
- joint ventures in which the entity is a joint venturer;
- key management personnel of the entity or its parent; and
- other related parties.

Examples of related party transactions (apart from remuneration of Key Management Personnel) include:

- short- and long-term borrowings;
- buying and selling of goods;
- guarantees;
- provision of management services.

There are exemptions from disclosure of related parties and related party transactions where the entities are government-related. This is to deal with situations such as that in China, where the government is heavily involved in all forms of business.

The issue of materiality is problematic for related party transactions. Director remuneration may be small in total in the context of the results of the entity, but the standard assumes that it will always be material to users (and indeed UK law takes the view that it must be disclosed precisely). For other transactions, there may be no or a very low transaction price. In effect, however, the standard assumes that the knowledge of the related party connection will always be material to users of accounts, and although similar transactions can be bundled together, disclosure will always be required.

Stop and think 7.2

What sort of information do you think would be useful in relation to a transaction with a related party? Would you be able to tell, from the information required by the standard, whether the transaction was carried out on an arms' length basis or not?

You can see the disclosure of the Marks & Spencer related party transactions in note 29 on page 121 of the 2016 ARA.

Chapter summary

- It is important to have an understanding of what constitutes a group for reporting purposes and the different levels of control and influence exist between investor and investee companies.
- The most important relationship is that of control between a parent and its subsidiaries. Control can be through a number of mechanisms but the standard is clear that certain criteria must always be present, including power over relevant activities and the ability to use that power to affect returns.
- A consolidation is a large adding-up exercise which involves taking out all intra-group transactions and balances so that only those with parties outside the group end up being aggregated into the consolidated accounts. There are rules on aligning reporting dates and accounting policies.
- Business is also carried on through joint arrangements and investments in associates, which are usually accounted for using the equity method of accounting. This is a one-line entry of the investment in the investee in the statement of financial position, and a one-line share of the profit of the investee in the investor's statement of profit or loss.
- There is sometimes a desire to structure investments to achieve particular outcomes, either to consolidate or not, depending on whether the parent wishes to include all the results of the investee in its group accounts or not.
- Businesses acquire stakes in other businesses in order to grow or move into new areas of business. Accounting standards require an acquirer to be identified and goodwill must be calculated by comparing the fair value of the assets and liabilities acquired with the fair value of the consideration given.
- It is important for users of financial statements to be able to see if transactions have been carried out between related parties. This may indicate they are not at an arms' length value.

Chapter eight
Financial ratio analysis

List of topics

1. Introduction
2. Profitability ratios
3. Liquidity ratios
4. Efficiency ratios
5. Gearing ratios
6. Earnings per share and other key investor ratios
7. Key performance indicators

1. Introduction

Financial ratios enable users of accounts to establish the relationship between items in the statement of financial position and statement of profit and loss, as well as the other statements, and provide users with meaningful indicators of the success or otherwise of a company's activities. Typical ratios will include those in respect of liquidity, profitability, earnings, leverage and financial stability. The ratios help analysts, shareholders and other stakeholders to identify financial strengths and weaknesses of a company, to benchmark companies against like companies in the same or similar industry and to compare performance and financial position over time. The high quality accounting standards that have been issued over the last 20 years have aided comparability of such ratios.

In this chapter, we will look at the main categories of ratio and what to consider when calculating and interpreting each type. We will look at how ratios are inter-related and the extent to which certain ratios are more important to some industries than others.

Care is required when looking at ratios presented by companies because of the amount of flexibility companies have in their calculation. Companies are required to disclose their key performance indicators (KPIs), which you may also see referred to as alternative performance measures (APMs); the 'alternative' is because they are usually not based on the statutory numbers. Nor are there any accounting standards that govern ratios or how their inputs are calculated. The only exception to this is the earnings per share (EPS) ratio, a shareholder investment ratio which is widely quoted in the press and used as an input into other quoted figures such as the price-earnings ratio. An experienced and knowledgeable eye on company accounts can make the best use of ratios, in terms of taking account of non-routine events during the year or abnormal external (possibly economic) events which have taken place. The skill often comes in interpreting ratios and deciding on what element is controllable and what is non-controllable. We will consider the red flags to look for when assessing company-generated numbers.

2. Profitability ratios

Profitability ratios measure a company's ability to generate revenue that is greater than expenditure. A high ratio indicates the company is performing well.

Ratios are used to compare a company's performance with other similar companies and to compare a company's performance in one period with a prior period. For example, a company might use profitability ratios to compare its fourth quarter performance with that of a competitor or it may compare its half year ratio with its own half year ratio in the prior year. Profitability ratios might also be used for half-year on half-year comparison (i.e. H1 v H2) but care must be taken of the impact of seasonal variations which can impact the figures, particularly in some industries.

For example, ice-cream sales in Britain in H2 (July to December) should always be better than H1 (January to June) ice-cream sales. It follows that comparing summer profitability with winter profitability may not provide as useful information as comparing like with like. It would be far more useful to compare profitability of H2 in 2017 with H2 in 2016.

2.1 Profit margins

Profit margins measures profit as a proportion of revenue. The higher the ratio, the more profit the business will make for each £1 of revenue. For example, a business with a 25% margin will make 25p for each £1 of revenue whereas a business with a margin of 10% will make 10p for each £1 of revenue. As with all ratios, the profit margin ratio of a company should be compared with like companies in the same industry as it enables investors to compare 'apples with apples' rather than 'apples with oranges'.

The profit figure that is compared with revenue can be taken at any level of the statement of profit or loss, but the most usual calculations are of gross profit margin and net profit margin.

2.2 Gross and net profit margin

The gross profit margin measures the gross profit a business makes on its sales and is calculated as follows:

$$\frac{\text{Gross profit \%}}{\text{Revenue}}$$

The formula for net profit margin is:

$$\frac{\text{Net profit before tax \%}}{\text{Revenue}}$$

The profit after tax figure is sometimes used in place of profit before tax to calculate the net profit margin. However, the profit before tax figure is often the more appropriate measure: the effects of taxation should usually be stripped out to provide a more meaningful comparison of either (i) two companies on different tax rates; or (ii) of a company's year on year net profit where there has been a change in the rate of taxation from one year to the next.

Note that an increase in gross profit margin will not necessarily lead to an increase in the net profit margin because of the varying impact of expenses outside cost of sales. Care should also be taken not to confuse increased profits of a company with increased profit margin. Whilst both measures are closely linked, a rise in profits does not always mean the profit margin is improving. The company may simply have sold more goods at the existing margin rather than the margin itself improving. Or revenues may have increased at a slower rate than the cost of goods sold because sales prices have been reduced in order to get more market share, thereby reducing the profit margin. One way of looking at this is to consider the ratio of expenses outside cost of sales to revenue, as shown in the following example:

Making it work 8.1

These are the headline profit figures for an entity for the year ended 31 March 2017 (with prior year comparatives):

	2017	2016
	£	£
Revenue	500,000	700,000
Cost of sales	(200,000)	(400,000)
Gross profit	300,000	300,000
Administration expenses	(50,000)	(60,000)
Legal fees	(60,000)	(20,000)
Other expenses	(90,000)	(80,000)
Net profit before tax	100,000	140,000

Gross profit margin = gross profit/revenue
2017: Gross profit margin = 300,000/500,000 = 60%
2016: Gross profit margin = 300,000/700,000 = 43%

Net profit margin = net profit/revenue
2017: Net profit margin = 100,000/500,000 = 20%
2016: Net profit margin = 140,000/700,000 = 20%

Expenses as a percentage of revenue:
2012: 200,000/500,000 × 100 = 40%
2011: 160,000/700,000 × 100 = 23%

The gross profit margin of the entity has increased from 43% to 60% because cost of sales has fallen relative to sales, which is a good sign. The increase in the gross profit margin has not translated into an increase in the net profit margin, however, because expenses have risen relative to sales (from 23% to 40%). In fact we can see here that the main reason for the increase in expenses has been due to a substantial increase in legal fees. This may be a one-off problem, but the user of the accounts will need more information from the entity to determine that and hence whether future profitability will be better.

2.3 Return on capital employed (ROCE)

ROCE is a measure of a company's success at achieving a return on capital invested. It is probably the most important profitability and efficiency ratio as it reflects how well an entity is using the resources it has. There are a number of ways of calculating ROCE but the most common method is to divide a company's return or earnings by net capital employed, treating long-term debt as capital, as well as equity. The ratio is calculated as follows:

$$\text{ROCE} = \frac{\text{Profit on ordinary activities before interest and taxation (PBIT) \%}}{\text{Total assets (TA) less current liabilities (CL)}}$$

= PBIT/(TA-CL) %

Using profit before interest and taxation (PBIT), sometimes also referred to as EBIT (earnings before interest and taxation), is preferred to profit after tax and interest because the latter will be affected by tax rate variations and also variations in how the entity is funded, rather than just operational results.

The ROCE formula might also be set out as:

$$\text{ROCE} = \frac{\text{Earnings \%}}{\text{Capital employed}}$$

$$= \frac{\text{Earnings \%}}{\text{Shareholders' funds + debt}}$$

ROCE also describes the relationship between profitability and asset turnover in that ROCE = operating profit margin × asset turnover (i.e. the company's revenue divided by the capital employed).

This means that the relationship between ROCE, profit margin and asset turnover may be described as:

$$\frac{\text{PBIT}}{\text{Capital employed}} = \frac{\text{PBIT}}{\text{Revenue}} \times \frac{\text{Sales}}{\text{Capital employed}}$$

Assuming all else stays the same, a company's ROCE will fall if either profit margin or asset turnover falls. Likewise, a company's ROCE will increase if either profit margin or asset turnover increases. However, if a company decides to increase its profit margin to make a greater return then it needs to be aware that selling goods at a higher value may lead to reduced revenue which could equally lead to a fall in ROCE or ROCE staying the same. Alternatively, in the hope of improving its return, a company might choose to boost asset turnover by reducing its profit margin and selling its products at a cheaper price.

Making it work 8.2

An entity has the following results for the year to 30 June 2016:

	£'000
Revenue	**5,000**
Profit before interest and tax	**200**
Capital employed	**1,500**

ROCE = 200/1,500 = 13.3%
Profit margin = 200/5,000 = 4%
Asset turnover = 5,000/1,500 = 3.3 times

The entity has a ROCE of 13.3% for the year ended 30 June 2016. In order to meet targets in the next year, the management team believes the best way to increase the company's return is by pushing up the prices of its products and operating at a much higher profit margin.

The figures for the year ended 30 June 2017 are as follows:

	£'000
Revenue	**2000**
Profit before interest and tax	**200**
Capital employed	**1,500**

ROCE = 200/1,500 = 13.3%
Profit margin = 200/2,000 = 10%
Net asset turnover = 2,000/1,500 = 1.3 times

The management strategy of the entity of putting up prices and operating at a higher profit margin has failed to improve the company's ROCE. This is because the higher prices led to reduced asset turnover. This example shows how ROCE, profit margin and asset turnover are interlinked.

The ROCE ratio may be presented in a number of different ways and in the examination you may be required to calculate ROCE from limited information. The profit before interest and tax figure may not be given but you will need to know how to calculate this using the profit after tax figure. If the total assets and current liabilities figures from the top half of the statement of financial position are not provided then you can instead use the figures from the bottom half of the statement of financial position (shareholders' funds and debt).
In addition, capital employed could be described as net capital employed or gross capital employed. The important distinction is that current liabilities are deducted from gross capital employed to get net capital employed because:

Gross capital employed = non-current assets + investments + current assets

and

Net capital employed = non-current assets + investments + current assets – current liabilities

= non-current assets + investments + working capital

= total assets less current liabilities

Further adjustments may also be made to make the calculation more meaningful. For example, intangible assets such as goodwill (see Chapters 5 and 7), should be deducted from non-current assets in calculating the ratio, unless the intangible asset has a market value and could be sold. Furthermore, long-term assets may be undervalued if they have not undergone a recent revaluation exercise or are being carried at cost. For example, if property is shown in the statement of financial position with a lower carrying cost than its true market value, the ROCE will show a higher percentage return. If a current value figure is available, it should be used instead of an older historical number.

Some calculations of ROCE measure the average of capital employed over the period by taking the average of the opening and closing balances. This may be helpful if capital employed is growing or falling substantially, but if it is fairly stable year on year then it may be unnecessary.

Worked example 8.1

Using the information provided, calculate the return on capital employed of this entity for the year ended 31 December 2017 and the prior period.

Statement of financial position as at 31 December

	2017	2017	2016	2016
	£'000	£'000	£'000	£'000
Property, plant and equipment		5,680		5,680
Current assets				
Inventory	200		350	
Debtors	1,250		300	
Cash at bank and in hand	50		350	
		1,500		1,000
Current payables		(300)		(400)
Net current assets		1,200		600
Total assets less current liabilities		6,880		6,280
Non-current payables				
8% loan stock 2024		(100)		(100)
Net assets		6,780		6,180

Share capital	**500**	**500**
Share premium	**50**	**50**
Retained earnings	**6,230**	**5,630**
Total equity	**6,780**	**6,180**

After taxation of £160,000 and dividends of £50,000 the retained profit for the year ended 31 December 2017 was £600,000. After taxation of £127,500 the retained profit was £500,000 for the year ended 31 December 2016 (there were no dividends for the year).

The entity's profitability has risen from 10.1% in 2016 to 11.9% in 2017. The entity appears to be performing efficiently with relative returns exceeding the 8% interest payable on the loan stock. This indicates that the entity might benefit from borrowing more long term money in order to generate greater returns. Further analysis should be undertaken to determine the reason for the 18% increase in profitability as measured by the increase in ROCE [(11.9%–10.1%)/10.1%]. Stakeholders should, therefore, review the full annual report and financial statements in order to establish if the company has taken on increased risk with a view to generating greater returns. A comparison should also be undertaken of ROCE of the company with the ROCE earned by similar sized companies in the same business sector.

Test yourself 8.1

What might cause the ROCE to vary from one year to another?

2.4 Return on investment

A variant on ROCE is return on investment or ROI. A widely used formula for determining the return of a particular investment is:

$$\text{ROI} = \frac{\text{Average annual accounting profit}}{\text{Investment}} \%$$

The average investment amount is usually used and is calculated by taking account of the scrap value of the investment at the end of its economic useful life:

$$\text{Average investment} = \frac{\text{Initial investment} + \text{scrap value}}{2}$$

If the expected rate of return on the investment is greater than the required rate of return then the investment should be undertaken. If, however, there are several mutually exclusive investment options which are all expected to generate a return above the entity's hurdle rate, then the investment which generates the highest rate of return should be chosen. If the investments are not mutually exclusive then the entity should, of course, consider undertaking all investments available where the expected rate of return exceeds the required rate of return.

2.5 Return on equity (ROE)

The return on equity ratio considers the return that equity shareholders get on their investment. The ratio is calculated as:

$$\frac{\text{Net income attributable to equity shareholders}}{\text{Equity}} \%$$

The ratio measures an entity's efficiency: the higher the ratio the more efficient and profitable the company is likely to be. The level of gearing of a company is likely to have an impact on ROE: companies which are highly geared, i.e. have a high proportion of debt to equity, are likely to have a higher ROE ratio. This may seem counter-intuitive, but by using debt, companies expand their capacity to earn profits and servicing debt is less expensive than servicing equity.

2.6 Return on assets (ROA)

ROA measures how well an entity's assets are being used to generate profit. The ratio is calculated by dividing net profit after tax by assets. Banks often find this ratio a useful measure of return because, unlike the return on equity ratio, it takes account of debt funding.

$$= \frac{\text{Net income attributable to equity shareholders}}{\text{Total assets}} \%$$

A high ratio indicates a well-run profitable business.

2.7 Earnings per share (EPS)

Earnings per share is a measure of income attributable to equity shareholders divided by the number of shares outstanding. It is a frequently used indicator of a company's profitability and is often used for comparing a company's financial health with a company with similar earnings. The EPS ratio is calculated as follows:

$$\text{EPS} = \frac{\text{Profit attributable to equity shareholders}}{\text{No of shares}}$$

See Section 5 for more information on EPS.

current ratio
This is a measure of short-term liquidity which shows a company's ability to meet short-term obligations from short-term assets.

quick ratio
This is a measurement of short-term liquidity which focusses on those items that can be turned into cash easily and quickly and therefore does not include stock which may not be easily realisable at full net book value.

3. Liquidity ratios

Liquidity ratios indicate a company's ability to pay its short term debt obligations by using its liquid assets. If a company's liquidity ratios show that a company has insufficient cover to meet its short-term obligations then it should take appropriate action which might include bringing this to the attention of its shareholders and other stakeholders such as the financial regulator (if the company is subject to supervisory oversight).

The most common liquidity ratios are the **current ratio** and the **quick ratio** ('acid test'). There are, however, a number of other liquidity ratios and the most common of these are discussed below.

3.1 Current ratio

The current ratio is a measure of a company's ability to repay short-term liabilities out of current assets. It is calculated by taking the current assets of a company and dividing them by the current liabilities. A ratio of 1 or greater means the company has full cover.

The formula is:

$$\frac{\text{Current assets}}{\text{Current liabilities}}$$

Worked example 8.2

The balance sheet of a company shows the following assets and liabilities:

	£'000	£'000
Current assets		
Inventories	**200**	
Trade debtors	**50**	
Cash at bank and in hand	**100**	
		350
Current liabilities		
Trade creditors	**70**	
Bank loan	**10**	
Accruals	**30**	
Tax	**50**	
		160
Net current assets		**190**

What is the company's current ratio and what does it indicate about the financial health of the company?

3.2 Quick ratio (or 'acid-test')

The quick ratio measures a company's ability to meet short-term liabilities out of the assets that are the most liquid and, therefore, the most quick and easy to realise (i.e. convert into cash). Inventories are not always considered to be quick and easy to realise and therefore they are deducted from the current assets figure in calculating the quick ratio. The quick ratio is, therefore, a more conservative ratio than the current ratio. Again, a ratio of 1 or greater means the company has full cover.

The formula is:

$$\frac{\text{Current assets} - \text{inventories}}{\text{Current liabilities}}$$

Worked example 8.3

Using the balance sheet figures for the company in worked example 8.2, calculate the quick ratio and consider what it means for the health of the company.

3.3 Liquidity ratio (or cash ratio)

The liquidity or cash ratio measures a company's ability to meet short-term liabilities out of cash and cash equivalents (including invested funds) and is an even more conservative measure of short-term liquidity compared with the current and quick ratio. This ratio is less frequently used by financial analysts compared with the current and quick ratio.

The formula for the liquidity or cash ratio is:

$$\frac{\text{Cash and cash equivalents}}{\text{Current liabilities}}$$

While liquidity is an important measure of a company's ability to meet short-term debt obligations, it is not realistic for a company to maintain high cash levels. A company is likely to generate better returns for its shareholders if it utilises its cash by reinvestment in the business; if it has no opportunity to do so it would be better to return cash to shareholders rather than leave it idle, which is a particular issue in a period of very low interest rates.

A ratio of 1 or greater means the company has full cover. As noted above, however, a very high ratio may not be good for shareholders as it could be an indicator of poor asset utilisation. A ratio of less than 1 does not necessarily mean a company has insufficient cover. For example, a company may have a significant level of other current assets which it deems to be sufficiently liquid to mitigate the risk of running out of funds. A company might also have a high level of non-current assets, such as a transport company, and may not need as much liquidity as a retail company. A liquidity ratio of 0.6 to 1.0 might be acceptable in the transport industry, whereas a ratio of greater than 1.0 to 1.5 would normally be required in the retail industry.

Test yourself 8.2

Why do you think a retail company might need greater liquidity than a logistics company?

Worked example 8.4

Using the balance sheet figures for the company in worked example 8.2, calculate the liquidity ratio.

3.4 Cash and cash equivalents/current assets

This is a measure of cash as a percentage of total current assets and is calculated by dividing cash by current assets:

$$\frac{\text{Cash and cash equivalents}}{\text{Current assets}} \%$$

Worked example 8.5

Using the balance sheet figures for the company in worked example 8.2, calculate the cash and cash equivalents as a percentage of current assets.

3.5 Cash flow ratio

This ratio measures a company's net cash inflow from operating activities as per the company's cash flow statement to its total debts and helps determine the cash position of the company compared with a prior period or with like companies. However, because the formula measures cash inflow to total debts, which includes liabilities falling due in over one year, it is perhaps less useful than cash ratios which are based on short-term liquidity requirements. It is calculated as:

$$\frac{\text{Net cash inflow from operating activities}}{\text{Total debts}} \%$$

4. Efficiency ratios

Efficiency ratios enable users of accounts to determine if a company is improving in efficiency. An improvement in efficiency usually results in increased profitability. Accordingly, some ratios may be described as both efficiency ratios and profitability ratios.

4.1 Return on capital employed (ROCE)

As explained in the earlier section on profitability ratios, **ROCE** is a measure of a company's ability to make returns from the level of resources it has available. It is probably the single most important profitability and efficiency ratio as it reflects the profit as a percentage of the amount of capital employed.

Please refer back to the more detailed description of ROCE covered in the section on profitability ratios.

return on capital employed (ROCE)
A measure of a company's success at achieving a return on capital invested. It is calculated by multiplying operating profit margin by net asset turnover.

4.2 Asset turnover

$$\text{Asset turnover} = \frac{\text{Revenue}}{\text{Net assets}} = \frac{\text{Revenue}}{\text{Capital employed}} = \text{X times}$$

This ratio is expressed as the number of times net assets are turned over and expresses the ability of a business to generate revenue from capital employed. A high number (relative to like companies in the same industry) might indicate more investment is needed whilst a low number indicates the business is not utilising its assets efficiently.

Test yourself 8.3

What is the relationship between operating profit margin, asset turnover and ROCE?

4.3 Non-current asset turnover

The non-current asset turnover ratio is a measurement of how effective a company is at generating revenue from the non-current assets (e.g. property, plant and equipment) at its disposal.

It is calculated by dividing revenue (which by definition under IFRS Standards will be after discounts, rebates, etc; see Chapter 5) by non-current assets to establish the multiple of non-current assets represented by revenue; in other words, how much revenue is generated for each £1 of investment in non-current assets.

$$\frac{\text{Revenue}}{\text{Non-current assets}}$$

This ratio is particularly relevant for manufacturing companies and others that have substantial investment in non-current assets. A fall in revenue is likely to result in a fall in the efficiency ratio (unless non-current assets also fall in value, e.g. due to depreciation or impairment; see Chapter 5). If revenue does not change from one year to the next and yet the ratio falls, it may indicate a fall in efficiency or that the company is over-invested in non-current assets which are failing to generate sufficient returns. It may also be a result of the company having upgraded its plant and equipment which may result in higher revenue being generated in future years.

Worked example 8.6

An entity had non-current assets on 31 August 2017 of £200,000 before depreciation. It invested £700,000 to upgrade plant and machinery on 1 June 2018. The annual depreciation charge is 25% of year end carrying value. Revenue for the years ended 31 August 2017 and 31 August 2018 was £1.5 million and £2 million respectively. Calculate the non-current asset turnover for the years ended 31 August 2017 and 31 August 2018.

4.4 Inventory turnover

Inventory turnover measures how efficient an entity is at converting inventory to revenues and shows how often inventory is turned over or used during the period under review. A quick rate (high ratio) indicates that inventory is tightly controlled or that cash may not be available to place larger inventory orders. A low rate may be a result of poor sales volumes or a relatively large order of inventory having previously been placed. Long turnover periods might mean excessive stocks leading to higher storage costs and increased risk of being left with obsolete stock which may never be sold. Low stock turnover implies either a downturn in trading or **overcapitalisation** which can lead to a lower return on investment.

overcapitalisation
An over investment in working capital which can lead to excessive stocks, high debtor/low creditor level and an unnecessarily large amount of cash. Overcapitalisation can result in a lower return on investment and unnecessary use of long-term funds to meet short-term obligations.

The inventory turnover formula used to calculate how many times the company has sold the value of its inventory during the year is:

$$\frac{\text{Cost of sales}}{\text{Inventory}}$$

The inventory days formula used to show the number of days it takes to turn over the inventory (i.e. the number of days that cash is tied up in inventory) is:

$$\text{Inventory days} = \frac{\text{Inventory}}{\text{Cost of sales}} \times 365 = \text{X days}$$

The average inventory (at cost) figure is used in the calculation. One method commonly used for calculating average inventory, where inventory movement is fairly consistent throughout the year, is to add the opening inventory value to closing inventory and divide by two:

$$\text{Average inventory} = \frac{\text{Opening inventory} + \text{Closing inventory}}{2}$$

Test yourself 8.4

What are the disadvantages of slow inventory turnover?

The manufacturing industry controls inventory turnover tightly by using **just in time procurement** methods. This minimises stockholding which reduces inventory costs and improves the quick ratio.

just in time procurement (JIT)
A term used to describe a procurement policy whereby stock is ordered just before it is needed. It relies on close customer and supplier relations to ensure the stock arrives 'just in time'. JIT production methods are commonly used in the motor industry and other manufacturing industries enabling flexible manufacturing processes which keep stock levels to a minimum.

4.5 Revenue to net working capital

The revenue to net working capital ratio shows the amount of net current assets required to generate revenue and, therefore, helps a business to control its cash levels. Whilst it is important for a business to have liquidity, any excess cash should be used to keep financing needs to a minimum and thereby reduce the overall cost of capital. If a company uses long-term capital to fund short-term obligations it should expect lower investment returns.

working capital
A company's current assets less its current liabilities and a term used to describe operational efficiency or the company's ability to pay its short-term liabilities.

The ratio is also known as net working capital turnover because it is a measure of how efficiently **working capital** is turned over.

The formula is:

$$\frac{\text{Revenue}}{\text{Net working capital}}\ \% = \frac{\text{Revenue}}{\text{CA-CL}}\ \%$$

Broadly speaking, a high ratio indicates the company has a strong ability to use working capital efficiently to maintain sales and a low ratio indicates inefficiency and overcapitalisation. As with the analysis of all ratios, other factors should be taken into account and ratios should not be looked at in isolation.

4.6 Debtor days

This is a measure of the average time it takes debtors to pay for goods they have received on credit. An increase in debtor days is a sign that the quality of the debtors is decreasing and could, if not addressed, lead to a business having cash flow difficulties. In a financial services company, debtor days which exceed 90 days usually have to be discounted for the purposes of short-term liquidity calculations as it becomes increasingly less certain the debtors will pay in full in a timely manner. In the retail clothing business, the average debtor payment period is often significantly shorter and credit terms of no more than 30 days are not unusual. Broadly speaking, the lower the debtor days, the better the cash position for the business. It is worth remembering that more companies go out of business because of cash flow problems than profitability issues.

A business with a tightly run credit control department will regularly monitor the average debtor payment period and look for movements in the trend so that increases in debtor days are effectively managed in a timely manner.

The ratio is calculated as follows:

$$\frac{\text{Trade receivables}}{\text{Revenue}} \times 365 = \text{X days}$$

4.7 Creditor days

This efficiency and performance ratio measures the average time it takes a business to pay its creditors. It is calculated by dividing trade payables by purchases.

$$\frac{\text{Trade payables}}{\text{Purchases}} \times 365 = \text{X days}$$

If the purchases figure is not available then the cost of sales figure or even the sales figure would be used.

If the ratio is over 90 days in, say, the financial services industry, it could mean that the business is struggling to generate sufficient cash to settle its invoices in a timely manner. It could also imply unethical practice, e.g. a major supermarket chain intentionally delaying payment to suppliers who are dependent on the supermarket for the business.

Test yourself 8.5

If a supermarket has purchases of £30 million and £5 million of trade payables, how long does it take on average to pay its suppliers?

Test yourself 8.6

What might the implications be if a company's creditor payment period were to decrease significantly from one year to the next?

5. Gearing ratios

Gearing ratios measure the solvency of a company and focus on the extent to which businesses use long-term **debt financing** compared with **equity financing**. **Gearing** is therefore a measurement of long-term debt to shareholders' funds. The various gearing ratios indicate the ability of a business to fund its debt and interest payments for its continuing operations. A company that is highly geared or leveraged has a high proportion of debt to equity whereas a company with a low gearing ratio has a relatively low level of debt compared with equity.

A highly geared company might be considered more risky than a company without gearing because the highly geared company will have regular interest payments to service the debt and, in times of increasing interest rates, businesses with high levels of borrowing with variable rate interest payments may find themselves faced with uncomfortably large monthly outgoings in order to service the debt. This means there is likely to be less money available for distribution to equity holders in the form of dividends, and even not enough to pay other creditors as they fall due.

A company that is funded only by equity will have no interest payments. Instead, it will pay out a dividend to the owners of the company but only if it can afford to do so. Dividends are paid out at the discretion of the board whilst interest payments on long-term debt financing are a contractual payment. While equity might be less risky than debt, it may prove more costly for the company to raise equity finance because equity is often more costly to service. In particular, interest payments on debt are tax deductible for the issuing entity, whereas dividends on equity are not. Many companies will be funded by both debt and equity. The merits and drawbacks of each type of financing would need to be taken into account should the company require further financing.

Lenders are particularly interested in a company's gearing ratios since a high gearing ratio might indicate a company's inability to repay debt. It is therefore not unusual for lenders to restrict a company's level of gearing through the use of loan covenants.

debt financing
Occurs when a company raises finance by issuing bonds, bills or notes and, in exchange, promises to repay the lender the interest and capital on the loan.

equity financing
Capital raised by selling shares in the company, typically by public offering. Investors buy the shares and become shareholders or owners of the company's equity.

gearing
A measurement of long-term debt to equity and measures the extent to which a company is leveraged by comparing borrowed funds to shareholder funds.

Test yourself 8.7

Can you think of any benefits of debt over equity as a source of financing?

There are a number of gearing ratios, the most commonly used ones being:

5.1 Debt to equity

Debt to equity is calculated as: $\frac{\text{Debt}}{\text{Equity}}$

This ratio measures debt to equity by taking the total debt figure from the statement of financial position and dividing it by the total equity. When comparing companies of similar nature and in the same industry, a low debt to equity ratio indicates less risk than a high debt to equity ratio.

5.2 Debt to debt plus equity (or debt ratio or gearing ratio)

This gearing ratio is much like the debt to equity ratio but measures debt to total assets.

$$\text{Gearing} = \frac{\text{Debt}}{\text{Debt + Equity}}\,\% = \frac{\text{Debt}}{\text{Total assets}}\,\%$$

This ratio might also be expressed as Debt/Total capital employed (%) and is often referred to as the main gearing ratio.

This measures debt as a proportion of total assets. Again, assuming everything else is equal, a lower gearing ratio indicates less risk. A high ratio indicates greater vulnerability to economic downturns because the company may have to continue to pay fixed interest payments on the debt when earnings fall.

5.3 Interest cover (or interest times covered)

$$\text{Interest cover} = \frac{\text{Profit before interest and taxation (PBIT)}}{\text{Interest paid}}$$

This ratio measures a company's ability to meet its interest payments from earnings. An interest cover of 4 indicates that a company has sufficient earnings to meet its interest payments four times. A ratio of 2 means the earnings will cover interest 2 times. A higher interest cover ratio, therefore, indicates a company is better placed to meet its interest obligations. Interest cover of less than 1 or slightly less than 1 means the company is likely to have difficulty in servicing its debt, particularly if interest rates rise.

When analysing leverage ratios, care should be taken not to state simply that a debt to equity ratio of, say, 180% means that a company is highly geared. A company's leverage should always be compared to that of similar companies in the same industry and commentary made in a relevant context. Analysts and users of financial statements should take into account the risk profile of the company and its investment policy. For example, it may not be unusual for a collective investment fund whose investment policy is specialist and alternative investments to be highly geared. The extent to which the fund company may be leveraged would be stated in the fund's **prospectus** or information memorandum (e.g. may not exceed 200%). A company with a high proportion of non-current assets is also more likely to have a high level of gearing, e.g. a construction company or a company that hires out plant and machinery, and so it would not be appropriate to compare the gearing of a plant hire company, which might have financial gearing of 200% or more, with that of a retail clothes store or financial services company which is less likely to need to raise finance to fund fixed asset investments and therefore might have a gearing level of no more than 100%.

prospectus
An information memorandum or offer document for subscriptions in a collective investment fund or investment company which sets out the terms of the offer and key information in respect of the fund. The document will include, among other things, risk warnings and details in connection with the investment policy and extent to which the company will use gearing.

6. Earnings per share and other key investor ratios

Earnings per share is a measure of profit after tax attributable to equity shareholders divided by the number of shares outstanding. It is a frequently used indicator of a company's profitability and is often used by shareholders for comparing a company's financial health with a company with similar earnings. It is the only such measure governed by an accounting standards, IAS 33 'Earnings Per Share'.

UK GAAP equivalent
UK accounting standards require companies whose shares are publicly traded to follow IAS 33 in reporting earnings per share. As untraded companies do not have to report EPS, the subject is not covered by FRS 102.

IAS 33 states that basic earnings per share is calculated by dividing profit or loss attributable to ordinary equity holders of the parent entity (the numerator) by the weighted average number of **ordinary shares** outstanding (the denominator) during the period. Earnings are after taking account of any preference share dividends or settlements if they have been reported as equity, but as most of these are usually reported as debt, they will already be adjusted for in the total profit after tax number.

ordinary share
An equity instrument (see Chapter 6) that is subordinate to all other classes of equity instruments.

The EPS ratio is calculated as follows:

$$\frac{\text{Earning (profit after tax)}}{\text{No of shares}}$$

Worked example 8.7

A company has net income of £19 million for the year ended 30 June 2018. The company has eight million shares at the start of the financial year and on 1 October 2017 issues a further two million shares. What is the EPS for the year?

Test yourself 8.8

Company A has earnings of £12 million and Company B has earnings of £11.5 million. Company A has four million shares in issue whereas Company B has four million shares in issue for the first half of the financial year and two million for the remaining six months. Which company has the highest earnings per share?

A company with greater overall earnings than another company is not necessarily more profitable because the company which has less earnings might have a higher EPS, i.e. it generates more earnings per share. Another consideration with profitability measures is to be aware that two companies may have the same EPS and so it is important for analysts and investors to take other factors and other profitability ratios into account when making an investment decision. For example, if Company A and Company B in the above example had the same EPS then the company with the least paid up share capital might be considered the better investment choice because it would have generated the same EPS despite less money having been invested in the company by the shareholders.

The Marks & Spencer EPS figures are stated, as required, at the bottom of the statement of comprehensive income on page 86 of the 2016 ARA.

Test yourself 8.9

Look at the Marks & Spencer results for 2016 and 2015, find the EPS figures and consider what they show about the company's profitability.

The calculation of diluted EPS is beyond the scope of this text, but basically dilution is a reduction in earnings per share or an increase in loss per share resulting from the assumption that convertible instruments are converted, that options or warrants are exercised, or that ordinary shares are issued upon the satisfaction of specified conditions. In other words, it takes account of all **potential ordinary shares**.

potential ordinary share
A financial instrument (see Chapters 5 and 6) or other contract that may entitle its holder to ordinary shares.

6.1 Price to earnings ratio (P/E ratio)

The price to earnings ratio is a measure of earnings growth and is calculated by dividing the market value per share by the EPS.

$$\text{P/E ratio} = \frac{\text{Market value per share}}{\text{EPS Earnings}} = \text{Market value per share} \times \text{number of shares}$$

$$= \frac{\text{Market capitalisation}}{\text{Earnings}}$$

Worked example 8.8

A listed company has the following trading figures for the year ended 31 March 2018.

	£'000
Operating profit	**50,000**
Tax	**(24,000)**
Profit after tax	**26,000**
Dividend for the year	**(10,000)**
Retained profit	**16,000**

The company has 10 million ordinary £1 shares in issue with a market value of 350p per share. Calculate the P/E ratio for the listed company.

The P/E ratio is viewed as an important measure that is used as a valuation tool for companies by considering the value of the shares as a multiple of their earnings. For example, if a company has a market capitalisation of £85 million and net profit of £5 million then the P/E ratio would be 17. As with many other ratios, the P/E ratio requires a comparative to be meaningful but, simplistically speaking, the P/E ratio would suggest, rightly or wrongly, to shareholders that it will take 17 years for their investment in the company to be paid off by earnings. However, other companies in the sector may be trading at a higher or lower P/E ratio, and investors and analysts will consider whether that is justified and may class the shares as over or under-valued as a consequence.

The P/E ratio is not without its shortcomings and one of the main drawbacks is that it is calculated using the earnings figure which could be subject to manipulation by management. Analysts may, therefore, use their own projection of future earnings in the calculation rather than relying on past performance as a measure of future performance.

A low P/E ratio of a company might indicate to investors that its shares are value for money but it could also mean that earnings are expected to fall, hence why analysts might use their own earnings forecasts to calculate the P/E ratio. Analysis of earnings growth should, therefore, take a number of financial and non-financial factors into account and not rely solely on the P/E ratio.

6.2 Dividend cover

The dividend cover ratio measures a company's ability to maintain dividend payments. It shows how many times the dividends could be paid out of profits. For example, a dividend cover of two times means that a company can afford to pay dividends twice out of profits. Put another way, it means profits attributable to shareholders were twice the dividend level.

Dividend cover is a key shareholder investment ratio because most shareholders like to receive regular and stable dividend payments. If the dividend cover falls then shareholders might become anxious if profits fall as this may mean their expected dividend payment is under threat.

Dividend cover = EPS/dividend per ordinary share
Or Earnings (profit after tax)/Total dividend

The ratio thus serves as a useful measure of sustained profitability, but some care is required. Dividends are paid out of *accumulated* profits not yet paid out, so if profit is down one year, or even if a loss is made, a company may be able to make a dividend payment that is as good as last year's if it still has a lot of past profits available. Listed companies will often do this and even increase their dividends in a bad year to show their confidence in future results and encourage shareholders to keep their shares. They also need cash to do this, but cash can also be borrowed.

Some companies, even with a lot of cash, do not pay dividends but rely on capital gains on shares to reward shareholders. High growth companies are often in this category and will not pay profits out as dividends until they become more stable and not as much cash is required for reinvestment in the business.

Case study 8.1

Apple Inc

In 2012 Apple announced the start of a dividend and share buy-back programme (which also allows money to be returned to shareholders in a tax-efficient way). The dividends were the first to be paid since 1995, when the company suspended its dividend due to trading difficulties. The company's cash pile by 2012 amounted to nearly $100 billion and it had come under pressure from some investors to start paying returns to shareholders to release some of that cash. CEO Tim Cook made it clear that such payments would not affect continuing investment in the business: 'We have used some of our cash to make great investments in our business through increased research and development, acquisitions, new retail store openings, strategic prepayments and capital expenditures in our supply chain, and building out our infrastructure. You'll see more of all of these in the future,' Mr Cook said, adding: 'Innovation is the most important objective at Apple and we will not lose sight of that. These [decisions] will not close any doors for us ...The pipeline is full of stuff and I think customers are going to be incredibly pleased with what's coming through.' (*Daily Telegraph*, 19 March 2012).

6.3 Dividend yield

Dividend yield is a key investor ratio as it highlights the return on the shares, i.e. how much an investor receives in dividend payments relative to his or her investment.

$$\text{Dividend yield} = \frac{\text{Annual dividend per ordinary share}}{\text{Market value of share}} \%$$

Worked example 8.9

A company's annual dividend is 80p per share and the ex-dividend share price is £16 per share. What is the company's dividend yield?

6.4 Dividend payout ratio

The dividend payout ratio measures the proportion of earnings paid out as dividends and is measured as:

$$\frac{\text{Total annual dividend}}{\text{Earnings (profit after tax)}} \%$$

$$\textit{Or}\ \frac{\text{Dividend per share}}{\text{EPS}} \%$$

7. Key performance indicators

In this chapter so far we have looked at fairly standardised measures of performance. However, UK company law requires company management to report on the measures they use to assess company performance and to judge how well their company is doing in their Strategic Report (see Chapter 1). These measures are called **key performance indicators (KPIs)**. Regulators often refer to them as alternative performance measures (APMs) as they are usually based on 'alternative' numbers to the statutory accounts figures.

Key performance indicators (KPIs)
Factors by reference to which the development, performance or position of an entity's business can be measured effectively

Companies have for many years reported their own version of company performance, which is different from the statutory numbers. The main aim is often to strip out one-off, non-recurring items to reveal underlying results. When done well, these figures can give great insight into how management are running the company and the things they think are really important. When done badly, however, they can mislead users of accounts, because the measures are not fully explained, the basis of calculation is changed too often, or potentially there is continual bias in how the figures are published to make the company look like it is doing better than it is.

When examining a set of company accounts, it is always worth looking at the company's KPIs, but then it is important to dig down into how they are calculated. The Marks & Spencer KPIs for 2016 are given on pages 18 to 21 of the 2016 ARA. Some of these are financial, including revenue growth and profit margins, which for retailers are very important. However, there are other KPIs that are non-financial, particularly around sustainability and also other strategic objectives.

The use of KPIs and APMs is becoming more heavily regulated, particularly for listed companies. They are expected to be calculated consistently and reconciled where appropriate to the statutory figures. This is important, but at the moment there is no need to have such figures audited, although the auditors will look at whether the information is consistent with the audited financial statements and what they have seen during their audit.

Stop and think 8.1

Do you think the Marks & Spencer KPIs are informative and helpful? How do they compare with the more standard ratios you can calculate from the statutory accounts?

Chapter summary

- For ratios to be meaningful, they should always be considered in context and compared with prior period ratios and/or with ratios of similar companies in the same industry sector. Key ratios cover profitability, liquidity, efficiency, gearing and shareholder returns measures, including earnings per share (EPS).
- Profitability measures are usually some level of profit compared to revenue, to estimate how much of revenue covers costs and how much generates profit.
- Liquidity ratios help to assess how much pressure the company is under to pay its short-term debts. One of the most important efficiency ratios is return on capital employed (which also deals with profitability), but there are others, including those that help to judge how well an entity is managing its working capital.
- Gearing (or leverage) ratios measure the solvency of a business and focus on the extent to which businesses use long-term debt financing compared with equity financing. An increase in gearing is usually linked to an increase in risk. Lenders often impose loan covenants on borrowers which restrict a company's gearing level and thereby help safeguard the loan.
- EPS and other investor ratios help investors assess the financial health of a company compared with a company with similar earnings because the company with greater overall earnings may have a lower EPS. The P/E ratio is a key shareholder investment ratio because it indicates how long it will be before they will receive back their initial investment in the company.

- Companies publish their own versions of important ratios, called key performance indicators (KPIs). These give important insights into how the company is being run and what management think is important. Managers are often rewarded through bonuses and other remuneration by reference to achieving targets in KPIs. Care is required, however, as the KPIs are not audited and there are no set rules on calculating them.

Part three

Chapter nine
Trust accounting

Chapter ten
Companies, partnerships and other vehicles

Trust accounts and other forms of entity

Overview

In this part you will learn about trust income and capital, and the significance of the income and capital split in the context of life interest trusts. You will also learn about the main financial statements comprising the accounts of a life interest trust and will gain an understanding of which accounting items might be classified as income and which might be treated as capital.

You will see the different types of company that may be formed in the UK, but also in offshore jurisdictions, where vehicles include cell companies and foundations. Different forms of partnership are also discussed. You will gain an understanding of how share and loan capital is created under UK company legislation and which legal reserves can be distributed to shareholders.

Learning outcomes

At the end of this part, you will be able to:

- Explain the concept of a trust
- Understand the role of the trustee of a trust
- Explain the difference between income and capital
- Explain what a discretionary trust is
- Outline the key features of a life interest trust
- Understand some of the key requirements of the UK Companies Act 2006 in relation to public and private companies
- Explain some key features of Jersey public and private companies
- Summarise the similarities and difference between Guernsey and British Virgin Island (BVI) companies
- Discuss the use of cell companies
- Summarise the key differences between trusts, companies, partnerships and foundations
- Describe the different forms of partnership that can exist, including both corporate and non-corporate vehicles
- Understand the different forms of share capital and explain the differences to loan capital.

Chapter nine
Trust accounting

List of topics

1. Introduction
2. Trusts, trust law and trustees
3. Income and capital
4. Preparation and interpretation of trust financial statements

1. Introduction

In this chapter, we will cover different types of trusts and the role and duties of trustees. Although this is not a comprehensive coverage of trusts, a complex area of law and accounting, you will gain an insight into discretionary trusts and life interest trusts, and in particular the importance of segregating income from capital. The chapter also explains what is meant by the terms 'life tenant' and 'remainderman' in the context of life interest trusts.

The chapter also introduces accounting for a life interest trust and you will learn how to prepare a life tenant's account and how to treat certain items of income and expenditure.

2. Trusts, trust law and trustees

2.1 What is a trust?

A **trust** is a legal arrangement whereby one or more persons, known as the trustee(s), are entrusted with the legal ownership of the assets of another party, the settlor, and to hold those assets (which might include property, investments and cash) 'on trust' for the benefit of one or more beneficiaries. In its simplest form, a trust is just a legal mechanism for separating the ownership of an asset into two parts: the 'legal' ownership, or title to the asset, on the one hand, and the 'beneficial' ownership on the other hand.

trust
A legal arrangement whereby one or more persons, known as the trustee(s), are entrusted with the legal ownership of the assets of another party, the settlor, and to hold those assets (which might include property, investments and cash) 'on trust' for the benefit of one or more beneficiaries.

2.2 Trust law and the use of trusts

Trusts have a long history and are usually found in common law jurisdiction such as the UK and USA. As well as the common law, there are also laws in statute governing trusts, which in areas have superseded the common law. Although the detail is beyond the scope of this text, the main Acts of Parliament in the UK are:

- Trustee Act 1925
- Trustee Investments Act 1961
- Recognition of Trusts Act 1987
- Financial Services and Markets Act 2000
- Pensions Acts 1995 and 2004
- Charities Act 2011.

There are also a large number of tax laws surrounding trusts, which are not covered in this text.

As can be seen from this list, trusts are used for a wide variety of purposes, including in financial services (for example in securitisation arrangements), pensions (where a trust usually holds the pension assets) and charities. Some of these more specialised trusts are governed by specific law and regulation, but in this chapter we will look at the more simple examples where individuals establish trusts to pass on assets in various forms to their relatives.

Trusts are often used for estate planning purposes, for example where a high net worth individual wishes their spouse and children to benefit from their estate, but wants to ensure that the spouse continues to enjoy the same level of income and that the capital is preserved for and passed onto the children or other descendants. Trusts are also used to keep money safe for children while they are young and, while perhaps providing for their education, to defer their receipt of the capital until they become adults, to ensure they are old enough to look after the inheritance they receive and use it wisely. Testamentary trusts may be created in wills, defining how money and property will be handled for children or other beneficiaries, but a trust can be set up to hold the property of someone still living.

A trust has no separate legal personality and therefore cannot contract in its own name. Instead, a trustee will be appointed to manage the affairs of the trust and contract in its name, i.e. as trustee of the trust. The assets, whether cash or other investments (including property) are settled on trust by the **settlor** and the trustees are empowered to invest the funds on behalf of the beneficiaries and make distributions of capital and/or income to them, at their own discretion or as set out in the **trust deed**.

Offshore trusts are also commonly used for the avoidance of **forced heirship**, for the avoidance of probate and for tax planning purposes.

settlor
The person (or persons) who creates the trust.

trust deed
A legal document setting out the terms of the trust and includes details of the interested parties, such as the settlor, trustees and beneficiaries as well as details of the trustee's powers – such as powers to invest and powers to distribute capital and income.

forced heirship
Essentially a feature of civil law jurisdictions and Islamic countries which do not recognise the full freedom of testation. This means, for example, that an individual making his will may not be able to leave an equal proportion of his assets to his surviving children and spouse. In order to prevent all the assets going to the eldest child, the individual may use a foundation or trust and thereby avoid the forced heirship rules.

2.3 Principles of trust law

As with contracts, there is no need for any formality to create a trust unless statute demands there should be, so for example for certain types of asset such as company shares, any transfer must be registered. Over the years case law has developed which means that trusts will only be deemed to have been created if certain conditions are satisfied. These include that the settlor should have had the intention to dispose of the assets in that particular way, although he or she does not need to be aware that they are actually creating a trust. There must also be certainty of subject, i.e. which assets are being settled, which can include a valid portion of a set of assets claimed by many people or a number of items that are fungible or interchangeable with each other as they are identical (e.g. '100 of my 500 shares in Company X'). Certainty of beneficiary is also important and in English law there has to be a person who is a beneficiary (unless it is a charitable trust).

The UK recognises the validity of offshore trusts, even if they are not consistent with English law, unless they are manifestly incompatible with public policy. In countries that are offshore financial centres, trusts can be created which serve no charitable function, or any function related to the good of society, so long as the trust document specifies someone to be an **enforcer** or protector of the trust. These include Jersey, the Isle of Mann, Bermuda, the British Virgin Islands and the Cayman Islands.

trust enforcer
A trust enforcer is the appointed overseer of the trust acting on behalf of the trust.

Offshore trusts
Offshore trusts are often used as part of the tax and financial planning of wealthy individuals and their families. Examples include:

- Errol Damelin, founder of Wonga, holds his shares through Castle Bridge Ventures, a trust based in the British Virgin Islands.
- The Enthoven family (behind Nando's restaurant chain) is reported to use trusts in the Channel Islands.

Offshore trusts also have many other uses:

- They are sometimes formed as unit trusts to operate as a mutual fund.
- They are often used as part of an orphan structure in capital markets or trade finance transactions.
- Pan-national non-governmental bodies are sometimes established as offshore trusts, e.g. the International Cricket Council is formed in the British Virgin Islands.

It is important to note that this area of law has seen substantial changes in recent times, and these changes are continuing, not least because of public concern on the use of trusts to evade tax or for money-laundering purposes. You will need to keep track of the latest developments in the jurisdictions you deal with.

2.4 Trustee

A trustee is an individual or corporate body (e.g. a limited liability company) which takes legal ownership of the assets of a trust fund and manages the trust fund for the benefit of the beneficiaries. A trust may have one or more trustees depending on the law governing the trust. For example, a Jersey trust may have one or more trustees, whereas in Guernsey the minimum requirement is two trustees. The trustee may be liable for damages if it does not carry out its **fiduciary duty** in a proper manner. A trustee is usually entitled to receive payment for its services and the terms will be set out in the trust deed.

fiduciary duty
The legal obligation of a fiduciary to act in the best interests of another party.

2.5 Types of trust

As noted above, trusts are used for many purposes and there are different types of trust. For the purposes of this text, we will focus on just two: discretionary trusts and life interest trusts.

Discretionary trusts
A discretionary trust is a trust where the trustees have absolute discretion over the trust funds and may determine how much of the trust fund may be paid out to one or more of the beneficiaries.

Life interest trusts
Life interest trusts (also known as interest-in-possession trusts) are often set up as part of estate planning, so that when a person dies his or her surviving spouse is entitled to the income from the trust fund for life and, thereafter, the capital is typically passed on to the children, who are known as the **remaindermen**. The beneficiary of the income is known as the **life tenant**, e.g. the surviving spouse, and is entitled to the income arising on the trust fund net of expenses, such as the trustee fees. The distinction between income and capital is discussed in the next section.

remaindermen
The term given to beneficiaries who receive the remaining capital upon termination of a life interest trust, e.g. after the death of the life tenant.

life tenant
A tenant who holds a life estate. A life tenant has all rights associated with ownership of real property, except the right to sell the property, until his/her (or someone else's) death. Upon the death of the life tenant, the property reverts back to the owner, or to a third party designated by the owner.

3. Income and capital

3.1 Introduction

One of the most significant issues in relation to accounting for trusts is the distinction between capital and income. This is important because of the way that trusts often allocate the benefits of income and capital to different beneficiaries.

3.2 Trust capital

Trust capital represents the cash and non-cash assets initially settled on trust as well as capital subsequently settled on trust. In other words, it is the money, investments, property and other assets put into the trust.

From an accounting perspective, capital is viewed as money spent to enhance the value of an asset. Capital expenditure might be money spent building an extension to trust property which will enhance its value and increase its future earnings potential by making it a more attractive property to rent out.

3.3 Trust income

Income describes the money earned from an asset while leaving the capital value of the asset intact.

Income arising on a trust might include, *inter alia*, bank deposit interest, dividends from shares held or property rental income. Revenue expenses typically include professional fees (e.g. legal fees, accountancy fees, registered office fees, company secretarial fees, trustee fees), bank charges and income distributed to the life tenant during the year.

3.4 Accounting for income and capital

By splitting out income and capital and ensuring capital is not eroded by only paying income, and not capital, to the life tenant, the trustees can ensure that the capital value of the trust fund is preserved for the surviving children. This is not to say that the trustees cannot pay capital to the life tenant – this will depend on the terms of the trust deed. Difficulties can arise when large expenses, such as trustee or legal fees, arise in respect of the trust. If the expenses are incurred in connection with income payments to the life tenant, for example, the remaindermen may expect to see the trustees paying such costs from the income of the trust fund and not from capital.

The balance due to the life tenant is included as an item within the income account and is shown in the balance sheet as a current liability. The balance sheet of a life interest trust is a snapshot of the trust's financial position, showing its assets and liabilities at a specific point in time, for example:

- fixed asset investments held by the trust such as freehold property and quoted investments;
- current assets such as debtors and cash at hand/bank; and
- creditors such as amount due to life tenant and other current liabilities.

4. Preparation and interpretation of trust financial statements

Trustees of a trust are responsible for ensuring accounting records are maintained and financial statements are prepared. The annual accounts for a trust typically include the following statements:

- Income account
- Capital account
- Statement of financial position (balance sheet)
- Schedule of investments.

The income account is mostly likely to show interest on bank deposits, property rental income and dividends received from investments. It will also show expenses paid out which are of an income nature such as bank charges, overdraft interest, legal fees, accountancy fees, administration and other professional fees. Any income distributions will also appear on the income statement. With life interest trusts, the income due to the life tenant is shown in the life tenant's account.

The capital account shows the cash and non-cash assets initially settled on trust as well as additional settled funds. It also shows the increase in capital from investments, including gains and losses on realisation, and items of capital expenditure such as capital gains tax and inheritance tax. Certain professional fees may also be charged to capital if they relate to expenditure of a capital nature, for example fees incurred in relation to the administration of an estate. Any capital distributions will also appear on the capital account. If a trust has separate funds (e.g. one for each beneficiary), the capital account should clearly show the capital balances by fund.

The statement of financial position shows fixed and current assets held by the trust including investments, property, bank balances and any debtors owing money to the trust (perhaps from a related party). It also shows the liabilities such as a bank overdraft, creditors and, in the case of a life interest trust, the amount due to the life tenant.

The schedule of assets typically lists quoted and other investments, the amount of shares held, the book value and market value of those shares, additions, disposals and gains and losses on disposal of the shares.

Worked example 9.1

The income account of a life interest trust showed an amount due to the life tenant of £100,000 as at 1 January 2016. The net income for the trust for the financial year ended 31 December 2016 was £15,000, of which £10,000 had already been distributed to the life tenant during the year.

Prepare the Life Tenant's Account for the year ended 31 December 2016 and state how much was due to the life tenant as at 31 December 2016.

Explain how this would be reflected in the statement of financial position of the life interest trust.

Worked example 9.2

The Liam Johnson Life Interest Trust was established on 7 June 2005 under the laws of Jersey. The appointed trustees are ABC Trustees Limited. The terms of the trust are to pay income to the life tenant, Mrs Linda Johnson, during her life and upon her death to pay the capital to the children, Miss Sinead Johnson, Mr Joseph Johnson and Mrs Sarah Lemmer.

The following balances have been extracted from the ledgers of the Life Interest Trust Account for the 12 months ending 5 April 2016.

	DR	CR
	£	£
Balances at 5 April 2016		
Quoted investments (market value)	500,000	
Freehold property (market value)	450,000	
Bank balances		
Capital	31,598	
Income	3,751	
Trust capital transactions for the reporting period		
Investment management expenses	1,500	
Legal fees	1,000	
Accountancy fees	1,200	
Gain on sale of investments		500
Trust revenue transactions for the reporting period		
Rental income		20,000
Income from quoted investments (dividends)		23,800
Bank interest		958
Trustee fees	2,500	
Accountancy fees	150	
Bank charges	175	
Distributions to life tenant	35,000	
Other balances b/f as at 6 April 2015		
Life interest trust fund		971,542
Due to life tenant		10,074
Totals	1,026,874	1,026,874

Assume, for the purposes of this example, that there is no taxation.

1 Prepare the income account for the Liam Johnson Life Interest Trust for the year ended 5 April 2016.

2 Prepare the life tenant's account as at 5 April 2016.

3 Prepare the capital account as at 5 April 2016.

4 Prepare the statement of financial position as at 5 April 2016.

Chapter summary

- A trust is a legal arrangement whereby one or more persons, known as the trustee(s), are entrusted with the legal ownership of the assets of another party, the settlor, to hold those assets (which might include property, investments and cash) 'on trust' for the benefit of one or more beneficiaries.
- A trust has no separate legal personality and therefore cannot contract in its own name. There is a long history of trusts and a lot of case law, but also statute covers various types of trust. There are differences between UK trusts and offshore trusts.
- There are different forms of trust, including discretionary trusts, where the trustees have absolute discretion over the trust funds and may determine how much of the trust fund may be paid out to one or more of the beneficiaries, and life interest trusts, where a life tenant has use of the assets of the trust but on his or her death these revert to the settlor or to the remaindermen.
- The distinction between income and capital is important, both for beneficiaries and, from an accounting perspective; capital is viewed as money spent to enhance the value of an asset. Capital expenditure might be money spent building an extension to trust property which will enhance its value and increase its future earnings potential by making it a more attractive property to rent out.
- The accounts of a life interest trust typically include an income statement, a capital statement and a statement of financial position (balance sheet).

Chapter ten

Companies, partnerships and other vehicles

List of topics

1. Introduction
2. UK corporate vehicles
3. Offshore corporate vehicles
4. Partnerships
5. Share and loan capital
6. Legal reserves

1. Introduction

Those wishing to run a business have a variety of means of doing so, depending on the legal jurisdiction within which they operate. In the UK and many other places, the main difference between corporate and non-corporate vehicles for running a business is that a corporate vehicle is entirely separate from its owners and provides the option for limitation of liability for the owners of the business. There are also wide-ranging differences in tax treatment.

In this chapter we will look at the key differences between public and private limited companies in the UK as well as the key features of limited companies in offshore jurisdictions such as Jersey, Guernsey and the British Virgin Islands. We will also look at cell companies and foundations, which are not available in the UK but are found in some offshore jurisdictions. The differences between general partnerships, limited partnerships and limited liability partnerships are discussed, both in the UK and offshore.

We will also consider the options to finance a business, considering the differences between share and loan capital. In relation to share capital we will look at what is meant by ordinary shares, preference shares, authorised share capital, issued share capital, called up share capital, paid up share capital, retained profits and share premium. The implications of gearing and taxation are discussed in the context of a company raising finance and the need for the directors to strike the balance of debt and equity finance. We will also consider the principle of capital maintenance and the way creditors are protected from making distributions to shareholders that would disadvantage creditors' claims on a company.

2. UK corporate vehicles

2.1 Introduction

Companies have their own legal personality which is separate from the legal personalities of the individuals who own and manage the company. Limited companies, therefore, offer protection to the owners of the business and this is why sole traders often form companies to limit their liability for debts. A company contracts in its own name.

Case law 10.1

***Salomon v A. Salomon & Co. Ltd* [1897]**

***Salomon v A. Salomon & Co. Ltd* is a landmark case in UK company law and established the principle of corporate personality. In other words, the company is liable for its own debts, not the owners or the directors.**

Mr Aron Salomon ran his own business as a sole trader manufacturing boots and shoes. He set up a limited company, A Salomon & Co Ltd and sold the business to the company in 1892 in return for £29,000 in cash, a £10,000 secured debenture and 20,001 shares in the company which was considered to be worth considerably more than the value of the business. There were seven subscribers in total, Mr Salomon, his wife and their five children. He made two of his sons directors of the company. The company went into liquidation a year later and there were £11,000 in trade creditors but Mr A Salomon was a secured creditor who had preferential rights over the trade creditors.

The creditors alleged the company was a sham and without substance. However, the House of Lords judgement stated that Mr Salomon was perfectly entitled to take advantage of the provisions and avail himself of the corporate veil and not be liable for the debts of the company.

In the judgement, Lord Macnaghten said:

'When the memorandum is duly signed and registered, though there be only seven shares taken, the subscribers are a body corporate 'capable forthwith', to use the words of the enactment, 'of exercising all the functions of an incorporated company. Those are strong words. The company attains maturity on its birth. There is no period of minority – no interval of incapacity. I cannot understand how a body corporate thus made 'capable' by statute can lose its individuality by issuing the bulk of its capital to one person, whether he be a subscriber to the memorandum or not. The company is at law a different person altogether from the subscribers to the memorandum; and, though it may be that after incorporation the business is precisely the same as it was before, and the same persons are managers, and the same hands receive the profits, the company is not in law the agent of the subscribers or trustee for them. Nor are the subscribers as members liable, in any shape or form, except to the extent and in the manner provided by the Act ...

The unsecured creditors of A. Salomon and Company Limited, may be entitled to sympathy, but they have only themselves to blame for their misfortunes. They trusted the company, I suppose, because they had long dealt with Mr. Salomon, and he had always paid his way; but they had full notice that they were no longer dealing with an individual, and they must be taken to have been cognisant of the memorandum and of the articles of association.'

It is possible to form an unlimited company but these are less common as the benefits, which include not having to file financial statements with Companies House, rarely outweigh the downside of unlimited liability.

In the UK, the CA2006 sets out the requirements of limited companies. Limited companies are either public or private and may be limited by shares or by guarantee, for example:

- Public limited companies (or plcs) may issue shares to the general public and each shareholder's liability is limited to the amount unpaid on the shares.
- Private companies limited by shares may only issue shares to a restricted circle of persons, which does not include the general public. Each member's liability is limited to the amount unpaid on their shares.
- Private companies limited by guarantee, unlike private companies limited by shares, do not have share capital. The members are guarantors whose liability is limited to the amount they undertake to contribute to the company's assets if it is wound up.

There are also other types of company – protected cell companies and incorporated cell companies – which offer limited liability, if desired, but they do not operate in the UK, only in certain offshore jurisdictions. These types of company are discussed later in this chapter in the section on offshore vehicles. The UK also has a form of company called a Community Interest Company (CIC) for civic or charitable purposes, but these are beyond the scope of this text.

2.2 UK public limited companies

As the shares of a public company are offered to the general public, many public companies choose to be listed on a stock exchange. The CA2006 sets out a number of requirements in respect of UK public companies, for example:

- The Articles of Association must state that the company is a public company.
- The certificate of incorporation, issued by Companies House, states that the company is a public company.
- The company's name must end with 'public limited company' or 'p.l.c.' or Welsh equivalent.
- There must be at least one share in issue and the minimum issued share capital requirement is £50,000 of which 25% of the nominal amount must be paid up on each share.

- There must be at least two directors.
- A public company is required to have a company secretary.
- A public company requires a trading certificate.

2.3 UK private limited companies

The CA2006 sets out a number of requirements in respect of UK private companies, for example:

- A private limited company is a company that is not a public company.
- Its name must end with 'limited' or 'ltd.' or Welsh equivalent. There are, however, exceptions to the rule, e.g. companies with charitable status or whose objects are the promotion of commerce, art, science, education, religion or similar have an exemption from this requirement and so long as they–
  - apply income to promote their objects;
  - prohibit the payment of dividends to members; and
  - require their assets on winding up to be transferred to another body with objects similar to their own or to a charitable organisation.
- A private company only requires one shareholder.
- A private company only needs one director.

2.4 Re-registration of a UK private company as public and vice versa

A private company may re-register as a public company limited by shares (with the Registrar of Companies at Companies House) provided certain conditions are met including requirements in respect of the company's share capital. The company would also need to make the necessary changes to its name and Articles of Association to reflect the fact that it will be a public company.

Similarly, a public company may re-register as a private limited company upon special resolution and filing of the necessary documents to the Registrar of Companies. The company must make the necessary changes to its name and Articles of Association to reflect the fact that it will be a private company limited by shares or limited by guarantee, as appropriate.

3. Offshore corporate vehicles

3.1 Introduction

There are various types of offshore vehicles such as limited companies, cell companies, partnerships (see Section 3), trusts (see Chapter 9), foundations as and other vehicles. Offshore structures are often a combination of more than one type of vehicle: for example, a trust with one or more underlying companies or partnerships (see Section 3).

While in the large majority of cases international finance centres in offshore jurisdictions are used for legitimate reasons by multinational organisations, families and private individuals (for tax and estate planning, wealth management, financial expertise etc), offshore jurisdictions are also, on occasions, used for tax evasion and other illegitimate purposes.

3.2 Offshore companies

Offshore companies are, in many ways, similar to UK companies, although companies limited by guarantee or unlimited companies are less common. It is beyond the scope of this text to outline all the different types of companies that exist in offshore jurisdictions, but some of the more important are outlined briefly below.

Jersey public limited companies

A Jersey public company is a company with:

- more than 30 members; or
- which has at least two members and states in the Memorandum of Association that it is a public company.

The company's name must end with the word 'Limited' or abbreviation 'Ltd' or with the words 'avec responsibilité limitée' or the abbreviation 'a.r.l.'. Alternatively, a public limited company may choose the name to end with the words 'public limited company' or with the abbreviation 'PLC' or 'plc'. A public company must have at least two directors. An important distinction between Companies (Jersey) Law 1991 and the CA2006 in the UK is that the minimum age requirement for a director in Jersey is 18, whereas it is only 16 in the UK.

A Jersey public company may issue an offering document (or prospectus) in respect of offering its shares for subscription to the general public. It is required to file audited financial statements with the Registrar of Companies within seven months of the financial period end. A Jersey public company undertaking a regulated activity, for example a public company which is a collective investment fund (as defined by Article 3 of the Collective Investment Funds (Jersey) Law 1988) will also be subject to additional requirements of the Jersey Financial Services Commission. Such requirements include adhering to any relevant certificate or permit conditions and Codes of Practice.

Jersey private limited companies

A Jersey private company is a company that is not a public company and whose Memorandum of Association states that it is a private company. A private company limited by shares requires only one member. The company's name must end with the word 'Limited' or abbreviation 'Ltd' or with the words 'avec responsibilité limitée' or the abbreviation 'a.r.l.'. Companies (Jersey) Law 1991 also states that a private company must have at least one director and, as is the requirement for public companies, they must have attained the age of 18 or over. There is no requirement for private companies to file audited financial statements with the Registrar of Companies but accounting records do need to be maintained and accounts prepared to enable the company to establish its financial position at any point in time. Unaudited financial statements may also need to be filed with the tax authorities.

Guernsey limited companies

Guernsey companies are governed by the Companies (Guernsey) Law 2008, which does not distinguish between public and private companies. As well as limited liability companies, it is possible to have a mixed liability company in Guernsey which can be a hybrid of guarantee members and shareholders. The shareholders can have either unlimited or limited liability. With limited companies, a member's liability is limited to the nominal value of his or her shares, as under English law. A company that is limited by shares must have the following words or abbreviations at the end of its name: 'Limited', 'With limited liability', 'Ltd.', 'Avec responsibilité limitée' or the abbreviation 'ARL'. A Guernsey company must have at least one director and at least one member and its objects are unrestricted unless otherwise specified in the company's Memorandum of Association. The accounts of the company must be audited unless the company is exempt under The Companies (Guernsey) Law 2008. Under Section 256(2)(b), the company is exempt if the members pass a waiver resolution in the financial year before the financial year to which it relates, or if it is in respect of the company's first financial year, in that financial year. The members may pass a waiver resolution relating either to a specific, or indefinite, number of financial years.

Test yourself 10.1

How might a Guernsey limited company seek an exemption under Companies (Guernsey) Law, 2008, from the requirement to have its financial statements audited?

British Virgin Islands limited companies

Companies in the British Virgin Islands (BVI) are governed by the British Virgin Islands Business Companies Act 2004. A BVI public company must have at least five members and the company name must end with the appropriate corporate suffix, e.g. 'Limited', 'Corporation', 'Incorporated', 'Société Anonyme', 'Sociedad Anonima' or abbreviations 'Ltd', 'Corp', 'Inc' or 'S.A.'. Private trust companies must also use the designation 'PTC' immediately before the suffix. Companies established for a charitable purpose or whose objects are non-commercial may apply for an exemption from having to use the corporate name ending. A key feature of BVI companies is that, with the exception of restricted purpose companies, they are not required to state their objects. This gives corporate capacity and flexibility and effectively removes the *ultra vires* doctrine. Directors are, nevertheless, required to act in good faith and exercise due care and skill in the exercise of their functions. BVI companies must have at least one director, although there is no requirement to have a director appointed immediately on registration.

3.3 Cell companies

A **cell company** is a private or public company which is able to segregate its assets and liabilities between different cells. Each cell may be used to carry out distinct and independent businesses. Whilst protected cells of a protected cell company have no separate legal personality, they are treated as separate legal entities limiting the ability of creditors from seeking the assets of one cell to pay off the debts of another. Whilst cell companies typically have limited liability, a cell company can be an unlimited or guarantee company.

cell company
A private or public company which is able to segregate its assets and liabilities between different cells. Each cell may be used to carry out distinct and independent businesses and the assets of each cell can be ring-fenced.

Protected cell companies (PCCs) were developed in Guernsey in the late 1990s and other offshore jurisdictions (including Cayman Islands, Jersey, Isle of Man, Mauritius, Bermuda and St Vincent and The Grenadines) have since developed their own types of cell companies such as segregated portfolio companies in the Cayman Islands and both incorporated cell companies (ICCs) and PCCs in Jersey.

Protected cells have no separate legal personality and therefore transact through the overarching cell company. The cells enable assets to be segregated and ring-fenced and are often used in collective investment schemes in preference to umbrella funds. They are also used frequently in captive insurance schemes. **Ring-fencing** is a protective measure to prevent the assets of a ring-fenced cell from being used to pay off the debts of another cell. With PCCs, it is usual for the directors to have a legal obligation to properly separate cellular assets. That said, the legislation in some jurisdictions, e.g. Jersey, permits a cell to invest in another cell of the same cell company (but not in the cell company itself).

ring-fencing
A protective measure to prevent the assets of a ring-fenced cell from being used to pay off the debts of another cell.

With incorporated cells (ICs) of an incorporated cell company, each cell has its own separate legal personality. Accordingly, each cell has its own board of directors (also permitted for cells of a PCC in some jurisdictions) and is able to contract and sue in its own name. The IC is not a subsidiary of the ICC. ICC structures, therefore, enable assets to be legally separated rather than relying on the actions of the directors to properly separate the cellular assets.

Having separate legal personality is an important factor for stakeholders to consider because an ICC/IC structure is less likely to face challenges from creditors than a PCC/PC structure whose ring-fencing capability is less substantive and might not be recognised by foreign court.

3.4 Foundations

A foundation is an organisation and is similar to a company in that it is a legal entity which can own assets and contract in its own name. Foundations are typically established by a one-off donation by an individual or business, known as the 'founder' and run by the foundation's 'council', in accordance with the foundation's charter, by-laws and regulations for non-profitable, charitable, scientific, humanitarian or philanthropic purposes. They are also used as an alternative vehicle to offshore trusts and companies.

Foundations are versatile offshore vehicles and have been a success story in a number of jurisdictions, particularly Liechtenstein, Panama, Malta and the Netherlands Antilles. Foundations may be established for a specified or unlimited period and, in some jurisdictions, the founder has the right to change the purpose of the foundation or revoke the foundation, although this may result in adverse tax implications.

In Liechtenstein, a foundation is known as a 'Stiftung' and in the Netherland Antilles as a 'Stichting'.

Benefits of foundations

- versatile offshore vehicles;
- protect the assets against creditor claims;
- simpler concept for clients to understand compared with trusts;
- can last for an indefinite period;
- confidentiality;
- succession planning;
- avoidance of forced heirship rules;
- protect assets in times of political instability to avoid expropriation of assets;
- probate may be avoided;
- the founder can also be the **guardian** and oversee the function of council, potentially influencing its decisions;
- often no fiduciary duty imposed on council (unlike for trusts and companies);
- can be used to mitigate tax liabilities.

guardian
The person who is empowered to oversee the foundation's council and performs a similar function to the protector of a trust. The founder might choose to appoint a guardian to a foundation, which may be himself, to ensure the foundation is run in an appropriate manner and in accordance with the foundations charter.

Drawbacks of foundations

- may have investment restrictions, e.g. a foundation might be prohibited from acquiring, holding or disposing of immoveable property in some jurisdictions;
- may not be able to carry out activities of a commercial nature if not incidental to the attainment of the foundation's objects;
- absence of court judgements and so tax mitigation is uncertain;
- founder surrenders ownership of assets;
- professional fees are incurred.

Table 10.1: Key differences between a foundation, trust and company.

Vehicle	Source of funds	Management	Benefit
Foundation	Founder**	Council	Beneficiaries*
Trust	Settlor	Trustee	Beneficiaries
Company	Subscribers	Directors	Shareholders

* A foundation can exist without beneficiaries and, unlike trusts, the beneficiaries of a foundation are not owed a fiduciary duty by the foundation council.
** As with a 'declaration of trust', the founder of a foundation may remain anonymous.

4. Partnerships

4.1 Introduction

Partnerships have been a form of business arrangement for a very long time. Before limited liability companies came into being it was common for business people to pool risk by going in to partnership with each other. This was the same as being a non-limited **sole trader** but gave additional security to creditors as there were more principals involved to whom recourse could be made if one of the other partners failed. Over more recent times different forms of partnerships have been developed to include some form of limitation of liability, but with different impacts for some or all partners, while retaining transparency for tax purposes, i.e. the partnership is not taxed but each of the partners is taxed on his or her share of the profits. Both UK and offshore forms of partnership are discussed here.

sole trader
A person who is the exclusive owner of a business, entitled to keep all profits after tax has been paid but liable for all losses.

4.2 General partnerships

A general partnership does not have a separate legal personality and each partner is responsible for losses and debts incurred by the partnership. Usually a partnership is governed by its own partnership agreement, a legal contract between all the partners about how the partnership should be run and the allocation of profits and losses to the partners. This allocation does not have to be in equal shares. However, if no partnership agreement exists, there are often statutory provisions which apply. In the UK, the Partnership Act 1890 is such an act, and this ensures that partnerships that are made without the formality of an agreement will operate in an appropriate manner. This is important as, if a business fails, the partners may attempt to deny a partnership existed and that therefore one or more of them should not be liable.

4.3 Limited partnerships

A limited partnership (LP) comprises limited partners, who invest in the partnership, and one or more **general partners (GPs)**, who manage the partnership. Generally speaking, LPs do not have their own separate legal personality and each partner is jointly and severally liable for losses and debts incurred by the LP, but only to the extent of the amount of capital committed less the amount already contributed. General partners also have unlimited liability for the debts of the partnership and, therefore, tend to be formed as limited liability companies in order to limit their liability. In the UK limited partnerships are governed by the Limited Partnerships Act 1907. In the UK, limited partnerships do not have to file accounts unless the partners themselves all have limited liability. In other words, the requirement to file accounts is connected to the ability of creditors to pursue at least one partner with unlimited liability.

general partner (GP)
The person who assumes the management responsibility for the limited partnership. The general partner has unlimited liability for the debts and obligations of the partnership and, therefore, is typically a limited company.

A number of offshore jurisdictions allow LPs to have their own separate legal identity and this type of partnership is favoured by promoters of private equity funds who, *inter alia*, prefer the LP's assets to be recorded in its own name. In Guernsey, the Limited Partnerships (Guernsey) Law 1995 allows LPs to elect to have a separate legal personality upon initial registration, meaning they are treated as body corporate in certain circumstances. In Jersey, the introduction of LP legislation in 2011 allowed for the formation of Separate Limited Partnerships (SLPs), which are not body corporates, and Incorporated Limited Partnerships (ILPs), which are body corporates. SLPs are governed by the Separate Limited Partnerships (Jersey) Law 2011 and ILPs are governed by the Incorporated Limited Partnerships (Jersey) Law 2011.

As mentioned above, LPs are used in fund structures (as an alternative investment vehicle to a company or unit trust), whereby limited partners invest through the LP and the GP, a limited company, undertakes the management function. LPs used as vehicles for collective investment schemes and undertaking regulated activities in the Channel Islands are required to be regulated under the relevant supervisory law(s), namely the Protection of Investors (Bailiwick of Guernsey) Law 1987 (if in Guernsey) and the Collective Investment Funds (Jersey) Law 1988 (if in Jersey). In Jersey, the LPs which are structured as collective investment schemes, are typically registered under the Limited Partnerships (Jersey) Law 1994 and have no separate legal personality. The limited partners have limited liability providing they remain passive investors and, subject to certain exceptions (e.g. a limited partner may act as a director of a corporate GP or may advise the GP in respect of the activities of the LP), do not participate in the management of the LP. The GP performs the management function and has unlimited liability. The GP is, therefore, usually formed as a Jersey limited company in which its shareholders have limited liability. The relationship between the limited partners and the GP is set out in the **limited partnership agreement (LPA)**.

limited partnership agreement (LPA)
A written document setting out the powers and obligations of the limited partners and of the GP. It will include the name of the LP and GP, will state the purpose for which the LP was formed, will set out how income and capital should be allocated, how distributions should be made, the various rights and obligations of both parties (e.g. the obligation of the GP to contribute to the debts of the LP) and the administrative arrangements.

4.4 Limited liability partnerships

Limited liability partnerships (LLPs) are a type of limited partnership which offers its partners limited liability as they would have if they were members of a limited company. LLPs are generally bodies corporate, so have their own legal personality. These vehicles are often used by accountancy and law firms and other employee owned businesses where it is not always appropriate or desirable to separate ownership and management. In some jurisdictions, such as the UK, LLPs are required to file accounts.

UK LLPs are governed by the Limited Liability Partnerships Act 2000 and many of the legal requirements in relation to LLPs track those of private limited companies in the CA2006. However, there are no capital maintenance rules for LLPs (see Section 5) and they are tax-transparent vehicles, i.e. the members are taxed directly on their share of the LLP profits rather than the LLP being taxed. A UK LLP is therefore very much a hybrid of a general partnership and limited liability company.

In offshore finance centres, the filing requirements for LLPs tend to be less onerous. For example, in Jersey, an LLP is not required to have its financial statements audited, unless required by the partnership agreement. However, various safeguards are set out in statute, namely the Limited Liability Partnerships (Jersey) Law 1997. The LLP must maintain sufficient accounting records (and keep them for at least ten years) in order to be able to disclose its financial position, with reasonable accuracy, at any time.

5. Share and loan capital

We will now consider how companies are financed and the legal formalities and tax treatment of different forms of finance.

Companies need to raise money in order to fund their operating and financing activities. Short-term financing is usually in the form of cash in the bank and at hand, bank overdrafts, supplier credit etc. Long-term financing is achieved by either issuing **equity shares** (to shareholders as members of the company) or issuing debt such as **loan stock** (to lenders as creditors of the company). The directors of the company need to consider carefully the implications of issuing equity or debt because this can affect, amongst other things, ownership and control, the level of gearing, risk and level of taxation.

equity shares
instruments issued by a company to give holders a residual interest in its assets and liabilities.

loan stock
shares of common or preferred stock that are used as collateral to secure a loan from another party. The loan earns a fixed interest rate, much like a standard loan, and can be secured or unsecured.

5.1 Share capital

Share capital represents the amount of cash and non-cash considerations raised by a company in return for issuing shares. Share capital is the investment in the company by its shareholders. There are different types of share capital and each type of share capital carries different rights and obligations, the most common of which are ordinary share capital and preference share capital. Importantly, shareholders cannot demand their capital back from a company; it is kept to protect creditors by subordinating shareholders' rights to the assets of the business to those of creditors. Although share capital can be redeemed or repaid, it can only be done so in specific circumstances where creditors are protected. This is discussed in Section 5.

Ordinary shares
Holders of ordinary (or equity) shares are members of a company who receive voting rights and dividend entitlements (which are not guaranteed and depend on the company's financial performance). Ordinary shareholders rank last in line for dividend payments and for the repayment of capital if the company goes into liquidation. As the holders of ordinary shares normally carry more risk than preference shareholders and lenders, they hope to benefit from dividend growth and increasing share prices. They also have more power through their voting rights, including in many jurisdictions the right to vote directors off the board and to vote on directors' remuneration, as we will see in Chapter 11.

Preference shares
Holders of preference shares are members of a company who are entitled to dividends (if declared) ahead of ordinary shareholders. The preference share dividends are usually fixed percentage dividends. For example, a 5% £1 preference share entitles the holder to a 5p dividend. Preference shares do not usually carry voting rights. They rank ahead of ordinary shareholders but after loan stock in the event of a liquidation.

Just because a preference share is a share, it does not mean that it is accounted for as equity under IFRS. IAS 32 (see Chapter 6) requires preference shares to be presented as a liability in a company's balance sheet if it contains an obligation to pay interest or capital because its holder is not taking the residual risk in the business. This is usually the case, which makes preference shares more akin to debt than equity. A company following IFRS Standards will therefore present the capital amount as a liability and dividends payable will be presented as interest in the statement of profit or loss, although legally they are still dividends. This is another example of the principle of 'substance over form'.

Authorised share capital

Authorised share capital represents the amount of share capital that a firm is allowed to issue. A company cannot issue more than the authorised amount of share capital, which for some companies is an unlimited number of shares. The concept of authorised share capital is less common than it used to be and many jurisdictions now allow companies to issue an unlimited number of shares if the company's Memorandum or Articles of Association permits. For example, this is now the case with BVI Business Companies under the BVI Business Companies Act 2004.

Issued share capital

The issued share capital is the nominal value of all shares which have actually been issued and taken up by the members. For example, a company that issues 100,000 shares of £1 each has an issued share capital of £100,000.

Called up share capital

Called up share capital is the amount that has been requested for payment in exchange for the shares that have been issued. This occurs when a company does not initially require all the funds from a share issue and so only calls up a set amount to begin with, e.g. 60% of the total. For example, a company issues 200,000 £1 shares but only calls up 60p per share. The issued share capital is £200,000 but the called up share capital is only £120,000. The company may call up the outstanding 40% when investments are identified or funds are required for other purposes.

Test yourself 10.2

A company allots 500,000 shares at £1 per share but only calls up 80p per share. What is the amount of called up share capital?

Paid up share capital

Paid up share capital is the amount of called up share capital that has been paid. If any called up capital has not been paid up then it is treated as a debtor on the asset side of the company's balance sheet (i.e. money owing to the company) and is termed 'Called up capital not paid'.

Capital requirements

Companies are sometimes required to maintain a minimum level of share capital to safeguard against risk and ensure they are better placed to survive reduced levels of business and exposure to market risk, operational risk and credit risk. For example, UK public companies must have a share capital of at least £50,000. A bank must maintain the minimum level of capital stipulated by the relevant supervisory authorities and these calculations can be complicated as capital may be ranked in different 'tiers' of safety, and the calculation may relate to how risky the assets of the bank are. A well-capitalised bank or financial institution is better placed to survive a market downturn or financial crisis than a bank with no safety buffer.

5.2 Loan capital

Loan capital is a type of long-term debt in the form of loan stock or debentures. A company may raise money by accepting loans from investors and issuing loan notes, bonds or debentures in return which entitle the lenders to a fixed interest payment. Debentures are secured loans which rank ahead of shareholders and trade creditors in the event the company enters into liquidation. Lenders therefore normally carry less risk than shareholders.

Loan capital is often preferred to equity because issuing debt does not affect ownership and control of the company. In other words, if a company issues more shares to raise finance, existing shareholders may find their shareholdings are diluted if they do not take up the share offer. Raising funds by issuing debt does not create this issue. It does, however, create gearing and tax implications which directors need to take into consideration when determining how to raise finance.

As we saw in Chapter 8, a company that is highly geared or leveraged has a high proportion of debt to equity whereas a company with a low gearing ratio has a relatively low level of debt compared with equity.

A highly geared company might be considered more risky than a company without gearing because the highly geared company will have regular interest payments to service the debt and, in times of increasing interest rates, businesses with high levels of borrowing with variable rate interest payments may find themselves faced with uncomfortably large monthly outgoings in order to service the debt. This means there is likely to be less money available for distribution to equity holders in the form of dividends.

Lenders of finance are particularly interested in a company's gearing ratios since a high gearing ratio might indicate a company's inability to repay the debt. It is therefore, not unusual, for lenders to restrict a company's level of gearing through the use of **financial covenants**. Most entities aim to strike a good balance of debt to equity which reflects their specific risk appetite and investment strategy.

financial covenants ratios that the borrower is required to stay above or below, but there are usually also often absolute restrictions on debt levels and minimum working capital requirements.

The interest element on debt is usually deductible for corporation tax purposes, which reduces the net rate of taxation and thereby the company's cost of capital.

5.3 Implications of gearing and taxation

The interest payments on debt instruments are allowable for corporation tax purposes which makes debt an attractive form of finance.

Companies raise finance in order to generate greater returns. The choice of equity or debt can influence a number of key investor ratios, such as return on equity and EPS (see Chapter 8). If a company chooses to issue ordinary shares to raise finance, rather than debt, there will be more shares in issue which means the earnings per share is likely to fall.

Issuing debt as a source of finance, however, leads to a company increasing its gearing. This can, however, have a positive impact on the company's EPS ratio. This is because the additional funds can be used to generate greater profits without increasing the number of shares in issue. Companies need to be able to service the interest charge on the debt and directors need to be mindful that the larger the interest charge, the less profit after interest (which will impact the return on equity ratio).

Companies which are highly geared are however at risk of not being able to pay their debts as they fall due and lenders of debt finance (e.g. banks) may impose loan covenants restricting the activities of the company if gearing exceeds a pre-determined limit.

6. Legal reserves

Alongside share capital, a company will show in equity various other reserves. These belong to shareholders as they are part of the residual equity balance remaining after liabilities are deducted from equity, but law or accounting requirements mean that the equity balance must be sub-divided into separate reserves.

Although this sub-division is shown in consolidated accounts, it is the division of equity into separate reserves in the individual accounts of a company that is important in legal terms. These accounts, as well as being important for tax purposes as tax is generally assessed on individual companies, are also relevant for determining which elements of equity are treated as permanent or semi-permanent share capital and which are instead treated as available for distribution to shareholders.

You can look at the reserves of the M&S parent company and the Statement of changes in Shareholders' Equity by looking at page 122 of the 2016 ARA.

distributable profits legally speaking, a company's accumulated realised profits (so far as not previously distributed or capitalised) less its accumulated realised losses (so far as not previously written off in a reduction or reorganisation of share capital).

Some of the main reserves (although you may occasionally see others) are discussed below in the context of UK company law and whether they are **distributable profits** or not; variations in practice are found in other jurisdictions. These are:

- Share capital
- Share premium account
- Revaluation reserve
- Profit and loss account/retained earnings

The requirement to preserve the portion of equity put in as share capital is known as the concept of capital maintenance, which acts to protect creditors of a limited company.

Case law 10.2

***Trevor* v *Whitworth* (1887)**

This is the way the concept is described in one of the most important earliest cases on the subject:

> **'One of the main objects contemplated by the legislature, in restricting the power of limited companies to reduce the amount of their capital as set forth in the memorandum, is to protect the interests of the outside public who may become their creditors. In my opinion the effect of these statutory restrictions is to prohibit every transaction between a company and a shareholder, by means of which the money already paid to the company in respect of his shares is returned to him, unless the Court has sanctioned the transaction. Paid-up capital may be diminished or lost in the course of the company's trading; that is a result which no legislation can prevent; but persons who deal with, and give credit to a limited company, naturally rely upon the fact that the company is trading with a certain amount of capital already paid, as well as upon the responsibility of its members for the capital remaining at call; and they are entitled to assume that no part of the capital which has been paid into the coffers of the company has been subsequently paid out, except in the legitimate course of its business.'**

12 App Cas 409, *per* Lord Watson.

6.1 Share capital

We have discussed share capital above in the context of comparing it with loan capital. In terms of its being a sub-division of equity, share capital is the aggregate nominal amount of the company's paid up share capital and is undistributable. Share capital cannot be given back to shareholders except by a reduction of capital or through a buy back or redemption of shares made in accordance with the CA2006 and these routes contain restrictions and tests to protect creditors.

If a company wishes to raise further capital from its shareholders, it will carry out a **rights issue**, asking its shareholders to subscribe for more capital. The shareholders can choose to sell those rights to other people, but they are often protected from their holding in the company being diluted through pre-emption rights. These rights mean that a company must ask its current shareholders to subscribe for more shares first, before offering them to third parties.

rights issue
an issue of shares offered at a special price by a company to its existing shareholders in proportion to their holding of old shares.

6.2 Share premium

Sometimes shares are issued at a premium. This means that shares are sold at a higher price than the nominal or carrying value. For example, if a company issues two million ordinary shares with nominal value of £1 each at £1.20 per share, the company will record cash of £2,400,000, share capital of £2,000,000 and share premium of £400,000.

Share premium is treated in a very similar way to share capital but can be applied in writing off the expenses of the relevant share issue and commissions relating to shares in respect of which the premium was created. It is undistributable but can be reduced or cancelled in the same way as share capital can under the CA2006.

Note that in some EU jurisdictions share premium is distributable.

6.3 Revaluation reserve

We looked at the choices companies have to revalue their long-term assets in Chapter 5. Accounting standards and the law require the uplift in value to be taken to a revaluation reserve. Thus, if a company has an asset at a carrying value of £100,000 and it is revalued to £500,000, the difference of £400,000 is recorded in the revaluation reserve.

In legal terms:

realised profit usually arises from a transaction for cash or when cash is expected to be received shortly with near certainty, although there are other circumstances where a profit may be classed as realised, for example if a debt is forgiven.

- It is a profit in accounting terms but not a **realised profit** although it can become realised in certain circumstances.
- It must be shown as a separate reserve.
- It cannot be distributed to shareholders.
- The revaluation reserve cannot be reduced/cancelled in a reduction of capital under the CA2006.
- But it can be used to pay up shares allotted to members as fully or partly paid bonus shares.

6.4 Retained profits

Retained profits are also a source of financing for companies and form part of shareholders' equity. Retained profits represent the net profits from prior periods of trading after dividends and taxation and which are available for reinvestment in the business or further distribution to shareholders.

6.5 Distributions and distributable profits

As noted above, the law restricts the extent to which shareholders can take profits from a company in order to protect creditors. This can be seen by looking at this representation of a company balance sheet, as seen in Figure 10.1.

Figure 10.1: Principle of capital maintenance by reference to balance sheet

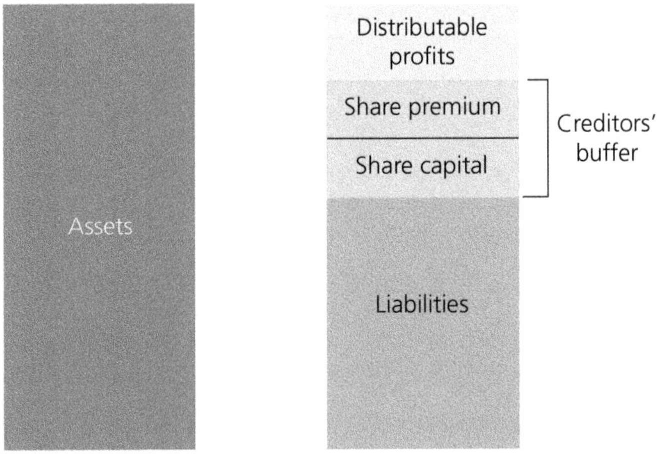

If the company could distribute assets equal to the value of all of the equity to shareholders, any fall in the value of its assets or the creation of trading losses would mean that not all the creditors could be repaid from the remaining assets. The law and accounting practice therefore specify that some of the balances in equity must be treated as unrealised and undistributable and these are sometimes known as the creditors' buffer.

In legal terms, a company may not make a distribution except out of profits available for the purpose. A distribution, which includes dividends, means every description of distribution of a company's assets to its members, whether in cash or otherwise, except a distribution by:

- issue of shares;
- redemption or purchase of own shares in accordance with the CA2006;
- reduction of share capital; or
- distribution of assets on a winding up.

A company's profits available for distribution are its accumulated, realised profits, so far as not previously utilised by distribution or capitalisation, less its accumulated realised losses, so far as not previously written off in a reduction of capital duly made. There are additional restrictions on distributable reserves for a public company.

Profits available for distribution must be measured by reference to 'relevant accounts', which will usually be the last statutory accounts of the company. Sometimes interim accounts are used, for example if a profit has been made since the last statutory accounts which the company wants to distribute. Those accounts must be properly prepared in order to assess the extent of distributable profits; public companies must file those individual accounts with the Registrar of Companies.

References in the CA2006 to 'realised profits' and 'realised losses', in relation to a company's accounts, are to profits or losses of the company as fall to be treated as realised in accordance with principles generally accepted, at the time when the accounts are prepared, with respect to the determination for accounting purposes of realised profits and losses. What this means is that accounting practice is important as well as the law. While it is generally accepted that profits will be treated as realised, for these purposes, only when realised in the form either of cash or other assets the ultimate cash realisation of which can be assessed with reasonable certainty, there is no requirement for accounts to disclose the breakdown of realised and unrealised profits.

In the light of this, the Institute of Chartered Accountants in England and Wales (ICAEW) and Institute of Chartered Accountants of Scotland (ICAS) produce joint guidance on this topic, which is authoritative, having been through a due process of development and been sanctioned by legal counsel under both English and Scottish law. This guidance is known as Tech 02/10 'Guidance on the Determination of Realised Profits and Losses in the Context of Distributions under the Companies Act 2006'. It contains important definitions, including of realised profits and losses, and looks to the substance of transactions when determining whether a profit is realised or not. This is particularly important when group companies or those related by other means trade with each other; if the transactions are artificial, profits arising will not be realised.

It is very important for directors not to make an unlawful distribution, for example making a distribution when the company has no or insufficient distributable reserves. If they do, it is a breach of their fiduciary duties (see Chapter 11) and they can be held personally liable.

Chapter summary

- Companies have their own legal personality which is separate from the legal personalities of the individuals who own and manage the company. Limited companies, therefore, offer protection to the owners of the business and this is why sole traders often form companies to limit their liability for debts. A company contracts in its own name.
- In the UK, the CA2006 sets out the requirements of limited companies. Limited companies are either public or private and may be limited by shares or by guarantee.
- Offshore jurisdictions also offer various forms of limited company, including cell companies, and other corporate vehicles such as foundations. The formalities and requirements to establish such entities vary between jurisdictions.
- A cell company is a private or public company which is able to segregate its assets and liabilities between different cells. Each cell may be used to carry out distinct and independent businesses.

- There are different forms of partnership, including general partnerships, limited partnerships (LP) and limited liability partnerships (LLPs). The way each operates in the UK and offshore jurisdictions will vary legally, although many principles remain the same.
- Long-term financing is achieved by either issuing equity shares (to shareholders as members of the company) or issuing debt such as loan stock (to the lenders as creditors of the company).
- Share capital represents the amount of cash and non-cash considerations raised by a company in return for issuing shares. Share capital is the investment in the company by its shareholders.
- Loan capital is often preferred to equity because issuing debt does not affect ownership and control of the company. Debentures are secured loans which rank ahead of shareholders and trade creditors in the event the company enters into liquidation. The interest element on debt is usually deductible for corporation tax purposes, which reduces the net rate of taxation and thereby the company's cost of capital.
- The principal of capital maintenance is important to protect creditors from over-distribution to shareholders. The UK rules on determining realised and distributable profits are based partly on the law but also additional accounting rules produced by the accounting profession.

Part four

Chapter eleven
Corporate governance and corporate responsibility

Corporate governance

Overview

In this final part, you will learn about the key issue of corporate governance and what is meant by that term. You will learn about agency theory, why it is necessary to institute good corporate governance to protect companies for the benefit of stakeholders and how governance failed in various ways during the financial crisis of 2008.

We will look at directors' duties which apply to all companies and which, while they are now in the CA2006, were originally part of the common law. That means there are many important cases on directors' duties, and we will consider some of the more important ones. You will learn about the development of additional corporate governance codes, which are more detailed and demanding, for listed companies and financial institutions, and cover board conduct and composition, board remuneration, the role of the audit and other board committees and internal controls. You will also learn about some of the key challenges surrounding directors' remuneration and how it is regulated in the UK.

The issue of wider corporate responsibility is discussed in the context of narrative reporting, and you will learn about initiatives such as that of the International Integrated Reporting Council to report more widely on the impact of company activity. We will also look at the wider international development of corporate governance regulation, including in the EU and US. This part finishes by looking at the role of audit and auditors in corporate governance.

Learning outcomes

At the end of this part, you will be able to:

- Understand the concept of agency theory and conflicts of interest
- Explain the duties of directors in the CA2006 and why the duties were brought into statute
- Discuss the common law cases *Re City Equitable Fire Insurance Co* [1925] and *Re D'Jan of London Ltd* [1994]
- Summarise the *Weavering* judgements of 2011 in the Cayman Islands and 2012 in the UK
- Understand the development of the UK FRC's Corporate Governance Code and its contents
- Explain how corporate governance codes have been developed for the fund industry and by offshore centres
- Discuss the increasing regulation of directors' remuneration and why it is controversial
- Appreciate the issue of wider corporate responsibility and the way it is reflected in initiatives on narrative reporting
- Understand and explain the work of the IIRC and initiatives in the EU on non-financial reporting
- Describe EU, US and international developments in corporate governance, including major US legislation
- Discuss the role of audit and auditors in corporate governance
- Explain the changes happening in regulation over auditing of public interest entities, including expanded audit reports.

Chapter eleven
Corporate governance and corporate responsibility

List of topics

1. Introduction

Companies and other businesses use the money of investors to trade and grow, yet the investors are often not the directors or managers who look after that process. Company law and other regulatory mechanisms place duties on directors to look after the interests of investors (and to some extent creditors) by requiring them to put the company's welfare ahead of their own. A good corporate governance framework inspires investor confidence and hence encourages further investment. If investors lose confidence in the level of governance and disclosure at a company, they will move their investment elsewhere, which is bad for the company, and if it is pervasive in a country, may be bad for that country.

Firstly, we will look at the conflicts arising between agents (who manage and control companies) and shareholders (who own companies). We will consider the requirements in company law in the UK around directors' duties, as well as the requirements for listed companies contained within the UK Corporate Governance Code, developed and maintained by the Financial Reporting Council.

Challenges around executive remuneration can be a cause of major corporate governance disputes at companies, and there have been substantial changes in this area recently in the UK. We will also look at the development of corporate social responsibility, sustainability reporting and integrated reporting, which bring into play the wider impacts of company activity on society.

We will look briefly at US regulation as this can have a substantial impacts on UK and offshore businesses that wish to do business in the US, as well as international regulatory co-operation that has resulted from the 2008 financial crisis. Finally, we will look at the important role of auditors in the governance of companies.

2. Corporate governance and agency theory

2.1 Introduction

Corporate governance is the process by which organisations are directed and controlled. It is through good corporate governance that the interests of investors and other stakeholders are safeguarded and, in so far as possible, aligned. Displaying sound governance is good for companies as it helps with their smooth running, attracts inward investment and helps raise finance.

Corporate governance encompasses the following areas:

- effective risk management systems and internal controls;
- timely financial reporting and annual audit, confirming that the financial statements give a true and fair view of the state of affairs and performance of the company;
- good communication, disseminating accurate and relevant information and dealing with shareholders in an open and honest manner to enable them to make informed decisions;
- transparency and disclosure, particularly in respect of directors' remuneration and the appointment of the remuneration committee;
- accountability;
- integrity;
- ethical behaviour and a culture that delivers the right outcomes;
- adequate span of control appropriate to the nature of the business;
- balance on the board (including between executive and **non-executive directors**) with a diverse mix of individuals possessing the relevant skills, knowledge and experience and who have clear lines of responsibility and who can exercise independence of judgement;
- fitness and propriety of directors;
- effective oversight by senior management and the board of directors; and
- compliance with regulatory standards and legislation.

non-executive directors
Member of a company's board of directors who are not part of the executive team. A non-executive director (NED) typically does not engage in the day-to-day management of the entity, but focusses on policy and strategy and holds the executive to account.

2.2 Ownership versus control

A problem arises when the directors, who manage and control the company, make decisions which are not consistent with the objective of maximising owner wealth. For example, directors may aim to please the market and influence the company's share price in the short term in order to boost their own bonuses where these are based on short-term company profits and/or share price. Shareholders, the owners, will welcome an increase in value of their company, but only if this is not achieved through aggressive accounting and unwanted risk and is therefore viable in the longer term. Imbalances in this respect can have catastrophic consequences, as was seen in the financial crisis, and the role of incentives given to those in control remains a controversial, and potentially worrying, aspect of corporate governance.

2.3 Goal congruence

Aligning the goals of owners and managers is an important means of helping overcome the agency problem and ensuring managers act in the best interests of the shareholders. It is controversial as to whether incentives such as performance-related pay further this aim or not. Performance-related benefits need to be carefully structured to ensure managers do not put their own personal gain ahead of the objective of maximising shareholder wealth. Good corporate governance seeks to address conflicts between managers and owners by the achievement of **goal congruence**. In other words, the company directors and other members of senior management need to be motivated to align their goals with the objectives of the company so that their behaviours and actions result in mutually beneficial outcomes.

goal congruence
Describes the alignment and harmonisation of goals and objectives. In the context of agency theory, this means matching the interests of the directors with the interests of shareholders so that directors are incentivised to act in the best interests of the company.

2.4 Asymmetry of information

Owners are not in a position to fully monitor the managers of the company as they do not have full knowledge of the business and access to all information. For example, shareholders will see the annual report but may often not have access to the management accounts and underlying information unless they are themselves involved in the company's management. This asymmetry of information puts managers in a position where they can, if they lack integrity and high moral standards, focus on their own wealth maximisation to the detriment of shareholder wealth maximisation without always being challenged. Managers may pursue their own goals of increasing their own rewards and bonuses and following their own agendas, including retaining their job for as long as possible. Shareholders, who may lack knowledge of the running of the business, may remain passive and unengaged in the business in which they invest.

After a number of corporate failures and financial scandals, there has been a move in recent years to encourage greater shareholder engagement with company management. Institutional shareholders, such as large pension funds, which typically hold large volumes of shares, can have a significant influence on how companies are run by challenging the board's decisions and ensuring the alignment of the objectives of the directors with their own objective of wealth maximisation for the longer term.

Targets can be set to reward managers for increasing shareholder returns, for example through improving the company's profitability or share price. Managers will lose motivation, however, if for example the required increase in share price looks unachievable. They may also lack drive to maximise the share price if they have already been rewarded for achieving a satisfactory return. Such behaviour

satisficing
Describes the behaviour of managers to do just enough to satisfy shareholders and achieve an adequate return on their investment rather than maximising the return for shareholders.

is known as **satisficing**. Profit-related incentives and share option schemes therefore need to be properly structured and regularly reviewed to ensure ongoing goal congruence of the interests of managers and the shareholders. We will look at executive pay in more detail in Section 4.

High standards of reporting and corporate governance provide comfort that managers are acting appropriately and with integrity and helps reduce the agency problem. In addition, in respect of the annual report and financial statements, the audit function acts as a safeguard for shareholders who may be concerned managers are achieving their goals with the help of aggressive accounting practice. This is discussed in Section 7.

As well as challenging corporate governance standards and how well a company is run, institutional shareholders are well placed to challenge investment decisions and financing decisions, especially where it is believed that directors may not be motivated to align their goals with the interests of the shareholders. This can be seen in the area of mergers and acquisitions, where investors have become much more robust in examining takeover activity due to the fact that they often destroy rather than create shareholder value. The tendency of chief executives of companies to 'empire build' through acquisition is more under the microscope than it has been in the past, and companies are now usually careful to ensure their major shareholders are supportive before making an offer. The Financial Reporting Council's Stewardship Code, discussed in Section 3, encourages investor engagement with companies.

Case study 11.1

In 2007 Royal Bank of Scotland (RBS, acting as part of a consortium) purchased Dutch bank ABN AMRO. Not long afterwards, RBS collapsed and had to be rescued by the British Government. In its report on why RBS failed, the Financial Services Authority (FSA) noted that the ABN AMRO transaction was only one element of the problems identified, but it nevertheless was a major factor. The takeover was the biggest in banking history and RBS, following a bidding battle with Barclays, was considered to have overpaid significantly, at three times the book value of ABN's net assets and on very little due diligence, even as the banking sector was starting to come under strain at the start of the financial crisis.

The FSA report indicates just how little information was available to the two banks at the time of their bid:

> **'On 29 April ABN AMRO provided two lever arch folders and one CD-ROM of information to the consortium and stated that this was the same information that had been provided to Barclays.... The information provided did not satisfy RBS's detailed request. RBS was largely unsuccessful in its attempts to obtain further information. Between 30 April and 3 May, RBS reviewed the information and met ABN AMRO personnel. While these meetings**

> provided a means of obtaining additional clarification and some comfort to RBS, only limited additional information was provided.'

Despite knowing little about what they were buying, executives at RBS were willing to press ahead. In an instructive interview with FSA investigators, Johnny Cameron, who at the time headed up RBS's global markets business, explained why the bank and its chief executive, Fred Goodwin, were willing to proceed:

> 'Fred had a well-honed approach to acquisitions and it all revolved around those two things—what are the revenue synergies and what are the cost synergies... it's sort of once the boat had been launched and you said these are the cost and revenue synergies, there was a bit of tidying up around the edges, but not a lot to be done.'

Broadly speaking, the takeover demonstrated various problems with corporate governance (as well as external regulation):

- Unrealistic integration plan: there was no clear strategic plan for what RBS would do if it eventually succeeded in the bid, in terms of integrating ABN into the group and making the whole work together.
- Overbearing chief executive: RBS's chief executive drove the transaction with unclear strategic motives and did not or would not change course, even when some of the main drivers of the transaction disappeared (ABN sold its US banking business La Salle, a key target for RBS, to Bank of America, before the RBS purchase went through).
- A supine board and executives: no RBS executive was prepared to say no to the CEO as to do so would have been seen as disloyal or even an attempt to take over his position. However, even the RBS non-executives on the board did not intervene.
- Poor due diligence: the process of investigating a target business is difficult if a takeover bid is 'hostile' (i.e. rejected by the board of the target), but therefore great care is required. RBS (and Barclays) had very little information to go on, but after the transaction, when given access to the ABN books, RBS did not find the value it expected.
- The 'winner's curse' and no brake applied by shareholders: RBS paid too much in a competitive auction for the target without a sensible appreciation of the true value of what was being purchased. Shareholders in RBS failed to object to the price paid or to stop the transaction and, once RBS was nationalised, they lost their investment.

3. UK Companies Act and directors' duties

3.1 Introduction

The CA2006 was introduced in Chapter 1. On the corporate governance front, the major change in the CA2006 was the incorporation into statute for the first time of the duties of directors. Until then these had been based on common law principles: that is, they had developed through accumulation of case law. One purpose of the move was to make the requirements more accessible to people becoming directors: they can read them in the CA2006 instead of having to look to case law (and potentially have a solicitor explain the duties to them). The system should also be more stable. The statutory rules are, however, not a direct codification of the existing common law and, even though the duties are now in statute, the law requires courts and others to take note of the common law and case history.

It is these duties that form the basis on which directors must act to ensure they are acting in the best interests of the company (and hence its shareholders) and this is the foundation for corporate governance in the UK. The additional requirements for listed companies are discussed over the next few pages, but the general duties of directors of all companies are set out in the CA2006 as follows:

- Section 171: Duty to act within powers;
- Section 172: Duty to promote the success of the company;
- Section 173: Duty to exercise independent judgement;
- Section 174: Duty to exercise reasonable care, skill and diligence;
- Section 175: Duty to avoid conflicts of interest;
- Section 176: Duty not to accept benefits from third parties;
- Section 177: Duty to declare interest in proposed transaction or arrangement.

Some of these duties require little further explanation, but others are discussed below.

3.2 Section 174 and the duty to exercise reasonable care, skill and diligence

The common law duties of care and skill are demonstrated by a number of company law cases, some of them now very old. Section 174 of the Companies Act 2006, however, introduced a more objective test for directors who, in carrying out their functions, have a duty to exercise reasonable care, skill and diligence, which overlays a subjective standard applying to the knowledge, skill and experience of that particular director.

Case law 11.1

***Re City Equitable Fire Insurance Co* [1925]**

In *Re City Equitable Fire Insurance Co* [1925] the company lost over £1 million due to underperforming investments and fraud perpetrated by a certain Mr Bevan, the company chairman. The liquidator sued Mr Bevan's fellow directors and, whilst it was found that some directors had breached their duty of care, they were held not liable by the Court of Appeal because their lack of care did not amount to gross negligence. They had acted honestly and the court held that in the performance of his duties, a director need not display a greater degree of skill than may reasonably be expected from a person of his knowledge and experience.

Case law 11.2

***Re D'Jan of London Ltd* [1994]**

A more recent landmark case, *Re D'Jan of London Ltd* [1994], which influenced Section 174 of the CA2006, demonstrates the tests used to determine if directors have acted with due skill, care and diligence. The case establishes that directors owe an objective standard of care based on what should reasonably be expected from a person in their position. The case concerns a director, Mr D'Jan, who signed an incorrectly completed insurance policy document without checking it. This led to the insurance company refusing to pay up when the company made a claim for fire damage. The company lost most of its stock and went into liquidation. The liquidators subsequently sued Mr D'Jan for negligence in order to recover creditors' funds. It was found that the common law duty of care owed by a director is the conduct of a reasonably diligent person having both:

- **the general knowledge, skill and experience that may reasonably be expected of a person carrying out the same functions as are carried out by that director in relation to the company; and**
- **the general knowledge, skill and experience that the director has.**
- **It was held that Mr D'Jan did not demonstrate reasonable diligence when he signed the insurance policy and was therefore in breach of his duty of care. The fact that it did not amount to a gross breach of duty (on the basis Mr D'Jan was found to be honest and reasonable) mitigated his damages and he was only held liable for an amount not exceeding any unpaid dividends to which he would otherwise be entitled as an unsecured creditor.**

Case law 11.3

Weavering

In *Re Weavering Capital (UK) Limited* [2012], Weavering Capital (UK) Limited and its liquidators sought relief under the Insolvency Act 1986. The judgement of the Weavering Case of 30 May 2012 refers to proceedings against two directors of a Cayman Islands hedge fund, the Weavering Macro Fixed Income Fund (the 'Macro Fund'), which was managed by Weavering Capital (UK) Limited. The two directors (Stefan Peterson and Hans Ekstrom) were the brother and stepfather of Magnus Peterson, who was the founder and driving force behind the investment manager and the fund.

The 2011 Cayman judgement on Weavering – *Weavering Macro Fixed Income Fund Limited (In Liquidation) v Stefan Peterson and Hans Ekstrom* [Grand Court of the Cayman Islands] found the two directors, both based in Sweden and one of whom was in his 80s, guilty of wilful neglect or default of their duties as directors of the Macro fund. The Cayman judgement found they had failed to detect that Mr Magnus Peterson of Weavering Capital (UK) Limited had 'dishonestly manipulated the Macro Fund's balance sheet and defrauded its investors.' Mr Peterson had failed to disclose the existence of risky over-the-counter (OTC) swap transactions which accounted for the majority of the value of the Macro Fund, despite it supposedly having a low-risk strategy 'to ensure a balanced and diversified risk profile'. In fact, reports sent to investors stated that the fund 'traded very little in OTC instruments' and failed to notify them that the swaps were with a related party. This allowed Mr Peterson to misuse his position and overstate the value of the investments.

The financial implications of the judgement against the negligent directors of the Cayman hedge fund amounted to US$111 million each. This was the first time the Cayman Islands took action against directors and, in this case, neither were based in the Cayman Islands.

In the UK, on 30 May 2012, the High Court of Justice awarded creditors of Weavering Capital (UK) Limited more than $450 million in civil damages. The judgement states that:

> 'Mr Peterson admittedly owed Weavering Capital (UK) Limited fiduciary duties as a director. For example, to act at all times in good faith and in Weavering Capital (UK) Limited's best interests, not to put himself in a position where his interests and duties conflicted, to act in accordance with Weavering Capital (UK) Limited's constitution, statutory duties under s.171–177 of the 2006 Act and duties to exercise reasonable care, skill and diligence in performing his duties as a director.'

3.3 Wider stakeholders and the impact of Section 172

Section 172 was debated heavily as it was developed, because it introduced the idea that, although the members were still the primary focus of the directors when considering the best interests of the company, the directors should also consider wider stakeholders. The CA2006 states that the directors should 'have regard to':

- the likely consequences of any decision in the long term;
- the interests of the company's employees;
- the need to foster the company's business relationships (e.g. with suppliers and customers);
- the impact of the company's operations on the community and the environment;
- the desirability of the company maintaining a reputation for high standards of business conduct; and
- the need to act fairly as between members of the company.

This approach, sometimes referred to as 'enlightened shareholder value' was a careful balance between pressure from those who think companies should have a wider corporate social responsibility mandate and the needs to satisfy the profit motive of shareholders. The underlying view was that by considering these factors companies would produce better returns for shareholders in the longer term. This approach is reflected in the requirements for quoted companies to report about such issues in their Strategic Report, but only to the extent that these issues are material to investors.

3.4 Sections 175–177 conflicts of interest

These sections are the main areas where the new statutory rules vary or add to the old common law rules, as follows.

- *Duty to avoid conflicts of interest* (except where they arise out of a proposed transaction or arrangement with the company, see below). Under the common law, a director must not allow their personal interests, or duties to another person, to conflict with their duty to the company. If they do, unless shareholders consent to the conflict, the company can avoid any relevant contract and the director must account to the company for any 'secret profit' they have made. The statutory duty replaces this old rule.
- *Duty not to accept benefits from third parties*. There is no express duty to this effect in common law. It appears to derive from the duties to act in the company's interests and the rule dealing with conflicts of interest.
- *Duty to declare any interest a director has in a proposed transaction or arrangement with the company to the company's other directors*. Under the common law, a conflict of interest arising out of a transaction or arrangement with the company is dealt with by the general rule on conflicts of interest, described above. Under the statutory arrangements, such a conflict (where it relates to a proposed transaction or arrangement with the company) is covered by this duty of disclosure.

There are fairly common situations which can cause problems in relation to conflicts of interest. For example, it is common for people to have multiple directorships, whether within the same group of companies or with completely unconnected companies. In such situations, the best course is immediate disclosure and authorisation, to avoid any potential conflicts arising. It is also possible to deal with conflicts in a company's articles of association. Directors may sometimes find it advisable to take independent legal advice in more complicated circumstances. Directors who are members of professional bodies themselves (such as The Chartered Governance Institute) as well as being governed also by their own professional body's standards, may also be able to seek advice from such bodies.

There are also strict rules in the Companies Act in relation to other issues that might give rise to a conflict of interest or a risk that directors might ask in their own self-interest. These must generally be approved by shareholders and include:

- service contracts for directors lasting longer than two years;
- loans or other credit given by a company to a director; and
- substantial property transactions, where the company sells a major asset to a director.

Although we have focused on only some of the duties here, they are all equally important. Upon joining the board of an offshore company, directors with a UK background should, as part of their induction, familiarise themselves with legal and regulatory requirements in that jurisdiction, e.g. Companies (Jersey) Law 1991; Companies (Guernsey) Law, 2008; BVI Business Companies Act, 2004; Companies Law 1961, as amended (Cayman). The company secretary, fellow directors and compliance officer should be able to assist in this respect. It is not sufficient to assume that the principles and requirements of the CA2006 will apply elsewhere.

Test yourself 11.1

Briefly explain the provisions of section 174 of the CA2006.

Test yourself 11.2

Why was it felt necessary to codify the existing common law rules on directors' duties into statutory law?

Test yourself 11.3

You are a director of Company A which is entering into a joint venture with Company B. The joint venture business is to be run from a company, Company C, to which Company A and Company B will appoint an equal number of directors. You will be one of those directors. What should you do to ensure you avoid conflicts of interest in relation both to Company A and Company C?

4. UK and offshore corporate governance codes

4.1 Introduction: development of the UK Corporate Governance Code

In 1991, in response to financial scandals (including the Bank of Credit and Commerce International, Maxwell Communications Corporation, the Mirror Group, Polly Peck and Guinness) and the resultant growing public concern over the management of large companies, the quality of their financial reporting, the apparent lack of accountability and the high levels of executive remuneration, Sir Adrian Cadbury was charged with conducting a review on the Financial Aspects of Corporate Governance. The Cadbury Committee, which was appointed by the Financial Reporting Council and the London Stock Exchange in conjunction with the accounting profession, issued its report and Codes of Best Practice on corporate governance in December 1992. The focus was entirely on **UK listed companies**.

UK listed company
A company with shares admitted to the Official List in the UK, but which may be incorporated anywhere. There is a choice between a Premium or Standard listing. Premium listed companies must meet higher standards than Standard listed companies, which need to meet only EU-mandated minimum criteria.

In its report, the Cadbury Committee defined corporate governance as 'the system by which companies are directed and controlled' and discussed the need for separating the role of management, which is about running the business, from the role of governance, which is about making sure the business is run properly. The result was the Cadbury Code on corporate governance, which was a voluntary code that listed companies were asked to follow, on the 'comply or explain' basis that still applies today (see below).

Following Cadbury, over time various reports were commissioned which led to changes and extensions to the original Cadbury Code. Some of these were prompted by new scandals or crises which indicated corporate governance needed to be revisited and some, particularly around remuneration, have been driven by public pressure.

- The Greenbury report on directors' remuneration was published in 1995. The report addressed the public concern over the directors of recently privatised companies who engineered significant salaries for themselves irrespective of their performance. This spread to cover the whole issue of directors' remuneration.

- The Hampel committee was charged with reviewing the implementation of the findings of the Cadbury and Greenbury committees and its final report was issued in 1998. The Committee drew up a list of corporate governance principles covering also the role of directors, directors' remuneration, the role of shareholders and accountability and audit, built on the findings of Cadbury and Greenbury.
- The Turnbull report of 1999 provided guidance to directors regarding good risk management and establishing a strong system of internal controls, following a risk-based approach and testing the effectiveness of the internal controls.
- Revisions were made following the Higgs review of the role and effectiveness of non-executive directors and the Smith review of audit committees in 2002–2003.
- Further reviews were undertaken in 2006 and in 2009, the latter review triggered by the financial crisis and to consider the recommendations of the Walker Review relating to banks, following a number of bank failings at the start of the global economic crisis.

All these developments, as well as more recent changes arising from new EU legislation on audit and audit committees, has culminated in the UK Corporate Governance Code.

In February 2017, the FRC announced a review to the 2016 Code and commenced a consultation on the proposed changes, which closed In February 2018. Subsequently, a substantially revised Code was published in July 2018, applying to accounting periods beginning on or after 1 January 2019.

The 2018 Code was designed by the FRC to improve corporate governance practices, governance reporting and to encourage constructive challenge in the boardroom. The 2018 Code emphasises the importance of a healthy corporate culture and the need for diversity. It also encourages stakeholder engagement, particularly with the workforce, and introduces new provisions in relation to the alignment of executive and workforce remuneration. The 2018 Code emphasises that long-term sustainable success can be achieved through good corporate governance practices, which may ultimately benefit the wider economy and society.

The 2018 Code takes a similar approach to the 2016 Code in terms of its structure; it is divided into five sections, each with a set of overall Principles supported by several underlying Provisions. This is discussed further in section 3.3.

4.2 Application of the UK Corporate Governance Code

The UK Corporate Governance Code is based on a 'comply or explain' approach to corporate governance, whereby the boards of companies should either comply with the principles of the Code or explain to shareholders the areas of non-compliance. Any company can choose to follow the UK Corporate Governance Code, but under the FCA's Listing, Disclosure and Transparency

Rules, the application of the the Code by UK premium listed companies is on a mandatory 'comply or explain' basis.

The Code is designed to help directors discharge their duties to shareholders by acting in their best interests. The Code recommends that the chair of a company reports personally to shareholders on board effectiveness and the application of the Code's principles in this respect.

While the Code encourages shareholder engagement and directors to report to shareholders on a 'comply or explain' basis, departures from the Code should not automatically be treated as breaches as it may be appropriate for certain complex companies to depart from the requirements of the Code in certain circumstances. Shareholders should consider the explanations given and engage with the board if they remain unconvinced with the reasons for departure from the requirements of the Code. A 'tick-box' approach Is discouraged, and there may be alternative ways that a company could apply the principles of the Code. Additionally, if a departure is described as 'time limited' then the explanation should also include when the company expects to be able to comply with the principle.

Departures from the principles of the Code are common for non-UK domiciled companies who have their shares admitted to trading on the Main Market of the London Stock Exchange, such as offshore investment companies domiciled in Guernsey or Jersey.

For example, these companies do not often have executive directors. The principles of the Code in relation to disclosure of certain executive remuneration arrangements or the division of the role of the chairman and chief executive office, will often not be applicable. The perceived non-compliance is therefore explained to shareholders in their annual report.

4.3 Content of the UK Corporate Governance Code

3.3.1 2016 Code: The Five Main Principles

The April 2016 Code was divided into a set of five 'Main Principles', which are outlined below. These 'Main Principles' were supported by provisions to provide guidance on how each of those principles could (or should) have been met.

Section A: Leadership

Section B: Effectiveness

Section C: Accountability

Section D: Remuneration

Section E: Relations with Shareholders

3.3.2 The 2018 Code: key considerations and disclosures

The introduction to the 2018 Code emphasises engagement with a wide range of stakeholders and the importance of promoting success over the long term. Culture, stakeholder engagement, diversity and proportionate remuneration set the framework of the 2018 Code.

The 2018 Code takes a similar approach to the 2016 Code in terms of its structure; it is divided into five sections, each with a set of overall Principles supported by several underlying Provisions. It also continues the 'comply or explain' approach but provides guidance on how some of its principles may be applied. The Provisions typically create additional disclosure requirements to be included in the annual report or otherwise disclosed by the company.

The Provisions are extensive; the key disclosure requirements of the Provisions in each section of the 2018 Code are included below and should be understood.

3.3.3 Section 1: Board Leadership and Company Purpose

This section places an expectation on boards to set and promote corporate culture, as well as engage with both shareholders and wider stakeholders. It is divided into five Principles and eight Provisions.The Principles state that the board should be accountable for ensuring that the long-term success of the company promotes value for shareholders and contributes to society. The board should establish the purpose, values and strategy of the company and be satisfied that these align with its culture. All directors must act with integrity, lead by example and promote the desired culture. The board must ensure adequate resources and controls are in place to meet and measure its objectives and enable effective risk management.

In addition, the board should engage with stakeholders and ensure that workforce policies and practices are aligned with the company's values and would support the long-term success of the company. The workforce should be able to raise any concerns in a safe environment.

The key disclosures to be made pursuant to the Provisions of Section 1 are:

- Details of the sustainability of the company's business model, how governance contributes to the company's strategy, and how the board have assessed opportunities and risks.
- An explanation of the board's activities, any action taken by them in relation thereto. It should include how the company invests in and rewards its workforce.
- A description of how the board have discussed and considered the interests of key stakeholders and the matters set out in s. 172 of the Companies Act 2008 when making decisions.
- An explanation if the board has chosen to engage with its workforce in an alternative way to one or more of the three ways recommended in the code, which are as follows:
  - through a director appointed from the workforce;
  - through a formal workforce advisory panel; and/or
  - through a designated non-executive director.

In addition to the disclosures in the annual report outlined above, Section 1 also imposes a requirement on companies to explain, when publishing the voting results of general meetings, what action it intends to take to consult shareholders to understand and address any resolutions which received a vote against of 20% or more of the total eligible voting rights for the general meeting.

4.3.4 Section 2: Division of Responsibilities

This section provides guidance on the division of duties within the board, the role of the non-executive directors, and how independence should be determined for the directors. It is divided into four Principles and eight Provisions.

The Principles outline the role of the chair of the board, which is to ensure effective and constructive relations between the board and to ensure that the non-executive directors contribute effectively to board discussions. The chair is also responsible for ensuring the board receive timely, accurate and clear information.

The role of non-executive directors is described in Provision 13 of the Code as providing constructive challenge, strategic guidance, specialist advice and to hold management to account. The role of a non-executive director includes:

- being involved in the appointment and removal of executive directors;
- scrutinising and holding management to account against agreed performance objectives; and
- meeting with the chairman without the executive directors present.

In addition, the board should be supported by the company secretary to ensure it is able to function effectively and efficiently. The board must be appropriately balanced between non-executive and executive directors (e.g. at least half of the board, excluding the chair, should be independent non-executive directors). There must be no dominant group or individual, combined with a clear division of responsibility between leadership of the board and executive leadership of the company's business.

It is worth noting that the Provisions of Section 2 set out the following criteria in relation to the independence of the chair of the board:

- the chair must be independent on appointment;
- the role of the chair and chief executive should not be performed by the same person, unless in exceptional circumstances in which case the majority shareholders should be consulted before the appointment is made and the reasons for the appointment disclosed in the annual report and on the company's website.

In addition, Provision 10 of Section 2 sets out the following criteria in relation to circumstances which could impair the independence of non-executive directors:

- having been an employee of the company or its group within the last five years;
- having had within the last three years, a material business relationship with the company;
- having received additional remuneration from the company apart from their fee for acting as non-executive director, including participating in

share options, performance related pay schemes or the company's pension scheme;

- having close family ties with any of the company's advisers, directors or senior employees;
- holding cross-directorships or having significant links with other directors through involvement in other companies or bodies;
- representing a significant shareholder; or
- having served on the board for more than nine years from the date of their first appointment.

The key disclosures to be made pursuant to the Provisions of Section 2 are:

- Whether each non-executive director is considered to be independent and, If applicable, an explanation of any divergence against the independence criteria set out at Provision 10 (as noted above).
- The number of meetings of the board and its committees, as well as the individual attendance of the directors at those meetings.
- The rationale for the approval by the board of any additional significant commitments of the directors.
- In either or both of the annual report and company website, a description of the responsibilities of the chair, chief executive, senior independent director, board and each of its committees.

4.3.5 Section 3: Composition, Succession and Evaluation

This section provides guidance on the formation of the nomination committee, how the board should consider its composition, its succession planning and the self-evaluation principles for the performance of the board. It is divided into three Principles and seven Provisions.

The Principles describe the recruitment process that the board should follow. It places an emphasis on appointments being made based on merit while still considering aspects of gender, ethnic, social and skill diversity. It also sets out guidance for the composition of the board and its committees, including tenure (for example, that the chair may not remain in such position for a period of more than nine years from first appointment).

In addition, the Principles outline the approach that should be taken when conducting self-evaluations of the performance of the board and its committees. For example, that the evaluation should be performed at least once per annum and that an external evaluator must be used at least once every three years (for FTSE 350 companies).

Section 3 also sets out the recommendation for establishment of a nomination committee responsible for overseeing the orderly succession of the board and senior management. Establishment of the committee is optional, but its absence should be explained in the annual report. It is unlikely that shareholders would deem it acceptable for UK domiciled issuers or larger companies (those in the FTSE 350 or above) to not have such a committee.

The nomination committee must be composed of a majority of independent non-executive directors. The chair of the board may be a member of the committee (or may chair the committee) but may not chair the committee when considering their own successor.

The key disclosures to be made pursuant to the Provisions of Section 3 are:

- All directors must be subject to annual re-election and, accordingly, the directors must set out in the papers (usually the AGM notice and agenda) the reasons why the contribution of those directors is to the benefit of the long-term success of the company.
- If the chair remains in office for more than nine years, a clear explanation must be disclosed (such as in the annual report), for example, if an extension of the nine-year period is to facilitate orderly succession.
- The use of an external search consultancy (for director recruitment) is encouraged. Where one is used, its details should be disclosed in the annual report, alongside a statement as to whether it has any other connection with the company.
- When an external evaluator is used for the annual evaluation of the board and its committees, its details should be disclosed in the annual report, alongside a statement as to whether it has any other connection with the company.
- The annual report must contain details of the work undertaken by the nomination committee, including, but not limited to:
  - the process used for director recruitment, the approach to succession planning and how diversity is supported;
  - the manner in which the board evaluation has been conducted (e.g. by way of internal or external evaluation) and the outcomes, actions and a summary of, the annual evaluation of the board and its committees;
  - the company's policy on diversity, how that policy is linked to the company's objectives, how it has been implemented and the progress on achieving the diversity objectives; and
  - details of the gender balance of those in senior management and their direct reports.

4.3.6 Section 4: Audit, Risk and Internal Control

This section provides guidance in relation to the formation of the audit committee, oversight of the internal and external audit function, and the procedures that should be followed to ensure management of principal risks. It is divided into three Principles and eight Provisions.

The Principles outline how the board should establish a framework for ensuring transparency, independence and effectiveness of the internal and external audit function to protect the integrity of its financial statements. It also encourages that the assessment of the financial position and prospectus of the company should be presented in an easily understandable manner.

In addition, the Principles recommend that the board should determine the nature and extent of the principal risks that the company should be willing to take to meet its long-term objectives and must have in place a framework that allows for effective risk management and oversight of internal controls.

Section 4 also sets out the recommendation for establishment of the audit committee, which is the only mandatory committee under the Code. The nomination and remuneration committees are not mandatory, but a company will need to explain their absence if the board have not appointed either.

The responsibilities of the audit committee are wide ranging. They include monitoring the integrity of the financial statements, reviewing any announcements of financial performance, providing advice to the board on whether the financial statements reflect a 'true and fair view', reviewing the internal control framework and assessing the effectiveness of the internal and external audit functions.

The audit committee must be comprised entirely of independent non-executive directors with a minimum membership minimum number of three (or two for smaller companies (those below the FTSE 350)). The chair of the board may not be a member of or chair the committee.

The key disclosures to be made pursuant to the Provisions of Section 4 are:

- An explanation from the directors for their responsibility for preparing the financial statements must be included in the annual report, including whether they consider them to be fair, balanced and understandable enough to inform shareholders of the financial position and prospects of the company.
- A statement from the board in the annual report that it is deemed appropriate to adopt the going concern basis of accounting and details of any uncertainties.
- An explanation from the board in the annual report of how they have assessed the viability (future prospects) of the company, over what period it has done so and why it considers that period appropriate (often referred to as the 'viability statement').
- A confirmation, in the annual report, that the board have undertaken at least an annual assessment of the company's principal risks, including a description of those risks and how they are being managed.
- A confirmation, in the annual report, that the board have undertaken at least an annual review of the internal control framework.
- A description of the work of the audit committee in the annual report, including, but not limited to, any significant issues and how they have been addressed, how the independence and effectiveness of the external auditor has been assessed, an explanation of why the board has not accepted their recommendations (if any), an explanation for the absence of an internal control function (if so) and an explanation of how the independence and objectivity of the external auditor has been safeguarded (if they provide non-audit services).

4.3.7 Section 5: Remuneration

This section provides guidance in relation to the formation of the remuneration committee and, principally, the structure of compensation and remuneration schemes for directors, with particular focus on executive remuneration. The code no longer implies or specifies any preference of one form of scheme over the other (e.g. long-term share incentive plans over short-term performance based cash bonuses).

The Principles detail how executive remuneration should be aligned to the purpose, values and long-term strategy or objectives of the company and that there must be a formal and transparent procedure for determining remuneration schemes. It also states that no director should be involved in discussions regarding their own remuneration.

In addition, the Principles recommend that the directors should exercise their judgement and discretion when setting remuneration policies, considering both the company and wider stakeholders (such as the workforce).

Section 5 also sets out the recommendation for the establishment of the remuneration committee responsible for determining director remuneration; and when setting executive director remuneration, consider the implications for the workforce in view of aligning remuneration with the company values and culture. Establishment of the committee is optional, but it's absence should be explained in the annual report. It is unlikely that shareholders would deem it acceptable for UK-domiciled issuers or larger companies (those in the FTSE 350 or above) to not have such a committee.

The committee must be comprised entirely of independent non-executive directors with a minimum membership of three (or two for smaller companies (those below the FTSE 350)). The chair of the board may be a member but may not chair the committee. The chair of the committee must have served as a member on a remuneration committee for at least 12 months.

The key disclosures to be made pursuant to the Provisions of Section 5 are:

- When a remuneration consultant Is appointed to assist the remuneration committee in its review of director remuneration schemes, its details should be disclosed in the annual report, alongside a statement as to whether it has any other connection with the company.

It is worth noting that Section 4 sets out specific details of how remuneration schemes should be constructed (the details of which are outside the scope of the syllabus) but when determining executive director remuneration policy, the remuneration committee should consider the following:

- Clarity; remuneration must be transparent and should promote effective engagement with shareholders and the workforce.
- Simplicity; remuneration schemes should not be complex and their rationale and operation should be easy to understand.
- Risk; remuneration schemes should not encourage excessive risk taking.
- Predictability; the range of possible values and/or rewards to directors should be explained at the time the policy is set.

Stop and think 11.1

As an example of how the disclosure requirements are addressed in practice, read through the Marks & Spencer governance disclosures in its 2019 annual report and audited financial statements, commencing from page 34 onwards. Go to the investor section of the company's website to find further governance information, under the headings of Corporate Governance, but also Shareholder Information.

4.4 UK Stewardship Code

Corporate governance is designed for the benefit of investors (and to some extent the wider business community) but those who invest in companies also have a role in the corporate governance system. This is not just through buying, holding or selling shares in companies, but also by engaging with companies to improve corporate governance and performance, to hold management to account and to vote responsibly on major issues such as appointment and reappointment of board directors, approving the annual report and the appointment of auditors, remuneration and so on. There has been criticism that some institutional investors do not play their part in an active enough manner, and that companies cannot be expected to improve their corporate governance without direct involvement by investors.

The UK Stewardship Code was borne out of the Walker Review and published first in 2010, establishing best practice in stewardship of UK listed companies by investors. It seeks to develop and improve engagement between institutional shareholders and the companies in which they invest. Compliance with the Code is not mandatory for everyone but all authorised asset managers and listed companies in the UK are required to either comply with the Code or explain any departures. The Stewardship Code is still relatively young compared to the Corporate Governance Code and the FRC is preparing to more actively monitor its signatories to ensure they are not merely paying lip service to the new Code's rules.

The FRC announced a consultation on proposed changes to the UK Stewardship Code at the beginning of 2019. The proposed revisions will aim to set higher expectations for investor stewardship policy and will focus on how effective stewardship delivers sustainable value for stakeholders. It will also set out more rigorous reporting requirements and address the demand for more effective stewardship and investment decision making that is aligned with the needs of institutional investors and their beneficiaries.

Test yourself 11.4

Why is it so important for an organisation to have a good system of corporate governance?

4.5 The AIC Codes of Corporate Governance

The Association of Investment Companies Code of Corporate Governance (the 'AIC Code') was originally published in 2003. The current version was published in February 2019 to reflect the changes to the UK Code of Corporate Governance. Its objective is to provide its members with best practice guidelines for the governance of investment companies, including guidance on practical application of the UK Corporate Governance Code for investment companies. It provides directors of investment companies with a one-stop approach to corporate governance to ensure they manage the issues pertinent to investment companies and meet the requirements of the UK Corporate Governance Code. It is a principles-based code and requires members to either comply with the principles or explain in their annual report why they do not comply. Alternatively, the directors of the investment company should set out the measures they intend to implement to ensure compliance with the principles going forward.

Prior to the February 2019 edition of the AIC Code, the AIC provided its members with a suite of codes specific to the UK, Jersey and Guernsey, along with a guide to mapping the principles of the AIC Code with the UK Corporate Governance Code.

Now, there is only one AIC Code covering all three jurisdictions and the mapping guide has been withdrawn on the basis that the AIC Code now closely reflects the Principles and Provisions of the UK Corporate Governance Code.

4.6 Guernsey Finance Sector Code of Corporate Governance

The current version of the Guernsey Finance Sector Code of Corporate Governance was issued by the Guernsey Financial Services Commission in September 2011 and took effect on 1 January 2012 (although it was also amended in February 2016 for insurers). It applies to companies subject to the Guernsey regulatory framework. The Code establishes eight key principles underpinned by best practice guidelines.

The eight principles are stated in the Code as follows:

1. *The board:* Companies should be headed by an effective board of directors which is responsible for governance.
2. *Directors:* Directors should take collective responsibility for directing and supervising the affairs of the business.
3. *Business conduct and ethics*: All directors should maintain good standards of business conduct, integrity and ethical behaviour and should operate with due care and diligence and at all times act honestly and openly.
4. *Accountability:* The board should have formal and transparent arrangements in place for presenting a balanced and understandable assessment of the company's position and prospects and for considering how they apply financial reporting and internal control principles.
5. *Risk management:* The board should provide suitable oversight of risk management and maintain a sound system of risk measurement and control.

6. *Disclosure and reporting:* The board should ensure the timely and balanced disclosure to shareholders and/or to regulators of all material matters concerning the company.
7. *Remuneration:* The board should ensure remuneration arrangements are structured fairly and responsibly and that remuneration policies are consistent with effective risk management.
8. *Shareholder relations:* The board should ensure that satisfactory shareholder communication takes place with shareholders and is based on the mutual understanding of needs, objectives and concerns.

Entities which comply with the UK Corporate Governance Code or the AIC Code of Corporate Governance are deemed by the Guernsey regulator to be in compliance with its own Code.

Companies subject to the Code are required to submit an annual assurance statement to the Guernsey Financial Services Commission confirming that its directors have considered the effectiveness of their corporate governance practices and are satisfied that they have applied with the principles of the Code in a manner commensurate with the nature, scale and complexity of their business activities. The assurance statement was originally a separate document but now forms part of the form used to submit the annual financial statements to the Guernsey Financial Services Commission, along with other compliance related matters.

Test yourself 11.5

What are the roles and responsibilities of non-executive directors?

Test yourself 11.6

Outline some strengths and weaknesses of the comply or explain approach of the UK Corporate Governance Code?

Test yourself 11.7

What are the eight principles of the Guernsey Finance Sector Code of Corporate Governance?

5. Directors' remuneration

5.1 Introduction

The issue of how much directors are paid has and continues to be a matter of great controversy, particularly for listed companies. Arguably the issue first came to great prominence in relation to the newly privatised companies such as British Gas, where the board directors saw their pay increase considerably. However, the issue, and public antipathy to the trend of pay for listed company directors increasing considerably while the pay of other workers has risen much more slowly or even remained static, continues today. For example, a study by a group called One Society noted in 2011 that the multiple of CEO pay to average employee pay had risen to 262:1 across FTSE 100 companies and the trend shows no signs of abating.

This has led to a gradual move from no regulation at all, through requirements in the Corporate Governance Code for the board to consider in relation to remuneration, through to the situation today where UK quoted companies must put their pay policies to a binding vote by shareholders every three years and an advisory vote on actual pay each year.

Note that the definition of a quoted company is wider than that of a UK listed company (see Section 3). A UK listed company can be incorporated anywhere but has shares on the UK Official List. Quoted companies include UK listed companies, but also those listed in another EEA member state and on the US Nasdaq exchange.

The issue of how directors are rewarded for their work is closely linked to the **agency theory** discussed in Section 1 of this chapter. There are still questions about the key drivers that should be used to measure corporate success and how these are translated into pay for directors. The overall effect of the changes in rules and greater scrutiny has tended to increase the complexity of remuneration arrangements. Generally, a listed company director's pay will be a combination of basic salary, annual bonus, pension payments and share options or shares, the latter usually given under a long-term incentive plan (LTIP). There is now greater emphasis on being able to claw back bonuses and shares from directors when companies subsequently fail, particularly in the financial sector.

agency theory
Predicated on the view that the managers of a company are appointed to act as agents of the owners of the company and that there is an inherent conflict of interest between the managers (who control the company) and the shareholders (who own the company).

IFRS Standards and UK GAAP
IAS 24 Related Party Disclosures deals with the disclosure of Key Management Personnel. Generally, UK company law requirements to disclose directors' remuneration will fulfil the requirements of the standard, but care is required if people who are other than directors fall into the category of Key Management Personnel (see Chapter 7). FRS 102 does not cover disclosure of KMP remuneration as it is governed by UK law.

5.2 UK Companies Act 2006 requirements

The UK government introduced a binding shareholder vote and greater transparency in relation to reporting requirements on directors' pay from 1 October 2013. This included new directors' remuneration reporting requirements for UK-incorporated quoted companies in respect of accounting periods ending on or after 30 September 2013, and new shareholder voting requirements in respect of directors' pay. Note that all companies must disclose directors' pay, but there are much more extensive requirements for quoted companies, which must produce a separate Directors' Remuneration Report, as well as having directors' pay voted on.

In summary the law requires the following to be produced and voted on by quoted companies:

- An annual statement by the chair of the remuneration committee, summarising the major decisions on directors' remuneration, any substantial changes relating to directors' remuneration made during the year and the context in which those changes and decisions occurred or were taken.
- An annual report on remuneration disclosing how the existing remuneration policy was implemented in the financial year being reported on, and setting out details of each director's remuneration in the last financial year. The remuneration for the period must be put to an annual advisory shareholder vote. It is not possible to make the vote binding as this would override the contractual arrangements between the company and its directors, but it gives an indication of whether shareholders are satisfied with the pay for the year.
- A directors' remuneration policy, which sets out the company's forward-looking policy on remuneration and potential payments (including its approach to exit payments), and which is subject to a binding shareholder vote a least once every three years. If the vote goes against the policy, the company must amend it and seek new approval from shareholders.

The Directors' Remuneration Report must be laid before members in general meeting and filed with the Registrar of Companies.

You can look at the Marks & Spencer plc 2016 Directors' Remuneration Report from page 50 onwards of the ARA. As you can see, the information provided is very extensive and detailed.

5.3 Impact in practice

The new legal requirements give much more power to shareholders to restrict the pay of directors than they had formerly. In practice, that power has been used in different ways, and also depending on what is happening overall in the corporate market. It is fair to say that, when companies are doing well and giving good returns to shareholders, there tend to be fewer complaints about executive pay. However, when profits and share prices fall but directors' remuneration does not, there can be significant rebellion against director pay policies.

In the first part of 2016 there were significant or majority shareholder votes against remuneration at WPP, BP, Shire and Weir Group. The vote at Weir was particularly damaging as it was a binding vote on pay policy and a large majority of shareholders voted against it. This means the company has to continue with its old remuneration policy until it can put a vote to shareholders on a revised policy.

Case study 11.2

There is much public comment on executive pay, from bodies such as the High Pay Centre, which monitors executive pay and lobbies against excessive remuneration: CEO pay continues to rise. Analysis of disclosures by 71 FTSE 100 companies which have reported on their FYE 2015 reveals that most CEOs have received an increase in the 'single figure' measure of CEO pay at the UK's largest listed companies.

The High Pay Centre has analysed the pay disclosures for 71 companies which have reported so far this year and are FTSE 100 members.

The HPC analysis shows that, out of 71 FTSE 100 companies, 40 reported a higher single figure for FY 2015 than the amount reported for FY 2014. Amongst the CEOs receiving a generous increase in take home pay were a CEO (Reckitt Benckiser) who got over £10 million more than their previous year's pay and one CEO (Shire) whose pay was over £12 million more than 2014.

Stefan Stern of the HPC said: 'The evidence which is coming directly from companies' own annual reports is that the 20-year rising trend in top company pay continues unabated. The UK's new disclosure rules now allow investors to observe this as it happens, but the latent power possessed by investors to call a halt to these excessive rewards remains unexercised.'

The High Pay Centre's analysis used the restated figures for 2014 for the purposes of comparison. Many of the 71 companies reported a higher figure for 2014 than was originally reported in their 2014 Annual Report. (Posted on the highpaycentre.org blog, 13 April 2016)

There have been examples of shareholders, rather than voting against a company's pay policy or actual pay for a year, choosing instead to vote against the reappointment of the chair of the remuneration committee or even the chair of the board. The reasoning is that, as non-executive directors, these people should be representing shareholder interests and curtailing excessive pay for the executives. This option is possible because under the existing Code, best practice is for all directors, both executive and non-executive, to stand for re-election each year.

The chair of the remuneration committee at BP was criticised by some shareholders in 2016 for allowing a significant pay increase for the chief executive. Some care is required, however. Alison Carnwath was heavily criticised as the chair of the remuneration committee at Barclays when the chief executive received a significant bonus in 2012, only for him to be ousted shortly afterwards, partly as a result of the Libor rate-fixing scandal. Many shareholders voted against Carnwath's reappointment as a non-executive. However, it later transpired when she gave evidence in front of a parliamentary select committee that she had been the only director to vote against the bonus. Until then, she had been bound by confidentiality and collective board responsibility principles from disclosing that fact.

6. Narrative reporting and corporate social responsibility

6.1 Introduction

We looked at the content of the ARA in Chapter 1. As noted there, reports of a narrative nature, outside but accompanying the audited financial statements, are required under company law and also under the Listing Rules. Smaller, unquoted companies also have to produce narrative reports, but with much less content required. Under current UK rules these narrative reports are broadly focused on investor information, giving insights into how the business is run and its future prospects.

There has been pressure from governments, non-governmental organisations and charities for companies to use their narrative reports as a means of communicating the company's impact on a wider range of stakeholders, such as employees, the community and the environment. There is an inherent tension in reporting to investors but where civil society demands greater insight into the impact on society at large of company activities. The tension is often resolved by companies reporting more in-depth information on issues such as sustainability or employee engagement outside the ARA, perhaps on its website. These reports are often voluntary but governments have moved to require other disclosures, for example on gender pay gaps, as discussed below. This leaves the ARA to cover such issues only to the extent they are material to investors.

6.2 UK company law

In the UK the primary focus of narrative reporting is on investors. Nevertheless, companies are required to produce a strategic report which looks to how the company's activities affect wider stakeholders, but only to the extent that this is material to investors. The CA2006 does this by linking the objective of the Strategic Report to the directors' duty under s. 172 of the CA2006 (see Section 2.3).

The requirements relating to the content of the Strategic Report state that the purpose of the strategic report is to inform members of the company and help them assess how the directors have performed their duty under s. 172 (duty to promote the success of the company). Smaller, unquoted companies can produce quite basic Strategic Reports. Larger companies, however, must describe their business model and strategy, future prospects, principal risks and KPIs (see Chapter 8), as well as information on gender diversity of the board and senior executives. Quoted companies must also, to the extent necessary for an understanding of the development, performance or position of the company's business, include information about environmental matters (including the impact of the company's business on the environment), the company's employees, and social, community and human rights issues, including information about any policies of the company in relation to those matters and the effectiveness of those policies.

This can be seen to bring in, at least to some extent, principles of corporate social responsibility (CSR), a term used to describe the processes an organisation uses to produce a positive impact on society through its activities. It is about the ongoing commitment of businesses to behave ethically and responsibly towards its employees, its customers, its competitors, the environment and the community at large, but on the basis that at the same time this will benefit investors in the longer term. Indeed, investors remain the key constituent and focus of the directors' duties. In a wider sense, CSR encompasses sustainable and responsible business decisions and development goals integrated with ethical values. Good CSR respects and embraces cultural differences and helps build the skills of the workforce.

The corporate governance principles which underpin CSR – transparency, accountability, integrity, corporate ethics, trust and respect – are important for the proper running of a business and therefore companies need to appreciate the potential benefits of adopting and investing in CSR. Good CSR practice is likely to lead to a well-run business that is successful in the long term from an investor viewpoint. A business can build long-term trust amongst staff and customers and society at large as a basis for a sustainable business model, which will help to create the right environment in which it can innovate and grow and various studies have been carried out – by academics and others – to demonstrate the positive relationship between good CSR and higher returns for shareholders. A company's board should therefore ensure that the values it has established and set for the company are upheld and adhered to throughout the company.

Test yourself 11.8

What do you think are the key principles and themes that underpin good CSR?

6.3 EU developments

Following the economic crisis, the European Commission published a new policy on CSR in October 2011 in order to address some of the social and ethical issues, which have been the focus of much attention. The aims include encouraging responsible business behaviour and the creation of favourable conditions for sustainable growth to help rebuild consumer confidence and levels of trust in business. The renewed EU strategy put forward by the European Commission is that:

> 'enterprises should have in place a process to integrate social, environmental, ethical, human rights and consumer concerns into their business operations and core strategy in close collaboration with their stakeholders, with the aim of:

- maximising the creation of shared value for their owners/shareholders and for their other stakeholders and society at large;
- identifying, preventing and mitigating their possible adverse impacts.'

As part of its work, the European Commission published a new directive (EU Directive 2014/95/EU) on Non-Financial Reporting, which applies mainly to larger listed companies. This legislation, in the process of being adopted into UK law by the UK government, follows a similar approach to the UK Strategic Report, in that it focuses on the information required by investors, but at the same time incorporates a wider CSR focus. The main addition to the UK disclosures will be in relation to anti-bribery and corruption policies and wider equality reporting, including gender, race, educational and professional background.

6.4 Other reporting requirements

The UK government does require wider CSR-related reporting, sometimes through the ARA, including company policies on employing disabled people, payment practices to small suppliers and so on. In recent years, however, there has been a recognition that this information can clutter up the ARA if it is not of direct interest to investors, or if it represents standing data that does not change much from one year to the next. The UK government has started to move to requiring these types of CSR disclosures separately on company websites, or simply allowing them to be filed as separate reports. Recent examples include:

- Modern Slavery Act 2015 supply chain disclosures;
- payment practices;
- gender pay gap reporting.

6.5 Internationally recognised principles and guidelines

For further information on CSR and its implementation within company policy, the company secretary can refer to various international standards and guidance, namely the:

- OECD Guidelines for Multinational Enterprises;
- Ten Principles of the United Nations Global Compact;
- ISO 26000 Guidance Standard on Social Responsibility;
- ILO Tri-partite Declaration of Principles Concerning Multinational Enterprises and Social Policy; and
- United Nations Guiding Principles on Business and Human Rights.

6.6 Sustainability reporting and integrated reporting

As climate change and its impacts have become better understood, pressure has been put on companies to give more information on the impact of climate change on the business's future prospects. Some companies, particularly in business areas considered central to climate change issues, such as oil and gas, coal mining and heavy manufacturing, often produce separate sustainability reports that deal with their impacts on the environment in much more detail than the Strategic Report. These will often contain a lot more technical material, but they may also lay out what the company is aiming to do to curtail its negative environmental impacts.

The International Integrated Reporting Council (IIRC) was set up to address this issue in more depth. As the IIRC says on its website:

'The International Integrated Reporting Council (IIRC) is a global coalition of regulators, investors, companies, standard setters, the accounting profession and NGOs. The coalition is promoting communication about value creation as the next step in the evolution of corporate reporting.

Mission
The IIRC's mission is to establish integrated reporting and thinking within mainstream business practice as the norm in the public and private sectors.

Vision
The IIRC's vision is to align capital allocation and corporate behaviour to wider goals of financial stability and sustainable development through the cycle of integrated reporting and thinking.'

The IIRC has developed **integrated reporting**, in which the approach is to suggest that company reporting, while still aimed broadly at investors, should be more holistic in its approach, considering all the kinds of capital a company uses: so not just financial capital, but natural resources, employees and so on. This form of reporting on multiple 'capitals' is seen as a much better representation of what a company is consuming to produce a profit, including where it does not have to pay a direct cost for the capital consumed, or where that cost does not represent the entire cost to society. For example, a company may pay for the water it consumes in its business, but the real cost may be greater because of the permanent over-utilisation of local water sources. These forms of 'capitals' are categorised as: financial capital, manufactured capital, intellectual capital, human capital, social and relationship capital, and natural capital.

integrated reporting (IR)
Is an evolution of corporate reporting, with a focus on conciseness, strategic relevance and future orientation. As well as improving the quality of information contained in the final report, IR makes the reporting process itself more productive, resulting in tangible benefits. IR requires and brings about integrated thinking, enabling a better understanding of the factors that materially affect an organisation's ability to create value over time. It can lead to behavioural changes and improvement in performance throughout an organisation.

Integrated reporting is becoming better known and there are moves towards the approach of the IIRC in both the public and private sectors in several countries, including the UK.

7. European, US and international regulation

7.1 Introduction

This section looks briefly at developments in EU and US legislation and regulation around corporate governance and finance to give an overview of the situation in what two of the biggest capital markets in the world. Those non-US companies that wish to list their shares in the USA will be subject to these rules and others, at least to some extent, as **Foreign Private Issuers (FPIs)**. While the UK is ahead of the curve on much corporate governance practice, EU developments can change the rules in the UK, particularly if they lead to legislation.

Foreign Private Issuers (FPIs)
A non-US company will qualify as a FPI if 50% or less of its outstanding voting securities are held by US residents; or if more than 50% of its outstanding voting securities are held by US residents and none of the following three circumstances applies: the majority of its executive officers or directors are US citizens or residents; more than 50% of the issuer's assets are located in the USA; or the issuer's business is administered principally in the USA.

7.2 EU projects related to corporate governance

Various reports were written for or by the European Commission as a reaction to the financial crisis that hit in 2007–2008. These reports have led to substantial regulatory action around company law but mainly the law and regulation governing banks and other financial institutions. These are beyond the scope of this text, but there are some ongoing initiatives around corporate governance that are of relevance, under various headings.

- *Directors*: includes studies on directors' duties and liabilities and a recommendation on the role of non-executive directors of listed companies, particularly on their independence and the role of board committees, such as remuneration, nominations and audit committees.
- *Shareholders*: proposals to revise the Shareholder Rights Directive as well as setting minimum standards for takeover bids to protect minority shareholders, employees through revisions to the Takeover Directive.
- *Employee share ownership*: rules to make it easier for companies to offer shares to employees, including across borders within the EU as employee engagement is seen as conducive to good governance.
- *Transparency around corporate governance arrangements*: including the introduction of a 'comply or explain' regime of governance similar to the UK, requirements to provide a corporate governance statement and non-financial information disclosures, discussed above.
- *Country-by-country reporting (financial institutions)*: banks and investment firms to publicly disclose certain information for every country where they operate (the type of activities, turnover, full-time employees, profit/loss before tax, tax paid, public subsidies received). This is now proposed to be extended to all listed companies.
- *Country-by-country reporting (extractive industries)*: oil, gas, mining and forestry companies to publicly disclose information on all payments to governments in the countries in which they operate. This is now law across the EU and may be in the US. It is designed to help citizens in developing countries hold their governments to account for monies they receive from mining royalties and so on.
- *Financial institutions' governance*: the Capital Requirements Directive lays down rules for banks and investment firms including effective risk management, board composition and pay structure (for executives and employees considered 'material risk takers') in the form of a 'bonus cap' (maximum ratio between variable and fixed compensation).

7.3 US Sarbanes-Oxley Act (2002)

The **Sarbanes-Oxley Act** has two official names (the 'Public Company Accounting Reform and Investor Protection Act' and the 'Corporate and Auditing Accountability and Responsibility Act', depending on which house of the US Congress is referring to it). It is more commonly referred to as SOX and was introduced in the US in 2002 following high-profile corporate scandals involving a number of US companies, including WorldCom (MCI Inc), the energy giant Enron and global auditing firm Arthur Andersen. In an attempt to restore public confidence in corporate governance, to combat accounting fraud and to protect the interests of investors, the US federal government enacted new and enhanced corporate governance standards with an increased focus on corporate disclosure. The legislation is wide reaching and applies to all US public companies, their management, their boards and their accountants. It also applies to non-US public companies carrying out business in the US. This effectively means that the Sarbanes-Oxley Act affects both UK and offshore public companies dealing with the US or processing transactions in US dollars.

The Sarbanes-Oxley Act (2002)
Legislation which was passed in the USA in 2002 in an attempt to restore public confidence, improve the transparency of financial statements and protect investor interests. The Act introduced new and more stringent measures for public companies in respect of corporate disclosure requirements and corporate governance.

The Act introduced a number of significant changes leading to much wider share ownership in the US and tighter regulation. Since the Act was passed in 2002, all US companies and companies dealing with the US have had to ensure compliance with the relevant provisions of the Act, which has driven up the costs of the compliance function for these entities. However, the increase in accountability for senior executives has led to enhanced reporting and improved disclosures to shareholders.

Publicly traded companies have been forced to make it a priority of their compliance function to review the provisions of the Act, which holds top executives more accountable for their actions. As well as leading to adverse publicity, failure to comply with the requirements or failure to accurately certify documents could lead to the offending officers of the company being extradited to the US to face charges. The Act imposes tough penalties which includes fines of up to US$5 million and/or imprisonment of not more than 20 years for certifying financial statements which do not comport with all the requirements.

The provisions of the Act include:

- improved accuracy, transparency and reliability of corporate disclosures;
- tightening of internal controls;
- increased corporate board responsibilities and holding of chief executive officers and chief financial officers personally liable for the accuracy and timeliness of financial reporting (CEOs and CFOs to review and certify quarterly and annual accounts);
- establishment of the **Public Company Accounting Oversight Board (PCAOB)** charged with the oversight and supervision of public company accounting firms providing audit services;
- auditor independence, auditor rotation and conflicts of interest;
- increased corporate board responsibilities;
- pre-certification of non-audit work by a firm's audit committee;

Public Company Accounting Oversight Board (PCAOB)
Charged with the oversight and supervision of public company accounting firms and oversees the audits of public companies in order to protect investor interests and further the public interest in the preparation of informative, accurate and independent audit reports.

- ban on loans to directors and officers;
- more timely reporting of insider trading;
- ban on insider trades during pension fund blackout periods;
- disgorgement of bonus and compensation payments;
- criminal and civil penalties for white collar crime, for non-compliance and for securities violations;
- disclosure of analyst conflicts of interest in order to restore investor confidence in reporting;
- protection for whistleblowers; and
- the powers of the **US Securities and Exchange Commission (SEC)** to censure or ban securities brokers, broker-dealers and advisors from the financial services industry.

US Securities and Exchange Commission (SEC)
One of the main financial services regulatory authorities in the US whose remit includes the protection of investor interests and the maintenance of fair, orderly, and efficient markets.

There have been legislative and regulatory reforms similar to the Sarbanes-Oxley legislation in other jurisdictions, such as France, Germany, Italy, Turkey, India, Japan, Canada, South Africa and Australia, focusing on enhanced corporate governance and disclosure requirements. The tangible benefits of these reforms may never be known with any degree of accuracy but the increase in market confidence (resulting from enhanced ethical standards, improved reporting, greater accountability and transparency) probably outweighs the costs of implementation and the on-going costs of compliance. Furthermore, companies which are able to demonstrate strong risk management and internal control systems can benefit from an increase in share price, due to improved investor confidence, and decreased borrowing costs as lenders of finance have greater confidence the loans will be repaid.

With regards to the offshore environment, a number of collective investment funds specifically preclude investments or dealings with the US because of the costs of compliance and the tough penalties that may be imposed on officers and senior executives under the Act. Offshore vehicles are still able to install investor confidence by locating themselves in highly regulated and reputable international finance centres such as the Crown Dependencies of Jersey and Guernsey. The directors and officers of these offshore vehicles still need to be aware, however, of the implications of the Act if they are transacting with the US.

Test yourself 11.9

Can you think of at least three benefits and three drawbacks of the increased requirements introduced by the Sarbanes-Oxley Act of 2002?

7.4 The US Dodd-Frank Act (2010)

The Dodd-Frank Wall Street Reform and Consumer Protection Act (the 'Dodd-Frank' Act) was passed in the US in 2010 in response to the 2008 global financial crisis with the collapse of large financial institutions, particularly in the US, the bailout of banks by governments across the world, and the downturn in global stock markets. The aim of the Dodd-Frank Act is, as its official name suggests, to reform the US regulatory framework and to protect consumer interests. This has been achieved by addressing a number of issues including the enhanced supervision of banking activities with a view to avoiding another major financial crisis.

The Dodd-Frank reform seeks to reduce dependence on large financial institutions, improve accountability and transparency in the financial system, end government bailouts by keeping the financial system under a closer watch and protect consumers from poor and abusive financial services practices. As well as addressing corporate governance issues and enhanced disclosure requirements, it covers a number of other key areas including:

- financial stability;
- orderly liquidation;
- proprietary trading;
- insurance;
- credit rating agencies;
- financial product regulation and trading restrictions; and
- whistleblowers and consumer protection.

The Dodd-Frank Act has also led to the creation of important new agencies, notably the Financial Stability Oversight Council (FSOC) which is attached to the US Treasury Department and whose role is to promote market discipline and to monitor, identify and assess systemic risk in the US financial system to ensure threats to financial stability are dealt with in an effective and timely manner.

Case study 11.3

Lehman Brothers began trading cotton in Alabama in the 1850s and the family developed the business into a commodities futures trading venture. The business was instrumental in setting up the New York Cotton Exchange before moving into merchant banking and later into investment banking under the company name Lehman Brothers Holdings, Inc.

Richard Fuld was appointed CEO in 1994 and it was not long before his aggressive risk taking had led to considerable exposure to the commercial real estate market in which Lehman Brothers had built up a significant portfolio. The company held positions in subprime mortgage tranches, was highly leveraged, held insufficient capital and began to run into liquidity difficulties. The bank was unable to provide sufficient collateral in respect of its positions in poor quality mortgage backed securities and was forced to sell off assets. With no credible and clear capital restoration and remediation plan, the bank was eventually downgraded by the credit rating agencies.

Despite offers to rescue the company, Lehman Brothers failed to agree terms with a merger partner. The Federal Reserve was not prepared to use taxpayers' money to bail out the bank. Lehman Brothers had foregone opportunities to save itself. The bank eventually filed for bankruptcy in September 2008 in what was to become the largest bankruptcy case in US history.

The board came under criticism for a number of failings, including:

- **Dominant CEO accused of putting his own interests ahead of those of the shareholders and for demoting those who challenged him. His aggressive behaviour led to management information being presented to him in a manner that did not show the true extent of the problems.**
- **No segregation of the roles of chair and CEO.**
- **Inexperienced board with an average age of nearly 70, with four of the ten members being over 75, and only one with current financial sector knowledge. The board had little knowledge of the banking and securities industry.**
- **Negligent risk committee which only met twice in both 2006 and 2007.**
- **Excessive leverage which was not clearly presented in the financial statements.**
- **Readiness to accept high risk in order to drive up earnings and increase executive bonuses.**
- **Excessive exposure to the US housing market and commercial real estate.**
- **Failure to fully understand the risks involved and the inherent weaknesses of its business model.**
- **Holding the riskiest sub-prime mortgage tranches.**
- **Poor risk management and internal control systems with little attention to the business as a whole.**
- **Insufficient liquidity and failure to inject capital despite senior executives being made aware of liquidity issues as early as January 2008.**
- **Dependent on its short-term obligations being funded by long-term capital.**
- **Compensation committee that gave rewards for poor performance including payouts totalling $75 million to the CEO, Richard Fuld, in the two years leading to the company's collapse and compensation payments to other executives even when the company was engaged in discussion with the US government over a rescue package.**

- **Lack of accountability for failings of the board and its members.**
- **Failure to save the company from bankruptcy because the board overestimated the value of the bank and refused to accept a merger deal that did not reflect its own valuation.**
- **Arrogance which led to analysts being ignored when they called for Lehman to inject more capital into the company.**
- **Failing to address the warning signs and have a clear strategy for recovery.**
- **Relying on the Federal Reserve to bail out the bank because it was 'too big to fail'.**

7.5 International regulation

Part of the reason for the global economic crisis which began in 2008 was that banks, insurance companies and major financial institutions were taking on the risk of a position without fully understanding the risk itself. Many were highly leveraged, had toxic assets, liquidity problems and no capital restoration plan. Dodd-Frank aims to prevent financial institutions getting themselves into such precarious positions and if they do, they should expect to face the consequences when it all goes wrong rather than be bailed out by the government. During the crisis, however, the US government helped bail out some financial institutions, such as the investment bank Bear Stearns, and yet allowed Lehman Brothers to collapse, and there were similarly uneven approaches in other countries. The considerations that came into play when dealing with a financial institution on the brink of failure have led to a realisation that there needs to be a more coherent and consistent response to failing financial institutions on an international basis.

The work of the **Financial Stability Board (FSB)** has been aimed at solving the problem of national regulators regulating global firms. In particular, there has been international agreement that some firms need to be designated as **systemically important financial institutions (SIFIs)** and therefore subject to greater regulation. The FSB's mandate includes:

- Monitor and advise on the best approach to regulatory standards.
- Co-ordination of regulation: the firms are global but the regulators are national so more cooperation is required.
- Advise on crisis management, including requiring firms to write so-called living wills, which consist of plans on how firms would be wound up if they failed, to make the process predetermined and therefore more orderly.

The FSB also co-operates with national regulators and other international regulators, such as the Bank for International Settlements (BIS), the Basel Committee on Banking Supervision and the International Monetary Fund. You can see more about the FSB on its website.

Financial Stability Board (FSB)
An international body that monitors and makes recommendations about the global financial system.

systemically important financial institutions (SIFIs)
Financial institutions whose distress or disorderly failure, because of their size, complexity and systemic interconnectedness, would cause significant disruption to the wider financial system and economic activity.

8. Audit and audit reporting

8.1 Introduction

Finally, we will look at another key component in the corporate governance and reporting system, namely the role of the auditors. One result of the agency problem, discussed in Section 1, was the idea that the shareholders of a company should receive accounts but also have those accounts checked by an independent third party, namely an auditor. Auditing as a profession has therefore developed alongside the introduction of limited liability companies with multiple outside investors who need someone to check on how the directors are managing the business. Auditing is now heavily regulated: to carry out a **statutory audit**, a person or firm must be a registered auditor and auditors are subject to substantial statutory and regulatory requirements.

statutory audit
A legally required review of the accuracy of an entity's financial records and financial statements.

audit
An objective examination and evaluation of the financial statements of an organisation to make sure that the records are a fair and accurate representation of the transactions they claim to represent. An external audit is done by an auditor or audit firm that is independent of the entity (a statutory auditor); an internal audit is carried out by employees of the entity (although it can be outsourced).

statutory auditor
An external auditor whose appointment is mandated by law.

8.2 Regulation of auditors

The CA2006 lays out the requirements for **audit** of UK companies in Part 16 and related schedules. All companies other than those that are small must have an audit on both their individual and (where they are prepared) consolidated accounts, although there are also some exemptions for dormant companies and subsidiaries within groups if the parent company guarantees the subsidiary's debts. The rules specify when auditors must be appointed, how their appointment and remuneration should be approved by shareholders, auditors' rights and duties and how they may stand down or be removed. In particular, it is a criminal offence for directors and employees of a company to mislead the auditors and the directors must make a statement in the Directors' Report that they have each individually given all relevant audit information to the auditors. The Listing Rules also require accounts to be audited, although half-yearly or interim financial statements do not have to be audited.

Part 42 of the Act deals with the regulation of **statutory auditors**, which is shared between the professional accountancy bodies, such as the Institute of Chartered Accountants in England and Wales (ICAEW) and the FRC. The FRC primarily deals with public interest, larger audits and auditors, but has oversight over how the accountancy bodies manage the rest. Although the law specifies some of the things auditors must do, in particular issuing an audit report on the audited company's financial statements, most of the detail about how audits are done are in auditing standards and related materials issued by the FRC:

- *International Standards on Auditing (UK & Ireland)*, ISAs, which are based on international standards but with some additions for UK and Irish legal and other issues.
- *Practice Notes* on audits of types of entity where there are special complexities or issues, for example for banks and insurers.
- *Bulletins* are for urgent or new issues that arise in practice where auditors need guidance, for example when IFRS Standards first came into force in the UK a special bulletin was issued.

As well as these instructions on how to carry out an audit, auditors and audit firms must also comply with strict ethical rules on independence and related issues. Independence is the key to auditing: if auditors are not independent of the company, their report is tainted and is of no value to the shareholders to whom the report is addressed. The FRC produces an Ethical Standard for Auditors, which covers:

- Overarching principles and supporting ethical provisions.
- General requirements and guidance relating to independence, objectivity and integrity.
- Financial, business, employment and personal relationships.
- Long association between auditors and companies.
- Fees, remuneration, gifts, hospitality and litigation.
- Non-audit and additional services (such as tax and consulting).

There are some derogations for audits of smaller and non-listed entities and the professional accountancy bodies also have their own ethical rules with which their members must comply.

There are inherent conflicts of interest in the system which drive the need for these rules. Directors generally choose the auditors and negotiate their remuneration, even though both must be approved by shareholders, but it is to shareholders that auditors report. Directors also have the gift of additional or other work that audit firms might carry out, such as tax services. Directors have a lot of power in getting rid of auditors, which may be to the detriment of shareholders if the auditors are trying to make the directors produce better financial information or to stop them misleading shareholders. Because of this, the law requires auditors leaving office to make public statements about the circumstances of them standing down.

8.3 Audit reporting

The auditors must issue an audit report on the financial statements, stating whether:

- the accounts show a true and fair view (discussed in Chapter 1);
- the accounts have been properly prepared in accordance with the Companies Act and any other relevant legislation;
- the accounts comply with the accounting standards that have been followed, e.g. IFRS Standards or UK accounting standards.

The auditors must also state whether the information accompanying the audited financial statements in the ARA (so all the narrative reports):

- are consistent with the financial statements;
- have been properly prepared in accordance with the relevant rules, e.g. the Companies Act; and

- nothing the auditors have seen in the course of their audit indicates that any of the information is misleading.

Auditors usually issue an unmodified or clean audit report, because the company's accounts comply with all the rules and the audit has not uncovered anything of concern. However, the auditors may draw attention to a significant problem by issuing an 'emphasis of matter' paragraph, for example if there are doubts about the entity's ability to continue as a going concern. More serious is a modified audit opinion, where either (1) the auditors disagree with a particular issue, but the rest of the accounts are fine, or (2) more seriously, the auditors do not agree the accounts show a true and fair view or have insufficient evidence that they do. Figure 11.1 indicates the different types of opinion:

Figure 11.1: Auditor's report: green, amber and red reports

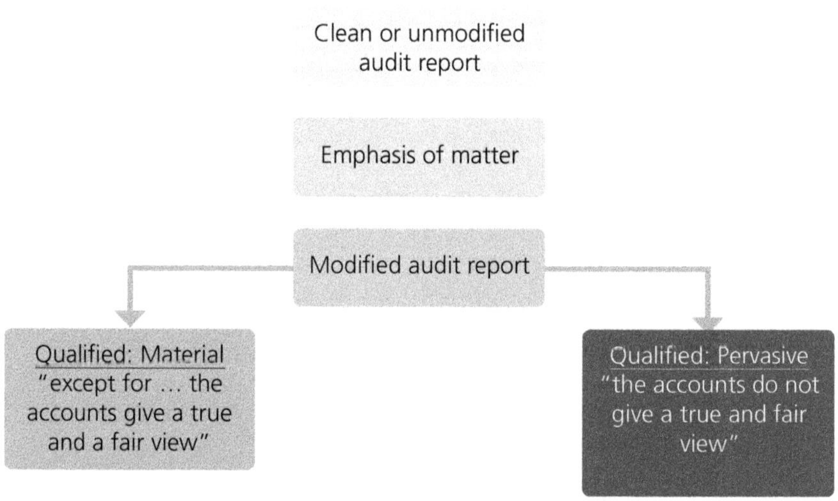

The FRC has also moved recently to require auditors of the largest companies to give more insight into the way the audit is conducted, the key areas of audit risk and the way auditors approach materiality. This has made audit reports much longer, but also more informative, and investors have generally welcomed the approach. You can look at the Marks & Spencer audit report by their auditors Deloitte on pages 78–85 of the 2016 ARA.

Note that one of the risks highlighted by Deloitte is supplier rebates, which are complex contractual mechanisms in which suppliers give volume and other rebates to a retailer, but also pay for advertising and prime store placement of products and other incentives may be involved. Accounting for these arrangements requires significant judgement. In the first year of the new audit reports, this became an issue that haunted Tesco plc, the major supermarket chain. Their auditors (PwC) also raised supplier rebates as a key issue in their report on Tesco's 2014 accounts. However, the Tesco audit committee disagreed with this assessment and went as far as to say in their own report, after listing out the significant financial reporting issues they had considered:

'The Committee notes that commercial income [i.e. supplier rebates] was an area of focus for the external auditors based on their assessment of gross risks. It is the Committee's view that whilst commercial income is a significant income for the Group and involves an element of judgement, management operates an appropriate control environment which minimises risks in this area. As a result, the Committee does not consider that this is a significant issue for disclosure in its report.'

Only a few months later, Tesco had to issue a revised earnings announcement when it transpired that supplier rebates had not been properly accounted for. This has led to investigations by the Serious Fraud Office, the Financial Conduct Authority and the FRC.

There was some criticism of auditors after the financial crisis, including that they had signed off clean audit reports just before banks had to raise new capital when they got into trouble, and also that they gave no indication of problems coming in the financial sector. The new audit reporting requirements, discussed above, were one response to these criticisms, although there has been no actual audit failure that has been prosecuted. Nevertheless, the European Commission has legislated to increase regulatory oversight over auditors across Europe and legislation is coming into force in mid-2016. For the first time, auditors of public interest entities (PIEs) are restricted to a maximum term (in the UK 20 years) and then must be replaced, thus dealing with familiarity issues. Provision of some non-audit fees by statutory auditors are prohibited and a cap placed on the fees that may be paid by PIEs. Audit committees have new statutory duties placed upon them. The oversight of auditors, carried out by the FRC, has been modified and strengthened.

In the context of listed companies, the role of the audit committee (a committee of the board) is important. The audit committee oversees the relationship between the auditors and the company, including negotiation and agreement of fees, the appointment and reappointment of auditors and examination of the findings of auditors to ensure that the executive has responded to audit concerns and prepared the financial statements properly.

Chapter summary

- According to agency theory, the managers of a company are appointed to act as agents of the owners of the company and there is an inherent conflict of interest between the managers (who control the company) and the shareholders (who own the company). A problem arises when the directors, who manage and control the company, make decisions which are not consistent with the objective of maximising owner wealth.
- Corporate governance is the process by which organisations are directed and controlled. Displaying sound governance is good for companies as it helps with their smooth running, attracts inward investment and helps raise finance. The basis for corporate governance in the UK (and in many other jurisdictions) is company law, which lays out directors' duties. These may also be found in common law, so arising from legal cases over time.

- The UK Corporate Governance Code combines and consolidates the recommendations of Cadbury, Greenbury, Hampel, Turnbull, Smith and Higgs to establish best practice principles and more detailed requirements in respect of board leadership and effectiveness, accountability, remuneration and shareholder relations. The application of the principles by UK listed companies is on a mandatory 'comply or explain' basis.
- In addition to the 'comply or explain' approach required by the UK Listing Rules, the Code lays down certain disclosure requirements in respect of information which should be included in the annual report, made available on the company's website or included in shareholder communications.
- Investors also have a role to play in corporate governance. The UK Stewardship Code was born out of the Walker Review and published in 2010 establishing best practice in stewardship of UK listed companies. By encouraging best practice, it seeks to develop and improve engagement between institutional shareholders and the companies in which they invest.
- There are other codes of governance, particularly for offshore companies, including the AIC Codes of Corporate Governance for directors of investment companies and the Guernsey Finance Sector Code of Corporate Governance.
- Corporate social responsibility (CSR) describes the processes an organisation uses to produce a positive impact on society through its activities. It is about ongoing commitment of businesses to behave ethically and responsibly towards its employees, its customers, the environment and the community at large. It is about doing business in a responsible and sustainable manner. Following good CSR can have a positive impact on corporate competitiveness as the public like to see large multi-national companies giving something back to the community.
- There have been various legal and regulatory initiatives to improve corporate governance and protect investors in the EU and US. Some of these are reactions to financial scandals and to the 2008 financial crisis. There is now more coordination internationally of regulation, through the Financial Stability Board and other international bodies.
- Audits and audit reporting are a key component of corporate governance and shareholders rely on the independent opinion given by auditors on company financial statements. Audit regulation and reporting has also been overhauled following the financial crisis and auditors now give much more detailed audit reports to help investors understand the key risks within companies.

Exercise answers

Chapter 1

Test yourself answers

Test yourself 1.1
Normally directors should follow accounting standards in order to show a true and fair view. Where there are choices in accounting, the directors should make the choice that is most appropriate to the company and should make sure the information is complete and unbiased. They should then consider whether any additional disclosures are required. Finally, if the accounting produced by accounting standards do not reflect the economic reality of the company's situation and the outcome was not anticipated by those standards, then the relevant standards should be overridden, but with full disclosure given of the impact and what would have been shown under the standards.

Test yourself 1.2
More standardisation, speed of change if new issues arise (vs the law), better comparability and consistency, less manipulation, more reliability for users.

Test yourself 1.3
Better comparability for international investors, easier cross-border finance raising for companies, reduced costs for accountants and analysts, reduced costs for companies, higher quality of standards overall if IFRS Standards maintains its quality marque.

Test yourself 1.4
FRS 100 describes the overall framework of application; FRS 101 is a reduced disclosure standard for use within IFRS Standards groups; FRS 102 is the main UK standard for groups and companies; FRS 103 is on insurance contracts; FRS 104 is for companies producing interim accounts under UK GAAP; FRS 105 is for micro-entities.

Chapter 2

Test yourself answers

Test yourself 2.1

Investors would probably look at information about the general state of the industry in which an entity operates, perhaps by looking at economic forecasts by industry bodies. They would also look at peer entities in the sector in order to decide which had the best prospects, lower cost base or lower risk profile. They might also assess whether the current share price of the entity indicates it is being undervalued, which would make it attractive to buy.

Test yourself 2.2

Error here is in the context of what is a material error, so it is not about trivial or meaningless errors. We will look at auditing in Chapter 11, but it is worth noting here that one of the main functions of an audit is to check for errors in financial statements. Auditing standards, which tell auditors how to carry out an audit, are therefore important in terms of how they require auditors to check for errors. International Standards on Auditing (ISAs), which auditors must follow when performing an audit, defines an error as 'An unintentional misstatement in financial statements, including the omission of an amount or a disclosure.'

Test yourself 2.3

1. The two fundamental concepts are relevance and faithful representation.
2. If a liability is deliberately overstated at the end of an accounting period, it may be reversed in the following period, creating a gain that was not actually made in the following period. This would be misleading and imprudent. See Chapter 6 for further detail.

Test yourself 2.4

The four enhancing qualitative characteristics are comparability, verifiability, timeliness and understandability.

Test yourself 2.5

Think about the salaries of the staff who run the accounts function and prepare the accounts, the cost of the auditors and management time spent on overseeing and checking the process. But how many of those costs would be incurred anyway in producing management information to run the business?

Test yourself 2.6

Recognition means capturing information to include it in the financial statements when it meets the definition of one of the elements of financial statements. The monetary amount of the item will be shown in the appropriate part of the relevant statement, accompanied by a description in words.

Test yourself 2.7

Historical cost measures assets and liabilities at cost and does not reflect changes in prices over time; however, it does deal with impairment/consumption of assets and fulfilment of liabilities. Current value reflects up-to-date prices for assets and liabilities.

Chapter 3

Test yourself answers

Test yourself 3.1

Statement of financial position, statement of comprehensive income, statement of changes in equity, statement of cash flows and notes to the accounts.

Test yourself 3.2

1. An estimate should be made of the month of electricity consumption not yet billed, and that amount should be accrued in the balance sheet as a liability and as a cost in the statement of profit or loss. If the bill is received after the year end but before the accounts are approved, the calculation of the amount to accrue can be made more accurately, but even without such a bill, an estimated amount must still be accrued.
2. The statement of cash flows.

Test yourself 3.3

In assets: inventories, trade receivables, prepaid expenses, cash and cash equivalents, derivative and other financial assets. In liabilities: borrowings due within one year, trade payables, salaries, benefits and other accrued expenses, taxation, derivatives and other financial liabilities.

Test yourself 3.4

1. Expenses classified by function are allocated to cost of sales and other expense headings. Expenses classified by nature are listed according to what they represent, without allocation to a function.
2. The extent to which each method is useful will depend on the type of business whose accounts are being prepared. For many, the functional method will give more information as it demonstrates what aspect of the business incurs expenses, so for example showing how much administration costs versus the selling function. For simpler businesses the by nature method may be more appropriate as it is easier to apply and it avoids what may be arbitrary allocation methods in the functional method.

Test yourself 3.5

If a company does not generate enough cash it may be unable to pay its debts as they fall due and could become insolvent. This is true of even very profitable businesses if it takes a long time to get cash from customers or if the business is expanding rapidly and cash is reinvested in a growing asset base.

Test yourself 3.6

Taxes attributable to income, such as corporation tax, are usually treated as operating cash flows unless they specifically relate to an investing or financing activity.

Test yourself 3.7
If the fall in value of the investments occurred after the year end it should be reported in the following accounting period.

Chapter 4

Test yourself answers

Test yourself 4.1
Management will need to determine first whether they item is material and, if it is, which accounting standards are relevant to accounting for it. Where there are choices within a standard, management must choose the accounting policy which provides the most faithful representation of the transaction or event. They will also need to consider what disclosures are required in the notes to explain the item. If there are no specific accounting standards, then management can look to other sources of guidance in IFRS Standards, including the Conceptual Framework, and in other accounting systems if these are consistent with IFRS Standards. Finally, if applying a relevant standard does not give a true and fair view (or fair presentation), the standard should be overridden to produce a true and fair view and full disclosure given of both treatments.

Test yourself 4.2
A change in accounting policy reflects a decision (or a requirement in a standard) to apply a new way of accounting for an item. It should be applied retrospectively if possible. A change in accounting estimate is a recalculation of the carrying value of an item due to new information and is applied prospectively.

Test yourself 4.3
Most mobile phone contracts will consist of a handset – the phone itself – and a contract for calls, data, texts and so on. The handset sale revenue will be recognised at the start of the contract as the phone is delivered to the customer. The revenue for the contract for calls and so on will be recognised over the life of the contract as the customer uses the phone. Some contracts may have other elements, for example an option to upgrade and/or trade in the old phone, whose accounting treatment may depend on the specific terms given.

Test yourself 4.4
1. The answer will depend on where you are based. Where there are no taxes on corporate profits, no accounting will be required for either current or deferred taxes.
2. Other types of taxes that are not treated as income taxes include all sales and value added taxes, taxes on production or taxes on other elements of an entity's financial results. For example, the UK bank levy is calculated as a percentage of the size of the bank's liabilities in its statement of financial position.

Worked example answers

Worked example 4.1

The revenue will be allocated as follows:

Performance obligation	Stand-alone price	Contract revenue
	£	£
A	40	100 × 40/120 = 33
B	60	100 × 60/120 = 50
C	20	100 × 20/120 = 17
Total	120	100

Chapter 5

Test yourself answers

Test yourself 5.1

Apple's expected capacity for future earnings is built into the share price and relates almost entirely to unrecognised intangible assets. These comprise not only the Apple brand, but all its internally generated intellectual property, including design features of its products, and the ability of its employees – technology innovators and inventors – as well as its know-how in delivering products to market.

Test yourself 5.2

As derivatives have a very low cost, likely not to be material to most entities, historical cost would give no information about a derivative until it matured, was sold or 'closed out' (i.e. settled). An entity's accounts and the potential risks associated with them might be very distorted if it had substantial derivatives which were off balance sheet. Fair value deals with this issue by requiring the current value to be shown at each accounting date.

Worked example answers

Worked example 5.1

2016: $\text{depreciation} = \dfrac{£120{,}000 - £20{,}000}{10\text{ years}} = £10{,}000$

Net book value = £120,000 – £10,000 = £110,000

2017: $\dfrac{£120{,}000 - £0 - £10{,}000}{9\text{ years}} = £12{,}222$

Net book value = £110,000 – £12,222 = £97,778

2018: $\dfrac{£120{,}000 - £0 - £22{,}222}{6\text{ years (note)}} = £16{,}296$

Net book value = £97,778 – £16,296 = £81,482

2019: Depreciation will be the same charge of £16,296 as there are no further changes in estimates. Net book value will continue to fall by the same amount until the end of the useful life.

Note: As the new total estimated useful life from 1.1.16 is 8 years, only 6 remain at 1.1.18.

Worked example 5.2

The basic rule is to recognise an impairment if the carrying amount exceeds the recoverable amount.

(1) Determine the carrying amount. The building has a cost of £2 million, useful life of 20 years and has been used for five years so far, so accumulated depreciation is £2m/20 × 5 years = £0.5m. So the carrying amount is £2m less £0.5m = £1.5m.

(2) Determine the recoverable amount, which is the higher of fair value less costs to sell and value in use. Fair value less costs to sell in this scenario is £1m minus £0.05m = £0.95m. Value in use is the present value of future cash flows which is £1.2m, so value in use is higher than fair value less costs to sell.

(3) Carrying amount is £1.5m while recoverable amount is £1.2m. An impairment loss of £0.3m is recognised (reduce the carrying value of the asset and recognise a loss in the statement of profit or loss).

Worked example 5.3

Units purchased	= 70 + 138 + 39 + 78		= 325
Units sold	= 95 + 118 + 62		= 275
Units in closing inventory	= 325 – 275		= 50
Cost of goods sold	Units	Unit Cost	Total £
Sales from 1 Jan b/f inventory	70	£16.00	1,120
Sales From 5 Jan purchase	138	£16.50	2,277
Sales From 11 Jan purchase	39	£17.00	663
Sales From 16 Jan purchase	28	£17.50	490
	275		4,550
Closing inventory	Units	Unit Cost	Total £
Inventory from 16 Jan purchase	50	£17.50	875

Chapter 6

Test yourself answers

Test yourself 6.1

An entity will be required to think about all the possible outcomes in relation to the provision and which is most likely to occur. It is possible that if the entity would settle for some middle amount, that may be the right value to use. If there is a portfolio of homogenous provisions, it may be possible to calculate an expected value across the whole portfolio.

Test yourself 6.2

A provision is a liability of uncertain timing and amount. It may arise from a legal or constructive obligation and must arise from a past event.

An example of a constructive obligation would be where an entity has no legal obligation to clear up certain environmental damage caused by its operations, but announces that it will do so publicly.

Test yourself 6.3

A provision is more certain than a contingent liability as it is more likely than not that the entity will have to pay something to settle it; contingent liabilities are only possible liabilities, where the threshold of probability of payment has not been reached. For some rare contingent liabilities, it may be probable that the entity will have to pay to settle it, but it is not possible to measure the obligation with sufficient certainty to record a provision.

Test yourself 6.4

As we will see in Chapter 8, where companies have significant operating leases, users of their accounts will sometimes add the disclosed off balance sheet obligations to the entity's actual liabilities to create a better picture of the total obligations and gearing of the company. They therefore need the disclosure of future commitments in order to perform the calculation accurately.

Worked example answers

Worked example 6.1

An entity assesses the probability of an outflow for the warranty obligations as a whole. The provision would therefore be calculated on an expected value of (75% of £nil) + (20% of £1m) + (5% of £4m) = £400,000.

Worked example 6.2

The liability component is measured first, and the difference between the proceeds of the bond issue and the fair value of the liability is assigned to the equity component. The present value of the liability component is calculated using a discount rate of 9%, the market interest rate for similar bonds having no conversion rights.

Present value of principal: £2m payable at the end of three years(1)	1,544,367
Present value of interest: £120,000 payable annually in arrears for three years(2)	303,755
Total liability component	1,848,122
Proceeds of the bond issue	2,000,000
Equity component (by deduction)	151,878

(1) $2{,}000{,}000/(1.09)^3$

(2) $120{,}000/(1.09) + 120{,}000/(1.09)^2 + 120{,}000/(1.09)^3$

If the bond is not converted to equity, the option will simply lapse and be reversed out of equity. If instead the bond is converted to equity, the outstanding liability is used to pay up the proceeds of the equity issued.

Chapter 7

Test yourself answers

Test yourself 7.1

A company might want to have a long-term strategic stake in a start-up business that is developing new products in its area. An investment at the level of control might be too expensive or risky, but a long-term stake would allow influence over the investee and the investing company may be able to increase its stake and even take control if it looks like the new business will be successful. The initial holding will give an advantage of early involvement, with lower risk.

Worked example answers

Worked example 7.1

	£	£
Fair value of consideration given		
Cash	1,000,000	
Shares: £10 × 100,000	1,000,000	
		2,000,000
Fair value of assets and liabilities acquired		(1,400,000)
Goodwill		600,000

Chapter 8

Test yourself answers

Test yourself 8.1

An entity might raise prices to gain more margin, or reduce prices to gain more volume sales. However, it might also increase sales without sacrificing margin by better marketing, reducing costs or breaking in to new markets. On the other hand, an entity may sell some of its assets if it believes they are not producing the required return; sales of inefficient assets should boost ROCE.

Test yourself 8.2

A retail company will have a lot of money tied up in inventory. Even though it may buy its inventory on credit and sell for cash or more immediate payment through credit cards, the amount of working capital tied up in inventory will offset this advantageous difference in credit periods. If the company is expanding, it may not be able to realise cash quickly enough from sales to purchase increasing amounts of inventory and it will be harder to arrange longer-term bank debt to cover purchases of short-term, low value inventory.

A logistics company will need warehouses, lorries and equipment, but these longer-term assets can be matched to longer term borrowings, which create more stability.

Test yourself 8.3

There is a trade-off between margin and asset turnover that means different businesses can produce the same ROCE. Low-margin businesses (such as food retailers) often have intensive asset usage, and produce a high volume of goods to sell but sell them at low prices. Higher margin businesses (for example, luxury jewellery producers) produce fewer goods but sell them at a high price. Many of these businesses are very labour intensive, rather than using a lot of machinery to produce their goods.

Test yourself 8.4

Cash is tied up in inventory so if it is slow to sell, the business may not get enough cash inflow to keep the company going. In addition, inventory may become obsolete if it becomes too old, depending on the type of business, and inventory storage costs may be high.

Test yourself 8.5

$$\text{Creditor days} = \frac{\text{Trade payables}}{\text{Purchases}} \times 365 = 5/30 \times 365 = 61 \text{ days}$$

Test yourself 8.6

The company may have chosen to implement a shorter period as a deliberate strategy, to ensure goodwill with suppliers. However, it might also be that the company's creditors have threatened to cease trading with it if it does not pay more promptly. Alternatively the cost of holding cash may have increased and so the business has decided to pay creditors earlier. It would normally be prudent only to shorten creditor days if there is a commensurate decrease in debtor days, i.e. the company is getting paid more promptly by its customers.

Test yourself 8.7

One of the main advantages of debt over equity is that interest on debt is deductible against corporate taxes in most jurisdictions, whereas dividends made to equity holders are not. However, this is becoming more restricted in some countries as a result of clamping down on corporate tax evasion.

Test yourself 8.8

Company A: EPS = £12m/4m = £3.00 per share
Company B: EPS = £11.5m/(4m × 6/12) + (2m × 6/12) = £3.83 per share
Company B therefore has the highest earnings per share.

Test yourself 8.9

You can find the EPS figures quoted at the foot of the income statement on page 86 of the ARA. M&S's basic EPS fell from 29.7 pence in 2015 to 24.9 pence in 2016, a fall of 16.2%, which would indicate lower profits for each shareholder. However, the company deducts items that it describes as non-underlying, to give what it believes are the ongoing underlying earnings of the business. On this basis, "Underlying EPS" has increased from 33.1 pence in 2015 to 35.0 pence in 2016, a rise of 5.7%. We will look at how companies use alternative measures to describe their results in Section 6.

Worked example answers

Worked example 8.1

31 December 2017:

$$\text{ROCE} = \frac{\text{Profit on ordinary activities before interest and taxation (PBIT)}}{\text{Total assets (TA) less current liabilities (CL)}} \%$$

$$= \frac{\text{Retained profit + dividends + taxation + interest (on loan stock)}}{\text{TA-CL}} \%$$

$$= \frac{£600{,}000 + £50{,}000 + £160{,}000 + £8{,}000^{(1)}}{£6{,}880{,}000} \%$$

$$= \frac{£818{,}000}{£6{,}880{,}000} \% = 11.9\%$$

(1) 8% loan stock 2018: 8% × £100,000 = £8,000

31 December 2016:

$$\text{ROCE} = \frac{\text{Profit on ordinary activities before interest and taxation (PBIT)}}{\text{Total assets (TA) less current liabilities (CL)}} \%$$

$$= \frac{£500{,}000 + £127{,}500 + £8{,}000}{£6{,}280{,}000} \%$$

$$= \frac{£635{,}500}{£6{,}280{,}000} \% = 10.1\%$$

Worked example 8.2

$$\frac{\text{Current assets}}{\text{Current liabilities}}$$

= 350/160 = 2.2:1

The ratio is over 1 which means the company has sufficient cover to meet its short-term liabilities. However, this ratio does not take account of the fact that inventories may not be easily converted into cash in a timely manner. If inventories cannot be easily sold then the quick ratio (or 'acid-test') may be a more reliable method of calculating a company's ability to meet creditors falling due within one year and other short-term liabilities.

Worked example 8.3

$$\frac{\text{Current assets – stock}}{\text{Current liabilities}}$$

$$= \frac{350–200}{160}$$

=150/160 = 0.9:1

The ratio is less than 1 which means the company, when subjected to the acid test, has insufficient cover to meet its short term liabilities. If inventories can be converted into cash in a timely manner then the company may still be able to demonstrate sufficient liquid cover to meet its short-term obligations, but this could be a warning flag that the company might have problem paying its debts if it came under any pressure, for example if it started to have problems collecting amounts due from receivables.

Worked example 8.4

$$\frac{\text{Cash and cash equivalents}}{\text{Current liabilities}}$$

=100/160 = 0.6:1

Worked example 8.5

$$\frac{\text{Cash and cash equivalents}}{\text{Current assets}}\ \% = 100/350\ \% = 28.6\%$$

Worked example 8.6

2017:

Non-current asset turnover = 1,500,000/(200,000 × 75%) = 1,500,000/150,000 = 10 times

The company has a high non-current asset: revenue ratio which indicates the company's assets are effective at generating turnover.

2018:

$$\text{Non-current asset turnover} = \frac{\text{Revenue}}{\text{Non-current assets}}$$

Non-current assets = (150,000 × 75%) + (700,000 – (700,000 × 25% × 3/12))

= 112,500 + 700,000 – 43,750 = £768,750

$$\frac{\text{Revenue}}{\text{Non-current assets}} = \frac{£2,000,000}{£768,750}$$

= 2.6 times

While the non-current asset turnover ratio has fallen significantly, implying a fall in efficiency, it is clear that the fall in the ratio is not due to a fall in revenue. It is possible that the fall in the efficiency ratio could be attributed to over-nvestment in plant and machinery, but it is perhaps more likely that the fall is due to the non-current asset investment being made in the final quarter of the financial year. The non-current assets figure has increased significantly year on year but the assets have not been held long enough to generate increased sales for the year ended 31 August 2018. In the case of this entity, it therefore cannot be assumed that efficiency has fallen simply because the fixed asset turnover ratio has fallen. The company should consider calculating the ratio for the nine months to 31 May 2018 and annualising the resultant figure which might be a fairer comparative on which to evaluate efficiency:

Non-current assets = (150,000 – (150,000 × 25% × 9/12))

= 150,000 – 28,125 (depreciation charge for the nine months) = £121,875

$$\frac{\text{Revenue}}{\text{Non-current assets}} = \frac{£2{,}000{,}000 \times 9/12}{£121{,}875} = 12.3 \text{ times}$$

In this example, we see that efficiency of the entity increased for the nine months ended 31 May 2018 when compared with the prior year.

Worked example 8.7

$$\text{EPS} = \frac{\text{Earnings}}{\text{No of shares}}$$

Earnings = £19m

Weighted average number of shares = (8m × 3/12) + ((8m + 2m) × 9/12)

$$\text{EPS} = \frac{£19\text{m}}{9.5\text{m}} = £2 \text{ per share}$$

Worked example 8.8

$$\text{EPS} = \frac{\text{Profit after tax}}{\text{No of shares}}$$

$$= \frac{£26{,}000{,}000}{10{,}000{,}000} = £2.60$$

P/E ratio = £3.50 / £2.60 = 1.3

Worked example 8.9
Dividend yield = £0.80/£16 = 5%.

Chapter 9

Worked example answers

Worked example 9.1
£100,000 + £15,000 – £10,000 = £105,000 would be due to the life tenant and this would be reflected as a current liability in the trust's statement of financial position as at 31 December 2016.

The Life Tenant's Account for the year ended 31 December 2016 would be:

	£
Balance as at 1 January 2016	100,000
Net income for the year	15,000
Amount available for distribution	115,000
Amount distributed in year	(10,000)
Balance as at 31 December 2016	105,000

Worked example 9.2

1

Liam Johnson Life Interest Trust
Income Account for the year ended 5 April 2016

	£	£
Income		
Rental income	20,000	
Income from quoted investments	23,800	
Bank interest	958	
		44,758
Expenses		
Trustee fees	2,500	
Accountancy fees	150	
Bank charges	175	
		(2,825)
Net income for the year		41,933

The figure for net income for the year is used for preparing the life tenant's account. The life tenant's account and the capital account are integral parts of the statement of financial position.

You will see from the life tenant's account below that the balance is £17,007. In other words, the trust has a liability to Mrs Linda Johnson of this amount. The trustees are, therefore, in a position to distribute more income to Mrs Linda Johnson if required.

2

Liam Johnson Life Interest Trust
Life tenant's account for year ended 5 April 2016 – Mrs Linda Johnson

	£
Balance as at 6 April 2015	10,074
Net income for the year	41,933
Less: Amount distributed during the year	35,000
Balance as at 5 April 2016	17,007

3

Liam Johnson Life Interest Trust
Capital account as at 5 April 2016

	£	£
Balance as at 6 April 2015	971,542	
Add: Gain on sale of investments	500	
		972,042
Less: Investment management expenses	1,500	
Legal fees	1,000	
Accountancy fees	1,200	
		(3,700)
Balance as at 5 April 2016		968,342

4

Liam Johnson Life Interest Trust
Statement of financial position as at 5 April 2016

	£
Capital account	968,342
Life tenant's account – Mrs Linda Johnson	17,007
	985,349
Represented by:	
Quoted investments	500,000
Freehold property	450,000
Bank balances	
Capital	31,598
Income	3,751
	985,349

The statement of financial position clearly shows the split between the capital account and income due to the life tenant. The bank balances are also separated out into capital and income.

Chapter 10

Test yourself answers

Test yourself 10.1
It can ask its members to pass a waiver resolution in the financial year before the financial year for which it wishes to obtain the exemption. The members can pass a waiver resolution relating either to a specific, or indefinite, number of financial years.

Test yourself 10.2
The amount of called up share capital is £400,000 (500,000 × 80 pence).

Chapter 11

Test yourself answers

Test yourself 11.1

Under s. 174 directors must carry out their duties using the skill, care and diligence that would be expected of any director, but also applying those they have in particular. This means that those with professional qualifications, such as Chartered Secretaries, will be held to a higher standard as they will be expected to use their knowledge and experience as Chartered Secretaries, beyond the tests of skill, care and diligence applied to directors in general.

Test yourself 11.2

There was a concern that directors did not have easy access to information as to what their duties are given that it had accumulated in case law over many years. Putting the duties on a statutory footing made them more accessible but also will allow them to be amended in future. Directors and the courts must still consider the body of case law, so directors may still need to take legal advice in difficult situations.

Test yourself 11.3

A director in this situation should declare any conflicts of interest and have them authorised by the shareholders. Preferably how such conflicts are dealt with should be laid out in the joint venture articles. When making decisions, directors will need to ensure they are acting in the best interests of the relevant company at the relevant time.

Test yourself 11.4

A good system of corporate governance will ensure that the directors are acting in the best interests of their shareholders at all times and will allow shareholders to hold directors accountable. This should reduce the risk of the company being run for the short-term interests of the directors and instead the focus will be on the longer-term sustainability of the business for the benefit of shareholders.

Test yourself 11.5

Non-executive directors focus on strategy and policy and will monitor the work of the executive to ensure they are acting in the best interests of the company and its shareholders. Non-executives are required under the UK Corporate Governance Code to make up a majority of the membership of board committees, such as the audit and remuneration committees.

Test yourself 11.6

The comply or explain approach is based on the premise that one size does not fit all and that flexibility is required to take into account individual company situations. By explaining the need to diverge from the rules, companies can keep shareholders properly informed of the reasons for non-compliance and shareholders can take an informed view of the departure. However, a downside is that directors can depart without regulatory sanction; and shareholders may not always be sufficiently engaged to object to the departure and/or may not be in a situation to coordinate with each other in order to take action if each shareholder has relatively little power on their own.

Test yourself 11.7

The eight principles are stated in the Code as follows:

1. The board: Companies should be headed by an effective board of directors which is responsible for governance.
2. Directors: Directors should take collective responsibility for directing and supervising the affairs of the business.
3. Business conduct and ethics: All directors should maintain good standards of business conduct, integrity and ethical behaviour and should operate with due care and diligence and at all times act honestly and openly.
4. Accountability: The board should have formal and transparent arrangements in place for presenting a balanced and understandable assessment of the company's position and prospects and for considering how they apply financial reporting and internal control principles.
5. Risk management: The board should provide suitable oversight of risk management and maintain a sound system of risk measurement and control.
6. Disclosure and reporting: The board should ensure the timely and balanced disclosure to shareholders and/or to regulators of all material matters concerning the company.
7. Remuneration: The board should ensure remuneration arrangements are structured fairly and responsibly and that remuneration policies are consistent with effective risk management.
8. Shareholder relations: The board should ensure that satisfactory shareholder communication takes place with shareholders and is based on the mutual understanding of needs, objectives and concerns.

Test yourself 11.8

The key theme is the long-term sustainability of the business, and the key principles will involve considering the company's impact on and interaction with all the stakeholders it relies upon. This will be not just shareholders, but also employees and the wider community, including the effect on the environment. By establishing good CSR principles, by definition the company will be better run, less risky and produce better returns to shareholders.

Test yourself 11.9

Advantages include (1) improved accuracy, transparency and reliability of corporate disclosures; (2) better internal controls; and (3) enhanced auditor independence. Disadvantages include (1) more costs of compliance and bureaucracy; (2) a consequential fall in companies listing in the US; and (3) an extra-territorial effect in that companies and auditors from other countries can be affected.

Directory of web resources

The AIC Codes of Corporate Governance
http://www.theaic.co.uk/aic-code-of-corporate-governance-0

Article on the connection between CSR and positive shareholder value in Business Ethics
http://business-ethics.com/2015/05/05/does-corporate-social-responsibility-increase-profits/

Companies Act 2006
http://www.legislation.gov.uk/ukpga/2006/46/contents

Equality Trust
www.equalitytrust.org.uk

European Financial Reporting Advisory Group
www.efrag.org

ESMA Guidelines on APMs
https://www.esma.europa.eu/sites/default/files/library/2015/10/2015-esma-1415en.pdf

EU work on corporate governance issues
http://ec.europa.eu/justice/civil/company-law/corporate-governance/index_en.htm

Financial Stability Board (FSB)
www.fsb.org/

Financial Reporting Council
www.frc.org.uk/

FRC Clear & Concise Reporting project
www.iasplus.com/en-gb/projects/frc-projects/clear-and-concise

FRC guidance on the Strategic Report, which also covers KPIs.
https://www.frc.org.uk/Our-Work/Publications/Accounting-and-Reporting-Policy/Guidance-on-the-Strategic-Report.pdf

GC100 Guidance on Directors' Conflicts of Interest
http://uk.practicallaw.com/8-380-1895

GC100 Guidance on Directors' Remuneration
http://uk.practicallaw.com/groups/uk-gc100-investor-group

The Guernsey Financial Services Commission Code of Governance Finance Sector Code of Practice
www.gfsc.gg/sites/default/files/20160218%20-%20Finance%20Sector%20Code%20of%20Corp%20%20Gov.pdf

International Accounting Standards Board
www.ifrs.org

The International Integrated Reporting Council
http://integratedreporting.org/

Public Company Accounting Oversight Board (PCAOB)
https://pcaobus.org/

UK Corporate Governance Code (April 2016)
www.frc.org.uk/Our-Work/Publications/Corporate-Governance/UK-Corporate-Governance-Code-April-2016.pdf

UK Stewardship Code (September 2012)
https://www.frc.org.uk/getattachment/d67933f9-ca38-4233-b603-3d24b2f62c5f/UK-Stewardship-Code-(September-2012).pdf

Glossary

12-month expected credit losses The portion of lifetime expected credit losses that represent the expected credit losses that result from default events on a financial instrument that are possible within the 12 months after the reporting date.

Accounting interpretations Statements issued by standard setters (e.g. IASB) to clarify how standards should be applied. Interpretations are typically published to address issues arising that were not foreseen when the standards were first set.

Accounting policies The specific principles, bases, conventions, rules and practices applied by an entity in preparing and presenting financial statements.

Accounting profit Profit or loss for a period before deducting tax expense.

Active market A market in which transactions for the asset or liability take place with sufficient frequency and volume to provide pricing information on an ongoing basis.

Acquiree The business or businesses that the acquirer obtains control of in a business combination.

Acquirer The entity that obtains control of the acquiree.

Acquisition date The date on which the acquirer obtains control of the acquiree.

Adjusting event An event after the reporting period that provides further evidence of conditions that existed at the end of the reporting period. An event that raises going concern issues for the entity is an adjusting event.

Agency theory Predicated on the view that the managers of a company are appointed to act as agents of the owners of the company and that there is an inherent conflict of interest between the managers (who control the company) and the shareholders (who own the company).

Aggregation A term used in IAS 1 to describe the grouping of immaterial assets and presenting the total as a single line item on the face of financial statements or in the notes. Aggregation is not permitted for material items or material classes of similar items.

Amortisation The systematic allocation of the depreciable amount of an intangible asset over its useful life.

Amortised cost of a financial asset The amount at which the financial asset is measured at initial recognition minus the principal repayments, plus or minus the cumulative amortisation using the effective interest method of any difference between that initial amount and the maturity amount and adjusted for any loss allowance.

Amortised cost of a financial liability The amount at which the financial liability is measured at initial recognition minus the principal repayments, plus or minus the cumulative amortisation using the effective interest method of any difference between that initial amount and the maturity amount.

Associate An entity over which the investor has significant influence.

Audit An objective examination and evaluation of the financial statements of an organisation to make sure that the records are a fair and accurate representation of the transactions they claim to represent. An external audit is done by an auditor or audit firm that is independent of the entity (a statutory auditor); an internal audit is carried out by employees of the entity (although it can be outsourced).

Business An integrated set of activities and assets that is capable of being conducted and managed for the purpose of providing a return in the form of dividends, lower costs or other economic benefits directly to investors or other owners, members or participants.

Business combination A transaction or other event in which an acquirer obtains control of one or more businesses.

Carrying amount The amount at which an asset is recognised in the statement of financial position after deducting any accumulated amortisation and accumulated impairment losses thereon.

Cash Comprises cash on hand and demand deposits.

Cash equivalents Short-term, highly liquid investments that are readily convertible to known amounts of cash and which are subject to an insignificant risk of changes in value.

Cash flow hedge A hedge of the exposure to variability in cash flows that is (i) attributable to a particular risk associated with a recognised asset or liability (such as all or some future interest payments on variable rate debt) or a highly probable forecast transaction; and (ii) could affect profit or loss.

Cash-settled share-based payment transaction A share-based payment transaction in which the entity acquires goods or services by incurring a liability to transfer cash or other assets to the supplier of those goods or services for amounts that are based on the price (or value) of equity instruments (including shares or share options) of the entity.

Cell company A private or public company which is able to segregate its assets and liabilities between different cells. Each cell may be used to carry out distinct and independent businesses and the assets of each cell can be ring-fenced.

Change in accounting estimate An adjustment of the carrying amount of an asset or a liability, or the amount of the periodic consumption of an asset, that results from the assessment of the present status of, and expected future benefits and obligations associated with, assets and liabilities. Changes in accounting estimates result from new information or new developments and, accordingly, are not corrections of errors.

Close family members of a person Those family members who may be expected to influence, or be influenced by, that person in their dealings with the entity and include that person's children and spouse or domestic partner, children of that person's spouse or domestic partner and dependants of that person or that person's spouse or domestic partner.

Comparability Enables users to identify and understand similarities in, and differences among, items.

Consolidated financial statements The financial statements of a group in which the assets, liabilities, equity, income, expenses and cash flows of the parent and its subsidiaries are presented as those of a single economic entity.

Constructive obligation An obligation that derives from an entity's actions where:

- by an established pattern of past practice, published policies or a sufficiently specific current statement, the entity has indicated to other parties that it will accept certain responsibilities; and
- as a result, the entity has created a valid expectation on the part of those other parties that it will discharge those responsibilities.

Contingent asset A possible asset that arises from past events and whose existence will be confirmed only by the occurrence or non-occurrence of uncertain future events not wholly within the entity's control.

Contingent consideration Usually, an obligation of the acquirer to transfer additional assets or equity interests to the former owners of an acquiree as part of the exchange for control of the acquiree if specified future events occur or conditions are met. However, contingent consideration also may give the acquirer the right to the return of previously transferred consideration if specified conditions are met.

Contingent liability A possible obligation to transfer economic benefit as a result of a past transaction or event and whose existence will be confirmed only by the occurrence or non-occurrence of uncertain future events not wholly within the entity's control. A contingent liability may also be a present obligation which is not recognised either because it is unlikely payment will be required to settle it or because the amount of the obligation cannot be measured with sufficient reliability.

Contract An agreement between two or more parties that creates enforceable rights and obligations.

Control The present ability to direct the use of an economic resource and obtain the economic benefits that flow from it.

Control of an investee An investor controls an investee when the investor is exposed, or has rights, to variable returns from its involvement with the investee and has the ability to affect those returns through its power over the investee.

Corporate social responsibility (CSR) A term used to describe the processes an organisation uses to produce a positive impact on society through its activities. It is about ongoing commitment of businesses to behave ethically and responsibly towards its employees, its customers, the environment and the community at large. It is about doing business in a responsible and sustainable manner.

Cost The amount of cash or cash equivalents paid or the fair value of the other consideration given to acquire an asset at the time of its acquisition or construction.

Costs of disposal Incremental costs directly attributable to the disposal of an asset or cash-generating unit, excluding finance costs and income tax expense.

Current assets Assets that are readily realisable and likely to be held for less than 12 months (e.g. stock, trade debtors, investments traded on a stock exchange, cash at bank and in hand).

Current liabilities Liabilities falling due in less than 12 months such as trade creditors or bank overdrafts.

Current ratio A measure of short-term liquidity which shows a company's ability to meet short-term obligations from short-term assets.

Current tax The amount of income taxes payable (or recoverable) in respect of the taxable profit (tax loss) for a period.

Current value A measure that provides monetary information about assets, liabilities, income and expenses using information that is updated to reflect conditions at the measurement date.

Customer A party that has contracted with an entity to obtain goods or services that are an output of the entity's ordinary activities in exchange for consideration.

Debt financing Occurs when a company raises finance by issuing bonds, bills or notes and, in exchange, promises to repay the lender the interest and capital on the loan.

Deferred tax assets The amounts of income taxes recoverable in future periods in respect of: differences between the carrying amount of an asset or liability in the statement of financial position and its tax base; the carry forward of unused tax losses; and the carry forward of unused tax credits.

Deferred tax liabilities The amounts of income taxes payable in future periods in respect of taxable temporary differences.

Defined benefit plans Post-employment benefit plans other than defined contribution plans.

Defined contribution plans Post-employment benefit plans under which an entity pays fixed contributions into a separate entity (a fund) and will have no legal or constructive obligation to pay further contributions if the fund does not hold sufficient assets to pay all employee benefits relating to employee service in the current and prior periods.

Depreciable amount The cost of an asset, or other amount substituted for cost, less its residual value.

Depreciation The systematic allocation of the depreciable amount of an asset over its useful life.

Derivative A financial instrument or other contract with all three of the following characteristics.

- Its value changes in response to the change in a specified interest rate, financial instrument price, commodity price, foreign exchange rate, index of prices or rates, credit rating or credit index, or other variable, provided in the case of a non-financial variable that the variable is not specific to a party to the contract (sometimes called the 'underlying').
- It requires no initial net investment or an initial net investment that is smaller than would be required for other types of contracts that would be expected to have a similar response to changes in market factors.
- It is settled at a future date.

Development The application of research findings or other knowledge to a plan or design for the production of new or substantially improved materials, devices, products, processes, systems or services before the start of commercial production or use.

Discontinued operation A component of an entity that either has been disposed of or is classified as held for sale and: represents a separate major line of business or geographical area of operations, is part of a single co-ordinated plan to dispose of a separate major line of business or geographical area of operations or is a subsidiary acquired exclusively with a view to resale.

Disposal group A group of assets to be disposed of, by sale or otherwise, together as a group in a single transaction, and liabilities directly associated with those assets that will be transferred in the transaction.

Distributable profits legally speaking, a company's accumulated realised profits (so far as not previously distributed or capitalised) less its accumulated realised losses (so far as not previously written off in a reduction or reorganisation of share capital).

Dividends Distributions of profits to holders of equity instruments in proportion to their holdings of a particular class of capital.

Earnings per share (EPS) A measure of income attributable to equity shareholders divided by the number of shares outstanding. It is used by shareholders for comparing a company's financial health with a company with similar earnings.

Effective interest method The method that is used in the calculation of the amortised cost of a financial asset or a financial liability and in the allocation and recognition of the interest revenue or interest expense in profit or loss over the relevant period.

Effective interest rate The rate that exactly discounts estimated future cash payments or receipts through the expected life of the financial asset or financial liability to the gross carrying amount of a financial asset or to the amortised cost of a financial liability.

Employee benefits All forms of consideration given by an entity in exchange for service rendered by employees or for the termination of employment.

Equity financing Capital raised by selling shares in the company, typically by public offering. Investors buy the shares and become shareholders or owners of the company's equity.

Equity instrument A contract that evidences a residual interest in the assets of an entity after deducting all of its liabilities.

Equity method A method of accounting whereby the investment is initially recognised at cost and adjusted thereafter for the post-acquisition change in the investor's share of the investee's net assets. The investor's profit or loss includes its share of the investee's profit or loss and the investor's other comprehensive income includes its share of the investee's other comprehensive income.

Equity-settled share-based payment transaction A share-based payment transaction in which the entity receives goods or services as consideration for its own equity instruments (including shares or share options) receives goods or services but has no obligation to settle the transaction with the supplier.

Equity shares instruments issued by a company to give holders a residual interest in its assets and liabilities.

Events after the Reporting Period Events, favourable or unfavourable, that have occurred between the date of the statement of financial position (i.e. the balance sheet date) and the date when the financial statements were authorised for issue.

Executory contract A contract under which neither party has performed any of its obligations or both parties have partially performed their obligations to an equal extent.

Exchange differences Gains and losses arising from settlement or from converting monetary items back to one currency from another, using different exchange rates to those used for the initial recognition.

Expected credit losses The weighted average of credit losses with the respective risks of a default occurring as the weights.

Fair presentation In the context of financial statements, means that an entity should adopt appropriate accounting policies and practices to ensure information presented in the financial statements is relevant, reliable, comparable and understandable. Where the adoption of IFRS Standards is insufficient to enable users to understand a specific transaction, additional disclosures should be given so ensure the financial statements give a fair representation of the results, financial position and cash flow.

Fair value The price that would be received to sell an asset or paid to transfer a liability in an orderly transaction between market participants at the measurement date.

Fair value hedge A hedge of the exposure to changes in fair value of a recognised asset or liability or an unrecognised firm commitment or an identified portion of such an asset, liability or firm commitment that is attributable to a particular risk and could affect profit or loss.

Faithful representation A faithful representation provides information about the substance of an economic phenomenon instead of merely providing information about its legal form. A perfectly faithful representation would be complete, neutral and free from error.

Fiduciary A legal person, such as an individual or body corporate, entrusted to look after the affairs and assets of another.

Fiduciary duty The legal obligation of a fiduciary to act in the best interests of another party.

Finance lease A lease that transfers substantially all the risks and rewards incidental to ownership of an asset. Title may or may not eventually be transferred.

Financial asset Any asset that is:

- cash;
- an equity instrument of another entity;
- a contractual right–
  - to receive cash or another financial asset from another entity; or
  - to exchange financial assets or financial liabilities with another entity under conditions that are potentially favourable to the entity; or
- a contract that will or may be settled in the entity's own equity instruments and is–
  - a non-derivative for which the entity is or may be obliged to receive a variable number of the entity's own equity instruments; or
  - a derivative that will or may be settled other than by the exchange of a fixed amount of cash or another financial asset for a fixed number of the entity's own equity instruments.

Financial covenants ratios that the borrower is required to stay above or below, but there are usually also often absolute restrictions on debt levels and minimum working capital requirements.

Financial instrument Any contract that gives rise to a financial asset of one entity and a financial liability or equity instrument of another entity.

Financial liability Any liability that is:

- a contractual obligation:
  - to deliver cash or another financial asset to another entity; or
  - to exchange financial assets or financial liabilities with another entity under conditions that are potentially unfavourable to the entity; or
- a contract that will or may be settled in the entity's own equity instruments and is:

- a non-derivative for which the entity is or may be obliged to deliver a variable number of the entity's own equity instruments; or
- a derivative that will or may be settled other than by the exchange of a fixed amount of cash or another financial asset for a fixed number of the entity's own equity instruments.

Financial Reporting Council (FRC) The UK's independent regulator responsible for promoting high quality corporate governance and reporting to foster investment. It also sets accounting and auditing standards for the UK.

Financial Stability Board (FSB) An international body that monitors and makes recommendations about the global financial system.

Financing activities Activities that result in changes in the size and composition of the contributed equity and borrowings of the entity.

Fixed production overheads Indirect costs of production that remain relatively constant regardless of the volume of production, such as depreciation and maintenance of factory buildings, equipment and right-of-use assets used in the production process, and the cost of factory management and administration.

Forced heirship A feature of civil law jurisdictions and Islamic countries which do not recognise the full freedom of testation. This means, for example, that an individual making his will may not be able to leave an equal proportion of his assets to his surviving children and spouse. In order to prevent all the assets going to the eldest child, the individual may use a foundation or trust and thereby avoid the forced heirship rules.

Foreign Private Issuers (FPIs) A non-US company will qualify as a FPI if 50% or less of its outstanding voting securities are held by US residents; or if more than 50% of its outstanding voting securities are held by US residents and none of the following three circumstances applies: the majority of its executive officers or directors are US citizens or residents; more than 50% of the issuer's assets are located in the USA; or the issuer's business is administered principally in the USA.

Gearing A measurement of long-term debt to equity and measures the extent to which a company is leveraged by comparing borrowed funds to shareholder funds.

General partner (GP) The person who assumes the management responsibility for the limited partnership. The general partner has unlimited liability for the debts and obligations of the partnership and, therefore, is typically a limited company.

General purpose financial reports A particular form of general purpose financial report that provides information (about the reporting entity's assets, liabilities, equity, income and expenses) that is useful to the primary users of those statements in assessing the prospects for future net cash inflows to the entity and in assessing management's stewardship of the entity's resources.

Generally Accepted Accounting Practice/Principles (GAAP) A common set of accounting standards regulatory rules and widely-followed practices used for the preparation and presentation of an entity's financial statements.

Goal congruence The alignment and harmonisation of goals and objectives. In the context of agency theory, this means matching the interests of the directors with the interests of shareholders so that directors are incentivised to act in the best interests of the company.

Going concern An entity should prepare its financial statements on a going concern basis, unless:
- the entity is being liquidated or has ceased trading, or
- the directors have no realistic alternative but to liquidate the entity or to cease trading,
- in which circumstances the entity may, if appropriate, prepare its financial statements on a basis other than that of a going concern.

Goodwill An asset representing the future economic benefits arising from other assets acquired in a business combination that are not individually identified and separately recognised.

Grant date The date at which the entity and another party (including an employee) agree to a share-based payment arrangement, being when the entity and the counterparty have a shared understanding of the terms and conditions of the arrangement. At grant date the entity confers on the counterparty the right to cash, other assets, or equity instruments of the entity, provided the specified vesting conditions, if any, are met. If that agreement is subject to an approval process (for example, by shareholders), grant date is the date when that approval is obtained.

Group A parent and its subsidiaries.

Group accounts A set of accounts which combine the results of a parent and all its subsidiary undertakings, eliminating all trading and balances between group members, thus presenting accounts that show transactions and balances only with those outside the group.

Guardian The person who is empowered to oversee the foundation's council and performs a similar function to the protector of a trust. The founder might choose to appoint a guardian to a foundation, which may be himself, to ensure the foundation is run in an appropriate manner and in accordance with the foundations charter.

Hedging A risk management strategy in which an investment is undertaken to offset a position and reduce exposure to price, currency or other fluctuations, e.g. a forward contract is used to hedge against changes in foreign currency exchange rates.

Historical cost A measure that provides monetary information about assets, liabilities, income and expenses using information derived from the transaction or event that created them. The historical cost measures of assets or liabilities do not reflect changes in prices. However, they do reflect changes such as consumption or impairment of assets and fulfilment of liabilities.

Identifiable An asset is identifiable if it either:

- is separable, i.e. capable of being separated or divided from the entity and sold, transferred, licensed, rented or exchanged, either individually or together with a related contract, identifiable asset or liability, regardless of whether the entity intends to do so; or
- arises from contractual or other legal rights, regardless of whether those rights are transferable or separable from the entity or from other rights and obligations.

Impairment loss The amount by which the carrying amount of an asset or a cash-generating unit exceeds its recoverable amount.

Impracticable Applying a requirement is impracticable when the entity cannot apply it after making every reasonable effort to do so, i.e, (a) if the effects of the retrospective treatment are not determinable; (b) the retrospective treatment requires assumptions about what management's intent would have been in that period; or (c) the retrospective treatment requires significant estimates of amounts and it is impossible to distinguish objectively information about those estimates that provides evidence of circumstances that existed on the date(s) as at which those amounts are to be recognised, measured or disclosed, and would have been available when the financial statements for that prior period were authorised for issue from other information.

Incurred loss model A model that assumes that all loans will be repaid until evidence to the contrary (known as a loss or trigger event) is identified.

Intangible asset An identifiable non-monetary asset without physical substance.

Integrated reporting (IR) An evolution of corporate reporting, with a focus on conciseness, strategic relevance and future orientation. As well as improving the quality of information contained in the final report, IR makes the reporting process itself more productive, resulting in tangible benefits. IR requires and brings about integrated thinking, enabling a better understanding of the factors that materially affect an organisation's ability to create value over time. It can lead to behavioural changes and improvement in performance throughout an organisation.

Interest rate implicit in the lease The discount rate that, at the inception of the lease, causes the aggregate present value of the minimum lease payments and any unguaranteed residual value (i.e. where the lessor has not assurance it) to be equal to the sum of the fair value of the leased asset and any initial direct costs of the lessor.

Investing activities The acquisition and disposal of long-term assets and other investments not included in cash equivalents.

Joint arrangement An arrangement of which two or more parties have joint control.

Joint control The contractually agreed sharing of control of an arrangement, which exists only when decisions about the relevant activities require the unanimous consent of the parties sharing control.

Joint operation A joint arrangement whereby the parties that have joint control of the arrangement have rights to the assets, and obligations for the liabilities, relating to the arrangement.

Joint venture A joint arrangement whereby the parties that have joint control of the arrangement have rights to the net assets of the arrangement.

Just in time procurement (JIT) A term used to describe a procurement policy whereby stock is ordered just before it is needed. It relies on close customer and supplier relations to ensure the stock arrives 'just in time'. JIT production methods are commonly used in the motor industry and other manufacturing industries enabling flexible manufacturing processes which keep stock levels to a minimum.

Key management personnel Those persons having authority and responsibility for planning, directing and controlling the activities of the entity, directly or indirectly, including any director (whether executive or otherwise) of that entity.

Key Performance Indicators (KPIs) Factors by reference to which the development, performance or position of an entity's business can be measured effectively

Lease An agreement whereby the lessor conveys to the lessee in return for a payment or series of payments the right to use an asset for an agreed period of time.

Legal obligation An obligation that derives from a contract (through its explicit or implicit terms, legislation or other operation of law).

Life tenant One who holds a life estate. A life tenant has all rights associated with ownership of real property, except the right to sell the property, until his/her (or someone else's) death. Upon the death of the life tenant, the property reverts back to the owner, or to a third party designated by the owner.

Lifetime expected credit losses The expected credit losses that result from all possible default events over the expected life of a financial instrument.

Limited partnership agreement (LPA) A written document setting out the powers and obligations of the limited partners and of the GP. It will include the name of the LP and GP, will state the purpose for which the LP was formed, will set out how income and capital should be allocated, how distributions should be made, the various rights and obligations of both parties (e.g. the obligation of the GP to contribute to the debts of the LP) and the administrative arrangements.

Loan covenant A restrictive clause in a loan agreement that is designed to protect the lender's interests by placing constraints on the borrower, such as limiting the borrower's ability to take on more debt without prior consent of the lender; imposing restrictions on leverage; or requiring working capital to be maintained at a minimum level.

Loan stock shares of common or preferred stock that are used as collateral to secure a loan from another party. The loan earns a fixed interest rate, much like a standard loan, and can be secured or unsecured.

Material Information whose omission or misstatement could influence decisions that the primary users of general purpose financial reports make on the basis of financial information about a specific reporting entity.

Minimum lease payments Payments over the lease term that the lessee is or can be required to make, excluding contingent rent (that is, rent dependent on a factor such as sales volumes, etc), costs for services and taxes to be paid by and reimbursed to the lessor, together with, for a lessee, any amounts guaranteed by the lessee or by a party related to the lessee.

Monetary items Units of currency held and assets and liabilities to be received or paid in a fixed or determinable number of units of currency.

Net realisable value The estimated selling price in the ordinary course of business less the estimated costs of completion and the estimated costs necessary to make the sale.

Non-adjusting event An event after the reporting period that is indicative of a condition that arose after the end of the reporting period.

Non-controlling interest Equity not attributable directly or indirectly to the parent company.

Non-current assets Assets that do not meet the definition of a current asset, so they are usually expected to be held and realised for more than 12 months (e.g. property, plant and equipment, intellectual property rights).

Non-current liabilities Liabilities falling due in more than 12 months such as longer-term bank loans and other financing arrangements.

Non-executive directors (NEDs) Members of a company's board of directors who are not part of the executive team. A non-executive director typically does not engage in the day-to-day management of the entity, but focusses on policy and strategy and holds the executive to account.

Normal capacity The production expected to be achieved on average over a number of periods or seasons under normal circumstances, taking into account the loss of capacity resulting from planned maintenance.

Onerous contract A present obligation where the unavoidable costs of fulfilling the contract are higher than the economic benefits that are expected to be received. Onerous contracts can arise where a firm undertakes a contract to supply a product or service and the cost of the raw materials or human resource costs more than originally anticipated.

Operating activities The main income producing activities of a business and other activities that are not investing or financing activities.

Operating cycle The period of time from the acquisition of assets (materials or services) to their realisation in cash receipts. For a retailer this is the length of time stock is held before receiving proceeds from its sale.

Operating lease A lease other than a finance lease. The inception of the lease is the earlier of the date of the lease agreement and the date of commitment by the parties to the principal provisions of the lease.

Ordinary share An equity instrument (see Chapter 6) that is subordinate to all other classes of equity instruments.

Other long-term employee benefits All employee benefits other than short-term employee benefits, post-employment benefits and termination benefits.

Overcapitalisation An over-investment in working capital which can lead to excessive stocks, high-debtor/ low creditor level and an unnecessarily large amount of cash. Overcapitalisation can result in a lower return on investment and unnecessary use of long-term funds to meet short-term obligations.

Parent An entity that controls one or more entities.

Parent company A company is a parent company of another company, its subsidiary, if it controls it through owning a majority of the voting shares, having the power to appoint the board, through a control contract or by a power in the subsidiary's governing document or through other mechanisms specified in the Companies Act.

Performance obligation A promise in a contract with a customer to transfer to the customer either: a good or service (or a bundle of goods or services) that is distinct; or a series of distinct goods or services that are substantially the same and that have the same pattern of transfer to the customer.

Post-employment benefits Employee benefits (other than termination benefits and short-term employee benefits) that are payable after the completion of employment.

Potential ordinary share A financial instrument (see Chapters 5 and 6) or other contract that may entitle its holder to ordinary shares.

Power Existing rights that give the current ability to direct the relevant activities.

Presentation currency The currency in which the financial statements are reported.

Prior period errors Omissions from, and misstatements in, the entity's financial statements for one or more prior periods arising from a failure to use, or misuse of, reliable information that:

- was available when financial statements for those periods were authorised for issue; and
- could reasonably be expected to have been obtained and taken into account in the preparation and presentation of those financial statements.
- Such errors include the effects of mathematical mistakes, mistakes in applying accounting policies, oversights or misinterpretations of facts, and fraud.

Probable obligation An obligation is probable if it is more likely than not to occur.

Property, plant and equipment Tangible items that:

- are held for use in the production or supply of goods or services, for rental to others, or for administrative purposes; and
- are expected to be used during more than one period.

Prospectus An information memorandum or offer document for subscriptions in a collective investment fund or investment company which sets out the terms of the offer and key information in respect of the fund. The document will include, amongst other things, risk warnings and details in connection with the investment policy and extent to which the company will use gearing.

Provision A liability of uncertain timing or amount.

Prudence The exercise of caution when making judgements under conditions of uncertainty.

Public companies Companies whose certificate of incorporation states they are a public company or which have converted to public company since incorporation and whose share capital is at least £50,000.

Public Company Accounting Oversight Board (PCAOB) Board charged with the oversight and supervision of public company accounting firms and oversees the audits of public companies in order to protect investor interests and further the public interest in the preparation of informative, accurate and independent audit reports.

Public Interest Entities (PIEs) Defined in EU law as listed companies, credit institutions and insurance undertakings. In addition, Member States can designate as PIEs other undertakings that are of significant public relevance, because of the nature of their business, their size or the number of their employees.

Quick ratio This is a measurement of short-term liquidity which focusses on those items that can be turned into cash easily and quickly and therefore does not include stock which may not be easily realisable at full net book value.

Quoted companies Companies whose equity share capital is listed on the main exchange in the UK, the EEA or the New York Stock Exchange or Nasdaq. AIM companies are not quoted.

Recognition The process of capturing, for inclusion in the statement of financial position or the statement(s) of financial performance, an item that meets the definition of an element. It involves depicting the item (either alone or as part of a line item) in words and by a monetary amount, and including that amount in totals in the relevant statement.

Recoverable amount Recoverable value of an asset or a cash-generating unit is the higher of its fair value less costs of disposal and its value in use.

Related party A person or entity that is related to the entity that is preparing its financial statements (the 'reporting entity'):

(a) a person or a close member of that person's family is related to a reporting entity if that person–
  (i) has control or joint control of the reporting entity;
  (ii) has significant influence over the reporting entity; or
  (iii) is a member of the key management personnel of the reporting entity or of a parent of the reporting entity.

(b) an entity is related to a reporting entity if any of the following conditions applies–

(i) the entity and the reporting entity are members of the same group (which means that each parent, subsidiary and fellow subsidiary is related to the others);
(ii) one entity is an associate or joint venture of the other entity (or an associate or joint venture of a member of a group of which the other entity is a member);
(iii) both entities are joint ventures of the same third party.
(iv) one entity is a joint venture of a third entity and the other entity is an associate of the third entity.
(v) the entity is a post-employment benefit plan for the benefit of employees of either the reporting entity or an entity related to the reporting entity. If the reporting entity is itself such a plan, the sponsoring employers are also related to the reporting entity.
(vi) the entity is controlled or jointly controlled by a person identified in (a);
(vii) a person identified in (a)(i) has significant influence over the entity or is a member of the key management personnel of the entity (or of a parent of the entity);
(viii) the entity, or any member of a group of which it is a part, provides key management personnel services to the reporting entity or to the parent of the reporting entity.

Related party transaction A transfer of resources, services or obligations between a reporting entity and a related party, regardless of whether a price is charged.

Relevant activities Activities of the investee that significantly affect the investee's returns.

Relevant financial information Financial information that is capable of making a difference in the decisions made by users.

Remaindermen The term given to beneficiaries who receive the remaining capital upon termination of a life interest trust, e.g. after the death of the life tenant.

Research Original and planned investigation undertaken with the prospect of gaining new scientific or technical knowledge and understanding.

Residual value The estimated amount of an asset that an entity would currently obtain from disposal of the asset, after deducting the estimated costs of disposal, if the asset were already of the age and in the condition expected at the end of its useful life.

Retrospective application is applying a new accounting policy to transactions, other events and conditions as if that policy had always been applied.

Return on capital employed (ROCE) A measure of a company's success at achieving a return on capital invested. It is calculated by multiplying operating profit margin by net asset turnover.

Retrospective restatement is correcting the recognition, measurement and disclosure of amounts of elements of financial statements as if a prior period error had never occurred.

Revenue Income arising in the course of an entity's ordinary activities.

Rights issue An issue of shares offered at a special price by a company to its existing shareholders in proportion to their holding of old shares.

Ring-fencing A protective measure to prevent the assets of a ring-fenced cell from being used to pay off the debts of another cell.

The Sarbanes-Oxley Act (2002) Legislation which was passed in the USA in 2002 in an attempt to restore public confidence, improve the transparency of financial statements and protect investor interests. The Act introduced new and more stringent measures for public companies in respect of corporate disclosure requirements and corporate governance.

Satisficing The behaviour of managers to do just enough to satisfy shareholders and achieve an adequate return on their investment rather than maximising the return for shareholders.

Secondary legislation Subordinate legislation which supplements primary law. It is enacted by a person or body, other than the legislature, who has been granted the relevant authority. This enables secondary legislation to be enacted in a timelier manner. For example, in Jersey primary legislation must be put before the UK's Privy Council whilst secondary legislation, such as an Order, may be approved locally by the relevant Minister, e.g. The Minister for Economic Development (for financial services secondary legislation).

Securitisation The process of taking an illiquid asset, or group of assets, and through financial engineering, transforming them into a security. A typical example of securitisation is a mortgage-backed security (MBS), which is a type of asset-backed security that is secured by a collection of mortgages.

Service cost comprises: (a) current service cost, which is the increase in the present value of the defined benefit obligation resulting from employee service in the current period; (b) past service cost, which is the change in the present value of the defined benefit obligation for employee service in prior periods, resulting from a plan amendment or a curtailment; and (c) any gain or loss on settlement.

Settlor The person (or persons) who creates a trust.

Share option A contract that gives the holder the right, but not the obligation, to subscribe to the entity's shares at a fixed or determinable price for a specified period of time.

Share-based payment transaction A transaction in which the entity receives goods or services from the supplier of those goods or services (including an employee) in a share-based payment arrangement.

Shareholders' funds All the assets of a company less all the liabilities. It is the equity amount in a company that is due to the owners (the shareholders).

Short-term employee benefits Employee benefits (other than termination benefits) that are expected to be settled wholly before 12 months after the end of the annual reporting period in which the employees render the related service.

Significant influence The power to participate in the financial and operating policy decisions of the investee but is not control or joint control of those policies.

Spot rate A foreign exchange is the market fx rate used in transactions with immediate delivery.

Sole trader A person who is the exclusive owner of a business, entitled to keep all profits after tax has been paid but liable for all losses.

Statutory audit A legally required review of the accuracy of an entity's financial records and financial statements.

Statutory auditor An external auditor whose appointment is mandated by law.

Subsidiary An entity that is controlled by another entity.

Subsidiary company A company that has a parent company.

Systemically important financial institutions (SIFIs) Financial institutions whose distress or disorderly failure, because of their size, complexity and systemic interconnectedness, would cause significant disruption to the wider financial system and economic activity.

Tax expense (or tax income) The aggregate amount included in the determination of profit or loss for the period in respect of current tax and deferred tax.

Taxable profit (or tax loss) The profit (or loss) for a period, determined in accordance with the rules established by the taxation authorities, upon which income taxes are payable (recoverable).

Termination benefits Employee benefits provided in exchange for the termination of an employee's employment as a result of either:

- an entity's decision to terminate an employee's employment before the normal retirement date; or
- an employee's decision to accept an offer of benefits in exchange for the termination of employment.

Timeliness Information that is timely is available to decision-makers in time to be capable of influencing their decisions.

Traded companies Companies with securities traded on a regulated market, such as the main London Stock Exchange.

Transaction price The amount of consideration to which an entity expects to be entitled in exchange for transferring promised goods or services to a customer, excluding amounts collected on behalf of third parties.

Treasury shares Shares in a company held in the company's own name.

True and fair view A legal concept. The question of whether accounts are true and fair can be decided only by a court, but the court will usually look to compliance with generally accepted accounting practice, particularly accounting standards, in force at the time the accounts were prepared as evidence that a true and fair view has been given.

Trust A legal arrangement whereby one or more persons, known as the trustee(s), are entrusted with the legal ownership of the assets of another party, the settlor, and to hold those assets (which might include property, investments and cash) 'on trust' for the benefit of one or more beneficiaries.

Trust deed A legal document setting out the terms of the trust and includes details of the interested parties, such as the settlor, trustees and beneficiaries as well as details of the trustee's powers – such as powers to invest and powers to distribute capital and income.

Trust enforcer The appointed overseer of the trust acting on behalf of the trust.

UK listed company A company with shares admitted to the Official List in the UK, but which may be incorporated anywhere. There is a choice between a Premium or Standard listing. Premium listed companies must meet higher standards than Standard listed companies, which need to meet only EU-mandated minimum criteria.

Understandability Financial information that is understandable is classified, characterised and presented clearly and concisely.

US Securities and Exchange Commission (SEC) One of the main financial services regulatory authorities in the US whose remit includes the protection of investor interests and the maintenance of fair, orderly, and efficient markets.

Useful life The period over which an asset is expected to be available for use by an entity, or the number of production or similar units expected to be obtained from the asset by an entity.

Value in use The present value of the future cash flows expected to be derived from an asset or cash-generating unit.

Variable production overheads Indirect costs of production that vary directly, or nearly directly, with the volume of production, such as indirect materials and indirect labour.

Verifiability Enables different knowledgeable and independent observers to reach consensus, although not necessarily complete agreement, that a particular depiction is a faithful representation.

Vesting condition A condition that determines whether the entity receives the services that entitle the counterparty to receive cash, other assets or equity instruments of the entity, under a share-based payment arrangement.

Vesting period The period during which all the specified vesting conditions of a share-based payment arrangement are to be satisfied.

Working capital A company's current assets less the current liabilities and is a term used to describe operational efficiency or the company's ability to pay its short-term liabilities.

Index

www.ingramcontent.com/pod-product-compliance
Ingram Content Group UK Ltd.
Pitfield, Milton Keynes, MK11 3LW, UK
UKHW051928100926
8556IPUK00022B/1437

9 781860 727818